VOCABULARY ASSESSMENT TO SUPPORT INSTRUCTION

Also Available

Bringing Reading Research to Life
Edited by Margaret G. McKeown and Linda Kucan

Bringing Words to Life, Second Edition:
Robust Vocabulary Instruction
Isabel L. Beck, Margaret G. McKeown, and Linda Kucan

Creating Robust Vocabulary:
Frequently Asked Questions and Extended Examples
Isabel L. Beck, Margaret G. McKeown, and Linda Kucan

Vocabulary Assessment to Support Instruction

Building Rich Word-Learning Experiences

Margaret G. McKeown
Paul D. Deane
Judith A. Scott
Robert Krovetz
René R. Lawless

THE GUILFORD PRESS
New York   London

Copyright © 2017 The Guilford Press
A Division of Guilford Publications, Inc.
370 Seventh Avenue, Suite 1200, New York, NY 10001
www.guilford.com

Printed in the United States of America

This book is printed on acid-free paper.

Last digit is print number: 9 8 7 6 5 4 3 2 1

Library of Congress Cataloging-in-Publication Data

Names: McKeown, Margaret G., author.
Title: Vocabulary assessment to support instruction ; building rich
  word-learning experiences / Margaret G. McKeown, Paul D. Deane,
  Judith A. Scott, Robert Krovetz, and René R. Lawless.
Description: New York : The Guilford Press, [2017] | Includes webography. |
  Includes bibliographical references and index.
Identifiers: LCCN 2017016465| ISBN 9781462530793 (paperback : acid-free
  paper) | ISBN 9781462530809 (hardcover : acid-free paper)
Subjects: LCSH: Vocabulary—Study and teaching—United States.
Classification: LCC LB1574.5 .M45 2017 | DDC 372.44—dc23
LC record available at *https://lccn.loc.gov/2017016465*

About the Authors

Margaret G. McKeown, PhD, is Clinical Professor of Education in the School of Education and a Senior Scientist at the Learning Research and Development Center at the University of Pittsburgh. Her work addresses practical, current problems that classroom teachers and their students face. Dr. McKeown has conducted research in the areas of instructional design and teacher professional development in reading comprehension and vocabulary. She is a recipient of the Outstanding Dissertation of the Year Award from the International Literacy Association (ILA) and a National Academy of Education Spencer Fellowship. Prior to her career in research, Dr. McKeown taught reading and language arts in elementary school. She is coauthor of books including *Bringing Words to Life, Second Edition*, and *Creating Robust Vocabulary.*

Paul D. Deane, PhD, is a Principal Research Scientist in Research and Development at Educational Testing Service (ETS). He has published extensively on lexical semantics, vocabulary assessment, writing assessment, and principles of assessment design. His research on vocabulary assessment has focused on developing methods to measure different aspects of vocabulary depth and breadth. During his career at ETS, Dr. Deane has also played a key role in the Cognitively Based Assessments of, for, and as Learning (CBAL) research initiative, where he led the development of learning progressions and assessment designs for English language arts, including vocabulary assessment.

Judith A. Scott, PhD, is Associate Professor in the Department of Education at the University of California, Santa Cruz. Her work addresses vocabulary acquisition and blending vocabulary instruction with effective teacher education within the context of language, literacy, and culture. Dr. Scott has been the lead researcher on three federally funded vocabulary research projects, including one focused on innovation in vocabulary assessment. She is a recipient of the John C. Manning Public School Service Award from the ILA. She also serves as a consultant for technology companies, helping them with educational applications and assessment.

Robert Krovetz, PhD, an independent researcher and consultant based in New Jersey, has consulted for ETS on projects to improve the assessment of vocabulary breadth and depth. He has published more than 30 papers, including one on morphology and information retrieval that has been cited by more than 700 other papers and was ranked by Citeseer as one of the 100 most-cited papers of the year in computer science. Dr. Krovetz has given invited talks at the American Society for Information Science and the Association for the Advancement of Artificial Intelligence symposium on Text-Based Intelligent Systems. Previously he was a scientist at the NEC Research Institute and a senior research scientist at Ask Jeeves.

René R. Lawless, EdM, is a Principal Research Associate in Research and Development at ETS. Her research has focused on the creation of measures of students' breadth and depth of vocabulary knowledge, second-language acquisition of vocabulary, evidence-centered design, and fairness across assessments. Ms. Lawless is currently working on fairness projects for cultural and linguistic minorities, for which she has coauthored multiple white papers, and is lead author of fairness guidelines for the International Test Commission.

Preface

If we are to understand the relationship between vocabulary and literacy, and support students' development of literacy, we need more powerful, precise, and meaningful assessments. In particular, assessments must have the range and flexibility to support classroom teachers as they make decisions about instruction. The germ of an idea that resulted in this book was that the authors were all engaged in programs of research on vocabulary that included creating new assessments. We thought it might be fun to pool our resources and initiate a project together, especially because we were taking different approaches and could benefit from each other's insights. As we began to talk about the dearth of appropriate resources for vocabulary assessment, we realized that fields such as educational research and measurement, linguistics, and computational linguistics approach this issue from different directions, and that blending these approaches could move policy in a productive direction. Conventional vocabulary assessments are simply not sensitive enough to assess gains in vocabulary and comprehension achieved through instruction.

The idea for a new, interdisciplinary project grew into a proposal to the American Educational Research Association's (AERA) Education Research Conference Program. Our proposal was accepted, and the conference was held at Educational Testing Service (ETS) in October 2014. So the first thing we want to do is express our gratitude to AERA for its sponsorship, to ETS for its hospitality and support, and most of all to the amazing colleagues who participated in the conference. This book would not have been possible without their contributions—reflections, discussions, and suggestions on the topics of vocabulary assessment and instruction.

The goal of the conference was to reimagine vocabulary assessment toward developing enhanced assessment practices in support of effective instruction. Conference participants represented three broad disciplines—education/measurement, linguistics, and computational linguistics—that rarely collaborated on a common vision. Within education and measurement, researchers represented classroom intervention, teacher development, early literacy, second-language learning, and large-scale assessment, with experience in major testing programs including the National Assessment for Educational Progress (NAEP), the Partnership for Assessment of Readiness for College and Careers (PARCC), and the Smarter Balanced Assessment Consortium (SBAC). Within linguistics, individuals represented psycholinguistics, lexical semantics, and language development, where the cognitive and psycholinguistic literatures support a richer set of distinctions within the construct of vocabulary than is represented in conventional vocabulary assessments. The computational linguists brought knowledge of technological solutions and methods to quantify and home in on students' vocabulary knowledge. Although individual researchers have been working on these issues, our conference created a unique opportunity to assemble relevant disciplines and benefit from their collective wisdom.

The event was conceived as a working conference where participants engaged in collaborative discussions leading to points of consensus and identified directions to proceed with future work. The conference was organized around a set of framing questions within three broad themes: defining the construct of vocabulary, assessment design, and educational impact of vocabulary assessments. Prior to the conference, participants submitted brief memoranda in response to one or more of the questions, which served as the basis of discussions. These memos and discussions culminated in the following set of recommendations:

- Vocabulary should receive greater prominence in education in the United States because it captures critical language skills that can make or break performance in reading comprehension, writing, and critical thinking.
- The construct of vocabulary should be conceptualized as including:
  - Metalinguistic awareness of words, such as understanding nuances of word meaning and use.
  - Conscious strategies for effective word learning, such as

morphological analysis and integration of word meaning and context.
  - o Tacit knowledge of generative patterns including characteristic grammatical constructions, patterns of polysemy, and morphological structure.
  - o Specific knowledge of words and phrases such as pronunciation, spelling, meanings, collocations, and connotations.
- Vocabulary assessment needs to be adapted to specific circumstances such as age, grade, and verbal proficiency; language proficiency and background (English learners/native English speakers; nonstandard dialects); and audience and purpose.
- For vocabulary assessments to support teaching and learning effectively, vocabulary knowledge needs to be measured through multiple item types and multiple modalities to assure:
  - o Measuring different kinds of lexical knowledge to fully represent the construct of vocabulary.
  - o Measuring incremental word learning both proximally and distally after instruction.
  - o Measuring both word knowledge and the ability to apply it to higher-order tasks (e.g., reading comprehension).
  - o Identifying patterns of strength or weakness that can be used to inform future instruction.
  - o Modeling effective classroom practices that teachers can use to strengthen vocabulary knowledge and build word consciousness.
- Technology can and should be used to create new, scalable forms of assessment that:
  - o Adaptively select assessment tasks through the creation of statistical models of vocabulary knowledge and word learning.
  - o Measure word knowledge and word learning dynamically within various instructional contexts.
  - o Create resources for instruction and professional development.
  - o Provide scaffolding support for at-risk students, formative (classroom) assessment, growth monitoring, and diagnostic assessment.

Using those recommendations as a template, the conference conveners (McKeown, Deane, Scott, Krovetz, and Lawless) developed this book, the goal of which is to contribute to advancements in vocabulary learning and assessment to help educators, administrators, policymakers, and researchers in better evaluating the results of vocabulary interventions and to more precisely understand the effects that vocabulary growth has on literacy outcomes. Furthermore, we hope that the book can lead to a better understanding of the outcomes of vocabulary instruction in school settings, and, in turn, to more effective implementation of vocabulary development in schools. Put another way, we aim to develop a nation of word learners!

In Chapter 1, we describe the role of vocabulary knowledge in providing key building blocks for learning in many domains and frame the problem of how the conventional use of the word *vocabulary* limits how vocabulary is taught and assessed.

In Chapter 2, we present a reconceptualization of the construct of vocabulary, drawing on perspectives from educational psychology, psycholinguistics, computational linguistics, and educational measurement. This framework encompasses multiword expressions and generative language patterns in addition to individual words.

In Chapter 3, we survey the current state of assessment, exploring the purposes of assessing vocabulary and the constructs that underlie conventional assessments. We point to the limitations of current assessments and explore what is on the horizon in state-of-the-art assessment development.

In Chapter 4, we suggest features of enhanced assessments, such as the types of words to include and a variety of item types and modalities. We discuss how to prioritize the words and word meanings that should be assessed and present a rationale for including multiword expressions and patterns of morphology (form and structure of words) and polysemy (multiple meanings of words) in vocabulary assessments.

Chapter 5 presents samples of novel assessment item types and formats for assessing various facets of vocabulary, including partial word knowledge and the ability to apply word knowledge in complex language tasks.

Chapter 6 addresses instruction and includes examples of a range of practices to strengthen students' knowledge and use of words and their ability to learn words, and to build their word consciousness. We also include suggestions for effective classroom assessment practices.

Chapter 7 turns to a discussion of the role of technology in creating adaptive and scalable assessments. This includes a discussion of dynamic assessments and tutoring systems.

Chapter 8 is essentially an annotated bibliography of resources that may be useful to educators, policymakers, and assessment developers. This includes a curated list of online resources for ideas for implementing effective vocabulary instruction, sites with tools for learning words, word games and puzzles, language blogs, reference sites specializing in words and word origins, and an annotated bibliography of published children's literature for use in developing word awareness.

We have also included a glossary of terminology because we realized that much of the vocabulary that we have used throughout the book may be unfamiliar to readers. The glossary provides a centralized location to look up the definitions of unfamiliar words that were encountered in previous chapters.

Throughout the book, we offer ample, robust examples of language constructs, assessments, instructional practices, and classroom interactions. These are intended to provide clarity and explanatory power, and to make this volume accessible to a diverse audience.

Acknowledgments

We gratefully acknowledge our colleagues who participated in the research conference on which this book is based:

Benjamin K. Bergen, University of California, San Diego
Camille Blachowicz, National Louis University
Kevyn Collins-Thompson, University of Michigan
Michael D. Coyne, University of Connecticut
William Croft, University of New Mexico
Amy C. Crosson, The Pennsylvania State University
Bonnie J. Dorr, Florida Institute for Human and Machine Cognition
Susan Leigh Flinspach, University of California, Santa Cruz
Gwen Frishkoff, Georgia State University
Elfrieda H. Hiebert, TextProject, Inc.
Michael J. Kieffer, New York University
Joshua F. Lawrence, University of California, Irvine
Diana McCallum, Institute of Education Sciences
William Nagy, Seattle Pacific University
P. David Pearson, University of California, Berkeley
Charles Perfetti, University of Pittsburgh
Jennifer Sullivan, Seneca College
Jack L. Vevea, University of California, Merced

The conference was supported by a grant from the Education Research Conference Program of the American Educational Research Association.

Contents

1. The Importance of Teaching and Assessing Vocabulary   1

*The Relationship between Vocabulary
and Reading Comprehension*   1

*The Relationship between Vocabulary
and Writing Quality*   2

*The Relationship among Expertise, Critical Thinking,
and Vocabulary Development*   3

*The Need for Greater Prominence of Vocabulary as a Topic
in American Education*   5

The Problem We Address in This Book   8

2. A New Perspective for Thinking about Vocabulary   9

The Word-Learning Burden   9

Complexities of Word Learning   11

Structural Regularities of Language   11

Tacit Knowledge of Generative Patterns   13

General Discussion of Generative Patterns   18

*The Importance of Context in Instruction
and Assessment*   19

Specific Knowledge of Words and Phrases   20

*Metalinguistic and Metacognitive Awareness of Words
and Their Properties*   22

The Role of Dictionaries in Vocabulary Learning 24
Final Thoughts 28

3. Surveying the State of Vocabulary Assessment   30

Multiple Purposes for Assessing Vocabulary 31
Issues Associated with Assessments 32
Traditional Vocabulary Assessment 34
The Receptive Assessment of Definitional Knowledge 37
*What Traditional Assessments Miss (and the Purposes
    for Which It Matters)* 38
What's on the Horizon in Assessment 40
The Impact of Recent Educational Reforms 45
*What We Do Not Yet See in Recently Developed
    Vocabulary Assessments* 50
Final Thoughts 51

4. Which Words and Word Meanings   52
   Should We Teach and Assess?

*Selecting Words, Word Patterns, and Contexts
    for Instruction* 53
*Selecting Words, Word Patterns, and Contexts
    for Assessment* 68
Final Thoughts 73

5. How Should We Assess Vocabulary?   75

Word-Learning Skill 76
Depth (or Richness) of Lexical Knowledge 82
Partial and Incremental Knowledge of Words 96
*Assessing the Impact of Vocabulary
    on Higher-Level Literacy* 103
Final Thoughts 105

6. Classroom Practices for Vocabulary Instruction   106

Establishing a Word-Conscious Classroom 107
Focused Vocabulary Instruction 119
*Building Metalinguistic Awareness
    of Generative Patterns* 126
Other Considerations 139

Aligning Instruction and Assessment   145
Final Thoughts   146

7. The Role of Technology to Support Adaptive, Flexible, and Scalable Assessments   148

   Automated Reading and Vocabulary Tutoring Systems   149
   The Technologies That Support Tutoring Systems   155
   Final Thoughts   175
   Appendix 7.1. Some Important Corpora   176

8. Resources for Developing a Nation of Word Learners   178

   Online Resources for Implementing Effective
      Vocabulary Instruction   178
   Selected Books for Developing Word Awareness   185
   Recommended Novels with Superb Gifts of Words   189
   Resources Authored by Our Conference Participants   192

Glossary   197

References   207

Index   242

CHAPTER 1

The Importance of Teaching and Assessing Vocabulary

Think of word knowledge, or vocabulary, as what you know about the words you know. That knowledge is critical not only to your mastery of the language you speak, but also to your ability to comprehend text, to learn from text, to express your thoughts in writing in coherent and convincing ways, and to engage in critical thinking. Research findings indicate, in multiple ways from myriad angles, the importance of developing strong vocabulary knowledge.

THE RELATIONSHIP BETWEEN VOCABULARY AND READING COMPREHENSION

Key to our understanding of the importance of vocabulary knowledge are numerous studies that have examined the relationship among components of reading. Some of the earliest studies analyzed factors underlying reading comprehension based on adults' assessment scores (Carroll, 1962; Davis, 1944; Hunt, 1957; Spearritt, 1972). This work indicated that word knowledge was the most significant predictor of reading comprehension.

Across the developmental span, vocabulary knowledge has been shown to play a key role in reading comprehension. For instance, Spira, Bracken, and Fischel (2005) found a relationship between kindergarten vocabulary and reading in grades 1 through 4; Snow, Tabors, Nicholson, and Kurland (1995) found that kindergarten vocabulary scores predicted reading comprehension as early as first grade; and Hart and

Risley (1995) found that the size of children's vocabulary at age 3 predicted their reading comprehension at age 9.

More recently, researchers have developed models of the reading process based on sophisticated contemporary statistical techniques. Vellutino, Tunmer, Jaccard, and Chen (2007) developed a model of reading comprehension for elementary and middle school students. This model linked reading comprehension to a variety of factors, including word identification, spelling, decoding, syntactic knowledge, vocabulary knowledge, and oral and text comprehension. However, after all these factors were accounted for, vocabulary knowledge remained an important determinant of language and reading comprehension. Cromley and Azevedo (2007) developed a model for reading comprehension among ninth graders that included such factors as background knowledge, inferences, comprehension strategies, vocabulary, and word reading. Their key finding was that vocabulary and background knowledge made the greatest contributions to comprehension.

More evidence of the relationship between vocabulary knowledge and reading comprehension comes from behavioral and neuroscience data in psychology. Studies employing both behavioral and neuroscience techniques led to Perfetti's lexical quality hypothesis, which holds that "successful comprehension depends on accessible, well-specified, and flexible knowledge of word forms and meanings" (Perfetti & Adlof, 2012, p. 12). Indeed, Perfetti and Stafura (2015) concluded that despite the complexity of comprehension processes, the lynchpin of deep comprehension is word knowledge. The role of accessible and flexible word knowledge in successful comprehension is rooted in the nature of reading. Reading is an interactive process, which means that a reader needs to coordinate lower-level processes such as word identification and higher-level processes such as transforming and connecting text statements (Rumelhart, 1994). A reader's ability to readily access the meanings of words in a text and understand their meanings flexibly is essential to keeping the reading process from breaking down (Perfetti, 2007).

THE RELATIONSHIP BETWEEN VOCABULARY AND WRITING QUALITY

Vocabulary is also related to writing quality. Stronger writers tend to produce a greater variety of words, which entails using rarer, longer, and more abstract words (Attali & Burstein, 2005; Deno, Marston, & Mirkin, 1982; Grobe, 1981; McNamara, Crossley, & McCarthy, 2009). This observation holds true across grade levels (Attali & Powers, 2008), although, of course, older students may draw on larger working vocabularies than their younger peers. Having control over a greater variety of words allows writers to express their meanings more clearly and precisely—and probably more fluently, since control of language helps free up cognitive resources needed to plan and evaluate one's own writing (McCutchen, 1996).

The particular facets of vocabulary that support writing ability change and develop as students progress through the grades. When the development of writing ability begins in the primary grades, writing quality is primarily driven by general oral language skills, as measured by tests such as the Peabody Picture Vocabulary Test (PPVT; Dunn & Dunn, 2007) (Abbott & Berninger, 1993; Dunsmuir & Blatchford, 2004; Kim et al., 2011). In later elementary school, the kinds of vocabulary that indicate strong writing ability begin to vary by genre, reflecting different expectations for different kinds of writing (Olinghouse & Graham, 2009; Olinghouse & Wilson, 2013). Vocabulary continues to play a critical role in secondary and postsecondary school writing, even though effective writing at those levels requires the writer to solve more complex, rhetorical, and conceptual problems.

The strong connection between writing quality and lexical diversity may be a by-product of a more general relationship between writing quality and linguistic fluency. One of the most influential theories of writing expertise, the capacity theory (McCutchen, 1996, 2011), posits that lack of linguistic fluency is a critical bottleneck in the development of writing expertise. According to this theory, there is a tradeoff between processes that require fluent language processing and processes that require deliberation and executive control. As a result, when language processes are less fluent, writers have fewer resources available to solve rhetorical and conceptual problems, and therefore produce lower-quality texts. Improving students' mastery of vocabulary and overall control of the language would thus seem like an important educational goal, since students who lack sufficient fluency in producing text may find themselves at a serious disadvantage when asked to solve the rhetorical and conceptual problems associated with academic writing.

THE RELATIONSHIP AMONG EXPERTISE, CRITICAL THINKING, AND VOCABULARY DEVELOPMENT

As the preceding sections indicate, vocabulary plays a crucial role in core reading and writing processes, with vocabulary size providing an important indicator of overall verbal skill. Unlike the extensive research on reading and writing, relatively little literature addresses the relationship between vocabulary and critical thinking. However, there are important reasons to suppose that vocabulary development can make it much easier for students to develop the metacognitive and metalinguistic skills they need to reason critically about their own and other people's ideas.

The literature gives us the following general picture of how expertise develops. When people develop any form of expertise, they learn new ways to categorize the world. Understanding these categorical distinctions fundamentally changes how they perceive situations within their area of expertise, which provides them with effective ways to represent and solve problems in different domains (Alexander, 2003; Boshuizen & Van de Wiel, 2014; Brown, Collins, & Duguid, 1989; Ericsson & Charness, 1994; Palmeri, Wong, & Gauthier, 2004; Sternberg, 1998). For example, chess players learn to recognize and label specific strategic and tactical concepts, sequences of moves that force an opponent to give up a piece (combinations), attacking two pieces at once (the fork), and situations where a piece cannot move without exposing a more important piece to attack (the pin). As this illustration emphasizes, there is an inherent connection between establishing new concepts and learning the labels for those concepts. Expertise depends on developing new ways to see and label the world. Thus there is a direct connection between acquiring expertise and acquiring the vocabulary that goes with it.

Experts not only learn how to categorize and solve problems in their domain; they also learn how to talk about the domain with other experts, which critically involves learning how to express those concepts in words. Education and training in a domain often include a heavy dose of domain-specific vocabulary, which involves both acquiring new technical terms and internalizing new uses and meanings for existing words. Thus as education proceeds and students develop richer conceptual understandings across a variety of domains, they must learn to use language more flexibly. Internalizing the language used to communicate about a domain is, of course, only one aspect of expertise, but it is a critical one, especially when dealing with words that have specialized meanings. For instance, words such as *combination, fork,* and *pin* have many different senses, depending on context, in ways that reflect expertise in different domains. Much of the vocabulary learning that happens in school involves words with multiple senses or with abstract meanings that have very different implications in different academic subjects. This typically academic vocabulary is at the core of vocabulary growth in the school years (Beck, McKeown, & Kucan, 2013) and is a critical prerequisite to developing expertise in the academic disciplines.

To sum up, the development of academic language goes hand in hand with developing the conceptual tools people need to think critically. Key critical thinking skills include self-reflection and the explicit representation and analysis of one's own ideas and the ideas of others, including the explicit analysis and evaluation of arguments (van Gelder,

2005). Argumentation skills are closely related to the ability to conduct oral academic conversations (Zwiers & Crawford, 2011), which depends, in turn, on mastery of academic vocabulary (Beck, McKeown, & Kucan, 2002; Francis, Rivera, Lesaux, Kieffer, & Rivera, 2006; Nagy & Townsend, 2012). Critical thinking involves forming conceptions of and talking about your own thinking, which has its own terminology, almost all of which is academic language.

THE NEED FOR GREATER PROMINENCE OF VOCABULARY AS A TOPIC IN AMERICAN EDUCATION

The well-confirmed role of word knowledge in language performance and achievement would indicate a prominent role for vocabulary in education, yet attention to vocabulary has received scant prominence in U.S. classrooms—indeed, at least until relatively recently, it has bordered on the invisible. However, recent educational reforms include a new emphasis on academic vocabulary (Common Core State Standards [CCSS]; National Governors Association Center for Best Practices & Council of Chief State School Officers [NGA & CCSSO], 2010), which may help to address this problem, although it is important to be aware of significant barriers to implementation (Fisher & Frey, 2014; Marzano & Simms, 2011; Neuman & Wright, 2015).

The lack of attention to vocabulary in American schools goes back decades. In 1978, Dolores Durkin documented a paucity of instructional time, observing that only 3% of the instruction allocated to either reading or social studies dealt with word meanings. That seemed to increase slightly in the 1980s and 1990s, with Blachowicz (1987) reporting that teachers spent 15–20% of their instructional interaction time during reading lessons on vocabulary learning; Blanton and Moorman (1990) documenting that 6% of observed reading time focused on vocabulary; and Watts (1995) recording vocabulary instruction in approximately 10% of her observations. However, a 2003 study comprising 308 hours of instruction in 23 ethnically diverse upper-elementary classrooms revealed that, on average, only 6% of each school day was devoted to vocabulary development of any kind, with only 1.4% devoted to vocabulary development in academic subjects such as math, science, art, and social studies (Scott, Jameison-Noel, & Asselin, 2003). More recently, researchers who studied 27 third-grade classrooms (Connor et al., 2014) found that teachers spent, on average, only 5 minutes per day engaged in oral language and vocabulary instruction.

Blachowicz, Fisher, Ogle, and Watts-Taffe (2006) discuss how interest in vocabulary knowledge and instruction has waxed and waned over many decades, and although research on the topic has also waxed and waned, classroom implementation has never kept pace with the resurgent periods of research in the area. Blachowicz et al. detected an interest in vocabulary heightening once again in 2006 as a result of studies that revealed a vocabulary gap between groups of children beginning in early childhood and persisting through schooling. Yet again, the authors noted, it seemed that classroom practice was not rising concomitantly.

This lack of focus on vocabulary is confirmed in a recent study of classroom instruction. Wright and Neuman (2014) observed 55 kindergarten classrooms at varying socioeconomic status (SES) levels to evaluate teachers' oral vocabulary instruction practice. They found that instruction was pretty much confined to occasional one-time, brief explanations of word meaning. They also found that there were fewer such occasions in lower-SES schools and the words addressed in those classrooms rarely represented sophisticated vocabulary beyond everyday conversational words.

The lack of attention to vocabulary seems to be at odds with teachers' recognition that vocabulary is often an obstacle because of the sizable vocabulary demands of reading materials in the classroom, especially by middle school. What may figure into this discrepancy is a tendency for teachers to think of vocabulary as separate from higher-order language processes, thus setting up an "either/or" situation in which teachers choose to focus on issues such as interpretation and critical thinking rather than vocabulary (Stahl & Nagy, 2006).

Another reason that Stahl and Nagy (2006) cite for the neglect of vocabulary is the tendency to think of vocabulary instruction as consisting of looking up definitions and writing isolated sentences containing the words. Wright and Neuman's findings confirm this, as does a study by McKeown, Beck, and Apthorp (2011), which examined transcripts from classrooms. McKeown et al.'s study was part of a larger project that evaluated the effects of a vocabulary intervention at four levels—kindergarten, first, third, and fourth grades (Apthorp et al., 2012). Randomly selected teachers in each grade were asked to audio-record a vocabulary lesson. A total of 56 lessons were provided, 30 from treatment classrooms and 26 from comparison classrooms. In lessons from the comparison classrooms, half of the talk devoted to vocabulary was the teacher providing rote information to the students, usually in the form of a brief definition. The other half of the time, teachers called on students to respond; however, the great majority of those opportunities consisted of the students responding to the teacher's request for a definition or a synonym. For less than 4% of the time were interactions more elaborated than these simple responses, such as asking students to provide a novel use of a given word or explain the word use or context. Other teachers tended to equate vocabulary instruction with spelling and had classrooms in which the only time students looked at word-level knowledge was when they learned spelling words for a weekly test.

Another reason for the discrepancy between the recognition of vocabulary as important and the instructional actions in classrooms may be that productive vocabulary instruction is hard to do. Productive instruction requires multiple encounters with contexts and is most effective if there are interactions around the contexts so that students have the opportunity to explore, play with, and reflect on word meanings and uses. Such instruction requires much more preparation time than presenting definitions—or merely having students look up the definitions themselves.

It is also the case that exactly how to carry out and sustain such instruction is not straightforward. Blachowicz and colleagues touch on this issue, saying that in their work they find that "many conscientious teachers" who want to attend to vocabulary needs are left with "many questions about how to design and implement effective instruction" (2006, p. 524). They characterize the available information for teachers on vocabulary as "rich but sometimes confusing" (p. 525). The notion of the difficulty of carrying out effective instruction is echoed through examples of activities in transcripts from McKeown and Beck's study. For example, in one classroom, the teacher launched an interaction with good potential, asking, "What famous person would you like to have a *conversation* with?" Students began to name their choices, such as John Legend or Will Smith, with eight students having turns. The teacher sometimes asked who these people were and sometimes commented about the person, but the word *conversation,* or the idea of talking to these people, never came up. Thus the potential for enriching or reinforcing the meaning of *conversation* was lost.

Likely contributing to the scarcity of effective vocabulary instruction is that resources for productive vocabulary instruction are not readily available in accessible forms. Try Googling "vocabulary lessons" and a great number of items appear—but most results are sets of commercially developed programmatic materials for purchase rather than something to which a teacher can gain immediate and cost-effective access. Many of the resources that are freely available focus on giving teachers ways to introduce and practice definitions. Many of these provide appealing, game-like formats, but the content is limited to definitional information (see, e.g., *www.proteacher.org/c/694_vocabulary_lesson_ideas.html*).

Another situation that makes it difficult to find effective materials is that teachers often have a set of words that they want students to learn, words that may come from what is being read in class, for example. Seeking instruction for a particular set of words further restricts availability of rich materials. The other important consideration is that, compared to focusing on definitions, productive vocabulary instruction occupies much more of a classroom's most precious commodity—time.

THE PROBLEM WE ADDRESS IN THIS BOOK

As our brief review indicates, strong vocabulary knowledge makes it easier for students to understand what they read, to express their ideas effectively in writing, and to think critically about what they have learned. And yet, very little effective vocabulary instruction seems to take place in classrooms. Moreover, the current conventional use of the word *vocabulary* does not capture what learners need to know about words and word learning. Vocabulary is taken to mean the stock of words that one can define—like a dictionary in our heads. That concept has limited the kind of instruction that is presented to most students to support their vocabulary development, and, as we will see later in this book, it has limited the kinds of assessments that are used to evaluate students' vocabulary development.

In contrast to the "dictionary in your head" notion, research in recent decades has led to the understanding that our mental organization of vocabulary knowledge is a network of connections among words and experiences built from multiple encounters with words in meaningful contexts—that is, contexts that reveal information about a word's meaning (Perfetti, 2007; Reichle & Perfetti, 2003). The greater the variety and meaningfulness of semantic encounters, the more likely that the semantic representations one develops will foster successful, efficient comprehension of text (Nagy & Scott, 2000; Perfetti & Hart, 2002).

The simple fact of the situation is that teaching and educational assessment practice have not caught up with the research literature. Far too often, teaching and assessment are still dominated by a paradigm that reduces vocabulary knowledge to a list of words (with associated definitions). We contend that vocabulary assessment can be made more nuanced—that the way we measure vocabulary can be made to reflect more closely the rich experiences that build effective word knowledge. If instructional and assessment practice work together, giving teachers a much richer framework within which to conceptualize vocabulary instruction, it may be possible to bring the results of the last 30 years of vocabulary research more strongly into practice.

CHAPTER 2

A New Perspective
for Thinking about Vocabulary

The *Merriam-Webster Collegiate Dictionary* (2014) defines vocabulary as "a list or collection of words or of words and phrases usually alphabetically arranged and explained or defined" or as "a sum or stock of words employed by a language, group, individual, or work or in a field of knowledge." But there is much more to vocabulary than a list of words to be learned. A realistic understanding of vocabulary requires that we understand just how complex vocabulary knowledge actually is.

In this chapter, we offer a new perspective on vocabulary that highlights the extent to which effective vocabulary knowledge comprises knowledge of language patterns, structures, and properties that go across words. We discuss: three generative patterns, morphology, syntax, and semantics; the influence of context on word learning; systematic properties of words and of multiword phrases; and the importance of metacognitive aspects of vocabulary knowledge. We conclude by examining the role of dictionaries in vocabulary learning, showing why, given the patterns and properties of words covered in the rest of the chapter, dictionaries are inadequate for the task.

THE WORD-LEARNING BURDEN

While a mastery of vocabulary knowledge is not acquired by just memorizing a list of words and their definitions, it is true that the size of vocabulary matters. The number of words needed for college and career readiness is a matter of debate, but a reasonable estimate is probably between 14,000 and 20,000 root words (Biemiller, 2001; Stahl, 1998). If anything, this estimate is a gross underestimate since it does not consider derived (i.e., morphologically complex) words formed by adding prefixes and suffixes to root words; compound words formed by combining two or more root words; and multiword expressions with independent meanings that cannot be predicted from the meaning of their component words. Nor does it consider the fact that common words can convey many different meanings, depending on context.

It is equally important to note that the challenge posed by vocabulary size escalates as students move through school. For example, native English-speaking first-grade students are estimated to know approximately 3,100 root words (and about 10,000 words total, including inflected and derived forms, plus idioms). By fifth grade, the number rises to 7,500 root words and about 40,000 words total, including inflected and derived forms, plus idioms (Anglin, Miller, & Wakefield, 1993). The core English oral vocabulary consists of at least a few thousand word families (Nation, 2006; Schmitt & Schmitt, 2014), in which approximately 5,000 individual words are needed to achieve a 96% vocabulary coverage of the words that appear in oral conversations (Adolphs & Schmitt, 2003). Complex morphology is rare, and prefixed forms are especially infrequent.

Even before most native speakers of English enter school, they are immersed in an English-speaking environment that presents them with multiple opportunities to learn words in this core lexicon. These words tend to be concrete and apply to people, things, and activities that are part of children's everyday lives. Children pick up words like *mother, father, ball, baby, dog, run,* and *sleep* readily because they hear them so often, and the words describe what is right in front of them.

However, starting in fourth grade, most of the words we acquire are learned by reading. This written vocabulary is qualitatively and quantitatively different from the vocabulary we use in everyday speech. Words that characterize written language tend to be abstract, without concrete referents in the physical world. Thus learning them relies on language itself rather than familiar surroundings. The total number of words is significantly larger, but most words are much, much rarer (Leech & Rayson, 2014). Words that appear primarily in writing, and not in informal oral usage, generally appear less than once every million words. This means that, during the school years, students have to master tens of thousands of words. Over the course of a 10-year period, a student may encounter each of these words once or a few times and then not see it again until they have read another million words.

COMPLEXITIES OF WORD LEARNING

The size of the vocabulary is not what makes word learning hard. It is the complexity of what people have to learn. Every word has at least one pronunciation and at least one spelling; but the spelling is not always phonetic, and sometimes there are alternative spellings or alternate pronunciations. In addition, some words can be divided into component parts—morphemes—such as prefixes and suffixes (*un-, re-, mis-, -ion, -er, -ize*), combining forms (*bio-, hydro-, -phobic, -logy*), and bound roots (e.g., *spect* [*inspect, spectacles, spectator*] or *consc* [*subconscious, unconscious, conscience*]). Many words can also be combined into higher-level units or multiword expressions, such as *hot dog, Civil War, put up with,* and *abject poverty.* Moreover, the same word can have many different meanings. When those meanings are related, such as a physical foundation for building and the foundation of a relationship, we call the resulting situation *polysemy*; when the meanings are not related, such as a river *bank* and a financial *bank,* we call the resulting situation *homonymy.*

These are all complexities of form or of the form–meaning correspondence. There are also complexities of meaning and usage. People may know how to use a word in a sentence without knowing exactly what it means. Conversely, people may know, roughly, what a word means without being able to use it correctly in sentence context. To develop a college-level vocabulary, students must master all of these complexities for the tens of thousands of words that they will encounter less than once for every million words they read (Nagy & Herman, 1987). Vocabulary learning would be overwhelming if people had to learn every word separately—but they do not. There is a structure to English vocabulary, and that structure creates redundancies in how words are understood and used. When language users with sensitivity to this structure encounter a new word in context, they are often already primed to learn it.

STRUCTURAL REGULARITIES OF LANGUAGE

In contemporary linguistic theory, the lexicon is understood to mean people's knowledge about vocabulary, including structural regularities about the way words are used. In early linguistic theories, the lexicon was basically thought of as a list of unrelated words, much like the definition of vocabulary given at the beginning of this chapter. This view is still reflected in many educational circles. More recent linguistic theories, however, emphasize that the lexicon has structure and generative mechanisms, which provide predictable patterns that reduce the burden on the learner. These generative mechanisms include a series of rules that make word meanings more flexible and more easily extended to new contexts (Pustejovsky, 1998). For example, many nouns can refer to either an *opening* or the physical structure that defines an *opening*—we can *walk through the door* and we can *paint the door*. In the first case, we are talking about a doorway and in the second, we refer to a physical door. The same pattern applies to *crawled through the window* and *broke the window* and to a whole series of similar examples. A comparable pattern applies to the meanings of verbs like *bake,* which can be used equally in phrases like *bake a potato* and *bake a cake.* In the first case, the potato undergoes a change of state but in the second case, the cake is coming into existence as a result of the baking. Similarly, words for locations often refer to an organization associated with that location (e.g., *I visited New York* vs. *New York raised the taxes yesterday*).

Learning a large vocabulary is an incredible achievement, and linguistic theory is centrally concerned with explaining how people manage that accomplishment. The key idea is that there are patterns regarding how words are constructed and used and that those patterns are widely shared among words. Thus people do not learn words in isolation; they learn them in the context of larger linguistic patterns. These include:

- *Morphological patterns (word families)*—how words are formed from their constituent parts.
- *Syntactic patterns (grammatical constructions)*—how words are fitted into a sentence (Goldberg, 1995a, 1995b).
- *Semantic patterns (polysemy)*—how word meanings are extended to further describe situations and senses.

As we gain repeated exposures to a word, we not only gain knowledge about the specific word or phrase, we also build up tacit knowledge of these generative patterns, which can be applied to new words, making them much easier to understand and remember. One of the great challenges of literacy education is that some students enter school with much of this learning machinery already in place, while others do not. More advanced students do not need much help in building their vocabulary. They want to read, and the more they read, the more quickly and efficiently they build their knowledge of the language; but some students start out with smaller English vocabularies, less tacit knowledge of academic language, and less metacognitive knowledge that could help them leverage what they already know. If we want to help these students, we must be sensitive to the structure of vocabulary knowledge and provide instruction that helps students understand this structure. People's tacit knowledge of this structure is a powerful engine for learning, and educators need to understand how it works. When people think of vocabulary in terms of lists of words and reduce word learning to the task of memorizing definitions, they are actually making the learner's job more difficult.

TACIT KNOWLEDGE OF GENERATIVE PATTERNS

> By trade he's a corn-chandler [said one character]. *And what*
> *is a corn-chandler?* Peggy asked crossly . . .
>   Lady Mear said: *A man who chandles corn, I suppose.*
> *Even my underrated intelligence can work that out.*
>   —BARBARA WORSLEY-GOUGH (1932, p. 149)

Generative patterns—whether morphological, syntactic, or semantic—facilitate inference and allow us to resolve ambiguity by appealing to the contextual information surrounding the word. For example, if a word is ambiguous between a people and a language, and the preceding word is *speak*, the word refers to a language. If a word such as *orange* is ambiguous between a substance and a color, and the preceding word is *vivid*, the word refers to a color. These kinds of patterns make language a much more flexible instrument than it would be otherwise. Lacking a word that expresses precisely what we have in mind, we have a wide range of resources that allows us to adapt the words we do know to the purpose at hand.

It is important to note that all aspects of meaning participate in tacit generative patterns (including connotation as well as denotation). These patterns range from very broad syntactic patterns to individual patterns of word combination (*collocations*) that implicitly support inferences about what specific words mean. For example, in the word pattern *abject* _____, the word that fills in the blank often has a negative connotation, with words such as *misery, poverty,* or *failure*. These kinds of inferences also tend to interact strongly with one's background knowledge about the world. For example, when a person begins a book, what are they beginning? The expected answer is reading, but the sentence never said so explicitly. More detailed real-world knowledge can modify such inferences. For instance, if we say *J. K. Rowling began a book*, the assumption is that she began writing it. In other words, tacit generative patterns support inference. Such inferences may draw upon knowledge of the words, how the words are combined, and the larger textual and social context in which they appear.

We now discuss three major patterns that allow generative learning to occur: morphological patterns (prefixes, roots, and suffixes), syntactic patterns (grammatical constructions), and semantic patterns (regular polysemy).

Morphological Patterns (Word Families)

As we build our knowledge of English, we learn that we can make a plural form by adding the letter *s*, and that we can convert a verb to past tense by adding *-ed*. Similarly, we learn that *un-*, *non-*, and *in-* negate the word they are added to, and that *-ion* turns a verb into a noun. Morphological patterns like these enable people to infer the meanings and grammatical properties of words they have never seen. That is, words with a common root form word families, and the meaning of each word in the family can be inferred by combining the meaning of the root with the meaning of the prefixes and suffixes attached to that root. For instance, none of the words derived from the root verb *interpret* should be particularly hard to understand. Like many other nouns ending in *-er*, an *interpreter* is an agent that interprets. Like any other noun ending in *-ion*, an *interpretation* is what results by performing the action named by the verb to which the suffix has been attached. Similarly, *misinterpret* involves a failure of the action, like other verbs beginning with *mis-*, and *reinterpret* involves repetition or duplication, like other verbs beginning with *re-*. As long as we know the meaning of the root and are familiar with the morphological pattern, we can infer the meanings of new words by analogy.

The ability to use morphology to recognize new words is particularly valuable when learning written or academic vocabulary. According to Anglin et al. (1993), one out of three words that students encounter for the first time is a derivational variant of a word they already know (and about half of the total if we include compounds). Similarly, Sullivan (2006) indicates that the majority of words acquired between the fourth and 12th grades are morphologically complex (i.e., an inflected word form, a compound, or a morphological derivative). As with many linguistic phenomena, a small number of common elements (in English, about 20 prefixes and 30 suffixes) accounts for the majority of derived forms (Graves, 2004; Krovetz, 1993). However, this observation may be misleading by itself, since knowing the affixes is not enough information to infer the meaning of a word; one must also know the meaning of the root word from which it was formed. To engage in morphological problem solving, you need to know the parts of the puzzle. For example, knowing the meaning of the prefix *mis-* is likely to help a third grader work out the meaning of *misunderstand*, but is less likely to prove helpful for *misapprehension*. The issue is further complicated by the fact that the relationship between a word and an affix may apply only for a particular sense of the word. For example, *gravitation* only applies to *gravity* in the sense of force of gravity, not in the sense of seriousness (gravity of a crime).

Syntactic Patterns

The regular patterns by which words are combined—syntactic patterns or grammatical constructions—are closely linked to word meaning. Some of these patterns are very general, such as the relationship between the active voice (*X greeted Y*) and passive voice (*Y was greeted by X*). Others apply to a narrower range of meanings. For instance, a sentence pattern like *X pulled Y out of Z* can be generalized to nearly any action verb that can be extended to mean causing motion. Thus we can understand sentences such as *The carpenter hammered the nail into the wood,* or even *Grandma tickled the children into bed.* Combined with other patterns, such as a metaphorical extension from motion to communication, the pattern can be extended to other types of verbs, producing expressions like *torture the secret out of someone.* The literature on grammatical constructions (Goldberg, 1995a, 1995b; Hoffmann & Trousdale, 2013) emphasizes the idea that words can be recruited into a construction by analogy with words that are already there. As a result, a great deal can be inferred about a word's usage and meaning from the grammatical contexts in which it appears.

It is precisely this feature of grammatical constructions that makes a poem like Lewis Carroll's "Jabberwocky" (Carroll & Tenniel, 1872) communicate effectively, even when most of the words are nonsense words (by definition, unknown to the reader):

> 'Twas brillig, and the slithy toves
> Did gyre and gimble in the wabe;
> All mimsy were the borogoves,
> And the mome raths outgrabe.

We know from morphology and syntax that *slithy, mimsy,* and *mome* are adjectives—and we know that *brillig* describes an environmental condition such as time of day (Lewis's intended meaning), that *toves* are living, moving creatures, and that a *wabe* is a place, and so on. For that matter, later in the poem, Carroll (Carroll & Tenniel, 1872) writes:

> One, two! One, two! And through and through
> The vorpal blade went snicker-snack!
> He left it dead, and with its head
> He went galumphing back.

A combination of morphological patterns and constraints on grammatical constructions makes it pretty clear that *snicker-snack* is the sound the blade makes and that *galumphing* is a manner of motion. In fact, *galumph* communicates so clearly that it has been adopted into the English language as meaning "to move in a clumsy manner."

Another pattern by which words combine results in what we can call "multiword expressions." For instance, compound nouns can be created by combining a modifying noun with a head noun (e.g., *bookstore, chessboard, fireman, houseboat*); phrasal verbs can be formed by combining a verb with an adverbial particle (e.g., *slow down, drink up, look up*); and idioms can be modified according to specific patterns (*kick the bucket* and *kicked the bucket,* but not *kick the buckets* or *kick the pail*). Multiword expressions are an important topic in their own right, as they are simultaneously syntactic combinations of two or more words and lexical content. Anglin et al. (1993) estimate that idioms and compounds (two major types of multiword expressions) comprise 25% of the total vocabulary, and that is probably an underestimate (a point we develop further below).

Semantic Patterns (Polysemy)

Polysemy—multiple but related meanings of the same word—exhibits regular patterns by which we extend word meanings, such as *door* meaning either a physical door or a doorway, as mentioned above. There is a large inventory of such regularities. For example, it is common for a word to mean both "a people" and "a language" (e.g., *English, Spanish, Chinese, Hungarian,* and many others). It is also common to have an ambiguity between a natural kind (something that occurs naturally such as flowers, elements, and minerals) and a color. Thus *violet, lavender, gold, silver, peach, amber, turquoise, cream,* and others can refer to a substance as well as a color associated with that substance. We can form verbs from nouns that name tools (e.g., *comb, brush,* and *mop*). These kinds of patterns fall into three major categories:

1. *Metonymy,* which is using the name of an object or concept to refer to a related object, such as referring to a businessperson as a *suit*.
2. *Metaphor,* in which concepts from one domain are applied to a different domain by analogy, such as *consume,* having a literal meaning of "use up," being applied more abstractly, such as to something that consumes attention. Such systems of conceptual metaphor play a key role in language (Gibbs, 2006; Lakoff & Johnson, 1980). For instance, words relevant to *war* have

extended senses that apply to the domain of argumentation: *he attacked their position; she demolished the argument; the criticism was right on target; they shot down everything I said.*
3. *Specialization (or generalization)*, where a word is applied more narrowly or more loosely than before. For instance, the word *alien* (meaning foreign or strange) has specialized meanings in which it means a noncitizen (i.e., foreigners and resident aliens), or in which it can mean a being from another planet.

Polysemy, like other generative patterns, varies in productivity. Some forms of polysemy, such as those discussed above, are highly productive. Practically any word for a substance can be used to describe a color, as long as the substance has a characteristic color. Other patterns are less productive, but still support inferences about newly encountered words. It is obvious enough, for example, if one reads *The captain ordered all hands to appear on deck* or *The ship went down with all hands,* that *hands* must refer to *sailors,* even though no other body part term is used in exactly that way.

Polysemy is one of the most important ways that the vocabulary grows. Sullivan (2006) observes that between fourth and 12th grades,

the number of new polysemous word meanings that students know increases exponentially, whereas the acquisition of new word meanings through less productive mechanisms is very gradual.

GENERAL DISCUSSION OF GENERATIVE PATTERNS

Interactions between Different Forms of Generative Knowledge

The previous section discussed morphology, syntactic patterns, and polysemy in isolation. There are several reasons to discuss their interaction. First, research suggests that instruction that integrates these types of information is more effective; for example, Bowers, Kirby, and Deacon (2010) found that teaching about morphology is more effective when embedded in broader literacy instruction. Second, we can show that generative patterns for morphology and polysemy apply not just to individual words, but also to multiword expressions. Third, by discussing the interactions among types of generative patterns, teachers can hope to increase metalinguistic awareness—the student's knowledge of linguistics structure—which supports their development of more effective strategies both for word learning and for reading comprehension.

Morphology interacts with other generative patterns because prefixes and suffixes can be related via the same types of relationships that hold between individual words. For example, prefixes and suffixes can display homonymy or polysemy. *In-* can be used in the sense "not" (*inappropriate*) or "in" (*inside, inpatient*). *De-* can be used to mean "remove" (*debone*) or "reduce" (*devalue*). The suffix *-er* can be used to refer to a person who performs an action (*teach/teacher*) or to a thing used to carry the action out (*toast/toaster*). The word *driver* can be used with both senses.

We see the same types of polysemy with multiword expressions that we do with individual words. For instance:

- *Milky Way*: either a type of candy bar, or the galaxy we live in (homonymy—very different).
- *Garbage collector*: either a person who picks up the trash, or a computer program that recycles memory that is no longer being used (metaphor).
- *New York*: either a location or a political entity (systematic polysemy).

Multiword expressions can also take prefixes and suffixes, following exactly the same patterns observed with individual words; thus from *New York*, we can form the phrase *New Yorker* (like *London/*

Londoner); similarly, from *East Timor,* we can form *East Timorese* (like *Vietnam/Vietnamese*).

Tacit Generative Patterns and Incidental Word Learning

Implicit in our discussion is the idea that knowledge of tacit generative patterns underlies incidental word learning. Incidental word learning has been extensively discussed in the literature since it involves the bulk of the word learning that happens for students who acquire a college-ready vocabulary. Swanborn and de Glopper's (1999) meta-analysis of incidental word-learning studies indicates that, for most students, acquisition of new vocabulary is incremental and partial, with proficient students typically learning enough to pass a test on approximately 15% of the new words they encounter during reading. There is evidence from psychological (psycholinguistic) studies of language learning that a single exposure to a word can generate a representation of what it means in its sentence context, although this effect primarily occurs with high-quality (highly constraining) sentence contexts (Borovsky, Elman, & Kutas, 2012). There is thus clear evidence that students will learn vocabulary more effectively if they have developed strong linguistic knowledge that supports this kind of tacit learning. But as we discuss in the next chapter, one should not conclude from this evidence that the direct teaching of generative patterns is an effective approach.

THE IMPORTANCE OF CONTEXT IN INSTRUCTION AND ASSESSMENT

As our discussion of generative mechanisms suggests, vocabulary is not something that we naturally learn in isolation. We learn our vocabulary from context, but often, when we are directly taught vocabulary, words are not presented within a context but instead as isolated items in a list. We are typically expected to learn how words and context work together to create meaning on our own, without any support.

Moreover, in natural contextual learning situations, individual contexts provide clues to the meaning of an unknown word to a greater or lesser extent. Thus multiple encounters with a word in a variety of contexts is typically needed in order to learn word meaning from context. Evidence of the benefits of multiple encounters has appeared in the literature for a long time (e.g., McKeown, Beck, Omanson, & Pople, 1985). Here we discuss some more recent examples. Bolger, Balass, Landen, and Perfetti (2008) provided learners with either varied contexts that contained an unfamiliar word or repeated exposures to the same context. They also explored the effect of adding definitions to both conditions. They found that varied contexts led to better learning and that adding definitions enhanced both conditions. Frankenberg-Garcia (2012) also investigated the impact of using a single context versus multiple contexts and the impact of using a dictionary in combination with the contexts. Her study used contexts drawn from existing language corpora (large collections of texts; singular corpus) to support improvements in vocabulary comprehension and production for English learners. She found that the presentation of words used in multiple contexts was at least as useful in helping students learn word meanings as looking up dictionary definitions. Moreover, using examples drawn from a large corpus was particularly helpful when students were asked to correct the usage of words that they understood but frequently misused (Frankenberg-Garcia, 2012, p. 289). Interestingly, she had to consult three different corpora in order to find appropriate instances for her experiment, which indicates the challenge of identifying rich contexts that will best promote student learning. Identifying rich contexts is one of the aims of current research, which we discuss further in Chapter 7.

Learners who have developed a love of reading for pleasure and have a strong enough command of the oral vocabulary can use repeated exposures to "flesh out" meanings of new words. Less motivated readers are much less likely to do so. Therefore, it may be particularly important to provide less avid readers with many rich contexts (McKeown, 1985)—that is, contexts that are richly informative about a word's morphological, syntactic, and semantic properties—and to provide opportunities to interrogate and respond to the contexts.

Currently, vocabulary assessments do not assess how quickly or easily students are able to infer new word meanings from context. We do not know for certain whether this is a skill that can be developed through instruction or whether it is largely a by-product of stronger language and reading skills. As things now stand, the current practices in vocabulary instruction and assessment do not make a sufficient connection between our ability to learn new words and our ability to understand what we read. As a field, we do not know the average ability or variations of abilities that students need in order to make these connections, and we do not have grade-appropriate instruments to measure that ability in anything but a superficial way.

SPECIFIC KNOWLEDGE OF WORDS AND PHRASES

Beyond tacit generative patterns, the process of learning word meanings requires the learner to acquire a wide range of specific facts about words. It is clear that when we have repeated exposures to specific senses of a word, we acquire knowledge about that sense incrementally (Nagy,

Anderson, & Herman, 1987). But we know relatively little about the details, in part because vocabulary knowledge is complex and involves multiple but related phenomena that can be difficult to isolate or fully distinguish in practice. Ideally, when someone has fully mastered a word, he or she knows (at least tacitly):

- How to pronounce a word (and thus things like how many syllables it has, and what it rhymes with).
- How to spell it.
- How many meanings it has and, if it has more than one meaning, how they are related.
- And for each meaning:
  - Its syntactic category or part of speech (e.g., noun or verb).
  - Its syntactic subcategories, such as the distinction between transitive and intransitive verbs (i.e., verbs with or without a direct object) or between count and mass nouns (*droplets* vs. *water*).
  - Its component morphemes (thus *disintegration* contains the root *integr-*, the prefix *dis-*, the [compound] suffix *-ation*).
  - How it is related to other words from the same word family (as *disintegration* is related to *integral, integrate,* and *disintegrate*).
  - Any idiom, collocation (e.g., *strong tea* but not *powerful tea*), or multiword expression (e.g., *hot dog* but not *warm dog*) in which it commonly appears.
  - Its register—for instance, *adolescent* is more academic than *teenager,* and *insect* is more academic than *bug.*
  - Its connotations—for instance, *steadfast* has a positive connotation. *Stubborn* is negative, but not as negative as *pigheaded.*
  - The major semantic category to which it belongs (e.g., a *convertible* is a car, from which we can infer other category memberships such as a *convertible* is a vehicle; a *convertible* is a physical object).
  - Other semantic relationships between words (e.g., a *car* has a *motor*; people drive or ride in a *car*; most *cars* have four wheels). This includes a variety of relationships such as antonyms: *hot* is the opposite of *cold.*
  - Selectional preferences (e.g., the object of the verb *to drink* should denote something liquid).
  - Other semantic constraints (e.g., *corpse* is used with people, and *carcass* with animals).

The kinds of knowledge learners have about the words they know can be presented in lists such as the one above, but a list does not reflect how information is arranged in our mental lexicon. Rather, our word knowledge is more like a complex network of connections among words that have features or associations in common. For example, if students learn the word *adolescent,* they might fit it into their network between *child* and *adult,* but also connect it to boy, girl, and to words such as *maturity, juvenile,* and ideas such as stages of development.

Individual words make up a large part of our vocabulary, but we also need to consider multiword expressions (MWEs), including compounds (*washing machine, hot dog*), phrasal verbs (*butter up, figure out*), idioms (*kick the bucket, cut to the chase*), and named entities (*United Nations, New York*). Although MWEs are important vocabulary elements, it is difficult to obtain basic information about what MWEs exist and about their frequency in English (Wray, 2002). As Wray also points out, even the terminology is variable, including such terms as "fixed expressions" and "formulaic language." Yet their importance is clear, since by the most conservative estimates there are tens of thousands of MWEs in English and they comprise at least 5% of running text (Moon, 1998), and probably much more, depending on genre (Conrad & Biber, 2004). The importance of MWEs is reflected in the wording of the CCSS for Language (NGA & CCSSO, 2010), which specify that students should "acquire and use accurately a range of general academic and domain-specific words *and phrases* [emphasis added] sufficient for reading, writing, speaking, and listening at the college and career readiness level."

Relatively little is known about how MWEs are learned and which ones should be taught. Given these complexities, it is far from clear how individuals move from initial learning to mastery, what the intermediate stages look like, or how those stages differ for students who are on track to achieve mastery, compared to students who are likely to lag behind.

METALINGUISTIC AND METACOGNITIVE AWARENESS OF WORDS AND THEIR PROPERTIES

A consistent theme in this chapter, and indeed throughout this book, is that the complexity of word learning requires a range and variety of knowledge, including the tacit knowledge of patterns. Two other types of knowledge essential for learning new words are metalinguistic and metacognitive knowledge. These types of knowledge refer to a learner's conscious awareness of knowledge and processes and the manipulation of that awareness to solve cognitive problems. Metalinguistic knowledge refers specifically to understandings about language, such as awareness of how words work in English and the ability to reflect on and manipulate that awareness. Metacognitive knowledge embodies the use of general cognitive processes involving strategic and procedural knowledge (Nagy, 2007; Nagy & Scott, 2000).

Shoe: © 2015 MacNelly, Inc. Distributed by King Features Syndicate Inc.
Reprinted by permission.

Metacognitive knowledge involves strategies such as cross-checking sources of information and activating background knowledge, which supports students' ability to recognize inconsistencies in language use and draw inferences about words. Thus metacognitive knowledge allows a learner to apply metalinguistic knowledge flexibly, to understand, for example, which sense of a word is appropriate in a particular context or recognize when specific word knowledge is necessary for comprehension.

No matter how large their reading vocabularies, students will routinely encounter words in print that they have never seen before. Both metacognitive and metalinguistic awareness are fundamental aspects of word learning needed to address this problem (Scott, Nagy, & Flinspach, 2008). For example, imagine a reader encountering the following sentence: *When they looked at their seat assignments, they knew that their trip was off to an auspicious start.* The reader might immediately understand that *auspicious* is describing something about the way in which the trip begins and that it connects to what seats they were assigned. Knowledge of seat assignments might then be drawn upon, with the reader considering possibilities including first class to coach class. If the reader recalls encountering the phrase *auspicious occasion* in relation to ceremonial events, this might prompt the realization that something *auspicious* must be something good, and thus the reader might hypothesize that the seat assignments were good ones. In turn, reflection on this encounter may add to the reader's understanding of *auspicious* as something reflecting good fortune.

Scott, Skobel, and Wells (2008) compared metalinguistic awareness to music or art appreciation. For example, it is easy to enjoy good music without metacognitive reflection on the elements involved. However, when listeners have knowledge about how the musician has combined elements to create a song, they develop a deeper understanding and appreciation of the composition. Being aware of the patterns and chords allows one to notice them in different songs and to use that knowledge to create new compositions. Similarly, an awareness of word patterns provides a parallel deeper understanding and appreciation of words that is central to word learning.

Metalinguistic awareness gives rise to the strategic knowledge that word learning requires, given the coordination of complex information necessary to that process. Proficient word learning calls for integrating multiple sources of information, evaluating their plausibility, and orchestrating metalinguistic knowledge with comprehension monitoring and other higher-level skills required to construct a coherent representation of a text. Because of the limitations of each potential source of information about a new word, learners must be able to apply word-learning strategies in combination. For instance, the use of a strategy such as morphological decomposition may supply only partial and not necessarily helpful information about the meaning of a new word. Consider a student reading that *the crowd at the rally became vociferous.* She might use knowledge of the root, *voc,* to understand that *vociferous* has something to do with speaking, but translating that context into "the crowd was speaking" would not capture the meaning. The student would need to combine the idea of speaking with her knowledge about the behavior of crowds to infer that the crowd became boisterously noisy. Thus students must learn to be flexible and reflective in applying their knowledge of language. When comprehension is the goal, students also need to coordinate word-learning strategies with a sophisticated level of comprehension monitoring. This strategic control over a variety of language processes will help them leverage what they know as they encounter new words.

These issues are important not just in comprehension but in production as well. Good writers will choose their words carefully, tailoring them for the intended audience, and leveraging what they know about connotation and inference as part of lexical choice.

THE ROLE OF DICTIONARIES IN VOCABULARY LEARNING

The perspective we have been developing requires us to reconsider the role of dictionaries in vocabulary learning. Dictionaries are the standard vocabulary resource used by teachers, students, professionals, and the general public. They are deeply embedded in our culture, but their successful use requires very high levels of metalinguistic awareness. In fact, dictionaries were not created to teach word meanings. Dictionaries were created to catalog the words in the language for the purpose of reference but not instruction per se (Landau, 1984). Over time, dictionaries were adapted to a wider range of purposes such as maintaining a historical record of the development of vocabulary (*Oxford English Dictionary;* Murray, 1884) or bilingual dictionaries to help with translation. The information contained in dictionaries and the conventions used to structure dictionary entries grew gradually, with an emphasis on achieving accuracy and completeness of the information presented—within the space constraints imposed by a particular dictionary's audience and publisher. As a result, the dictionary format tends toward brevity and presupposes a great deal of metalinguistic knowledge.

This point is worth expanding on. By definition, a dictionary must capture a great deal of specific information about each word. Learners must be able to use this information effectively. This means, for instance, that they must be able to identify the correct definition for the word they are looking up and that they must be able to know how to use all of the ancillary information that is supplied alongside the definition, such as syllable boundaries and pronunciation guides; part of speech information; information about roots, prefixes, and suffixes; lists of common collocations; or example sentences. Much of this information is very difficult for novice learners to use. Roughly speaking, the more

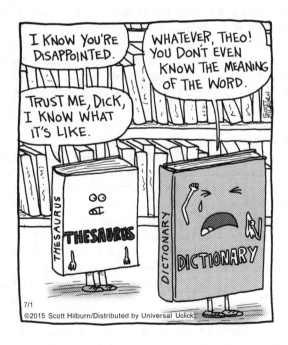

Copyright ©2015 Scott Hilburn/Distributed by Universal Uclick.
Reprinted by permission.

accurate and complete a dictionary is, the higher the level of metalinguistic knowledge that it requires.

Yet even a very complete dictionary may not express all the information the lexicographer would like to communicate. No dictionary captures all of the multiword expressions used in English; there are too many, appearing in too many contexts and domains. Dictionaries also tend to be inconsistent in dividing a word into its different senses. When word meanings are very different from each other (as with *river bank* and *savings bank*), people will agree they are different, but when word meanings are related to each other, people will disagree about whether the two senses differ (Panman, 1982). For example, does the sense of *compatible* differ if we are describing *compatible people* versus *compatible theories* versus *compatible software*?

As a consequence, in any given dictionary, some words will have related senses separated into two distinct entries, some words will use only one sense to cover the same ground, and some words will be defined with an additional remark (e.g., *waltz*—[the music of] a type of dance). Very different decisions may be made about these issues in different dictionaries. Each dictionary must establish its own priorities and conventions about handling difficult cases, and interpreting the results can be difficult for a novice with little metalinguistic awareness. Consider morphologically related words, for instance. In a large reference dictionary, the word *teacher* may be listed separately (with a cross-reference back to *teach*). In a more compressed dictionary, the existence of *teacher* may be reduced to the notation -*er* near the end of the entry for *teach*. In effect, such a dictionary reduces the number of entries by requiring a higher level of metalinguistic knowledge from its users.

These kinds of issues can cause a dictionary either to be overwhelming if the information in an entry is long and complex, or potentially misleading to someone who is in the early stages of developing English literacy if information has been left out to make the entry more concise. For example, students may produce sentences like *My family erodes a lot* and *Mrs. Morrow stimulated the soup* because they only use a fragment of a dictionary definition as the meaning of the word, such as "eat out" for *erode*, or "stir up" for *stimulate* (Miller & Gildea, 1987; Scott & Nagy, 1997). This problem may be exacerbated in shorter dictionaries and lexicons, which leave out information about usage and collocational patterns. For example, the word *ameliorate* is defined in WordNet (Fellbaum, 1998) as part of the synonym set *better, improve, amend,* and *ameliorate*. However, the sample sentences provided—*The editor improved the manuscript* (for the transitive usage), and *The weather improved* (for the intransitive usage)—only work for the word *improve*. We cannot naturally say *We ameliorated the weather* or *The weather ameliorated.* The verb requires a different object—a problem or something that can be construed as a problem. Such quirks are not unusual, but they are hard to address without including large numbers of example sentences. As mentioned earlier, dictionaries are more useful as an aid to comprehension than in selecting which words to use in writing (Frankenberg-Garcia, 2012).

All of this helps to clarify exactly why "common sense" can be problematic when it comes to teaching and assessing vocabulary knowledge. It might seem like common sense to teach vocabulary by asking students to memorize lists of words and definitions and to assess vocabulary by checking whether students can match the right words with the right definition, but a list of words and definitions is a bare-bones dictionary, and like any such dictionary, successful use requires a lot of metalinguistic knowledge. This explains why students, who often lack that kind of metalinguistic knowledge, can have many problems learning words from dictionary definitions. These problems have been demonstrated in several studies, as described below.

Miller and Gildea (1985) examined how students used dictionary definitions and observed that students typically ignored grammatical information, looked at the wrong meaning of a word (or even a different definition entirely), and tended to extract only part of the information in a definition while ignoring other components that were necessary for correct comprehension and production. For example, the definition for the word *transitory,* "passing soon or quickly," yielded sentences such as *The train was transitory.* Scott and Nagy (1997) tested fourth- and sixth-grade students' ability to extract information from dictionary definitions to see whether the format of the definition affected this ability. They found that extracting information from definitions was a significant problem for both grades—students did indeed focus on only a fragment of the definition. For example, given a definition for *exotic* of "foreign; strange; not native" one student wrote *The colonists were exotic in America.* True, the colonists were not native to America, but that is not the sense of "not native" entailed by the word *exotic.*

However, students were able to recognize that correct definitions were more compatible with correct contexts, and this ability improved from fourth to sixth grade. Students were also able to recognize when a context was semantically unrelated to the definition, and this ability also improved by grade; but given a context that was compatible with only a fragment of the definition, the results were no different from chance. Neither the format of the definition nor the presence of an example sentence made a significant difference in student behavior.

McKeown (1993) focused on identifying problems that fifth-grade students had with definitions and creating revised formats for definitions to ameliorate those difficulties. Her results showed that students were able to produce more accurate sentences with the words when definitions:

- Characterized prototypical understandings of the words (compare definitions for *conspicuous*: dictionary definition—"easily seen"—and revised definition—"describes something you notice right away because it stands out").
- Were written in natural, accessible language (compare definitions for *disrupt*: dictionary definition—"break up; split"—and revised definition—"to cause difficulties that prevent something from continuing easily or peacefully").

Although revised formats produced better results, students' responses were far from perfect. About 60% of the sentences produced from dictionary definitions were unacceptable, while about 30% of the revised definitions led to unacceptable sentences.

All of these results make perfect sense once we recognize how much metalinguistic knowledge is built into a dictionary. A dictionary is an adequate tool for a sophisticated user who already has the necessary metalinguistic knowledge. One of the goals of literacy instruction is to turn students into that kind of sophisticated user. But using a dictionary effectively is much more challenging than learning words in rich contexts where it is possible to build on preexisting (though tacit) knowledge about the language.

FINAL THOUGHTS

In this chapter, we have presented an enhanced vision of the vocabulary construct, emphasizing the multiplicity of ways that vocabulary knowledge goes beyond the memorization of definitions. We have sketched how vocabulary growth not only depends on building stronger knowledge about root words, but also on knowledge of structural regularities and generative mechanisms for word learning; on increasing metalinguistic awareness and metacognitive knowledge; and on learning how to coordinate these different forms of knowledge to infer word meanings in context. The default "commonsense" understandings of vocabulary that most people bring with them to teaching may fail to address the importance of tacit understandings and systemic regularities, and may underestimate the work needed to develop metalinguistic awareness and support the use of metacognitive strategies in word learning. Diagnostically, it would be useful for teachers to know whether students can exploit morphological knowledge, whether they can infer word meanings efficiently from rich contexts, and whether they can use words flexibly to mean different things in different contexts. Clearly, teachers need to expose students to words—and contexts—that give students the opportunity to develop those skills.

This understanding of vocabulary knowledge suggests that it may be all too easy to oversimplify the problem and fail to address the full richness of vocabulary learning. We need to think about whether we are exposing and testing words that tell us about students' knowledge of prefixes, suffixes, and roots. We need to pay close attention not just to how many words students are learning, but also to how many contexts they have experienced those words in. We need to ask ourselves whether they have been exposed to secondary meanings of words and whether they are even aware that those words are being used in unusual ways. We need to worry about multiword expressions, idioms, and collocations—and, more generally, about all the richness of usage that supports the development of rich knowledge about words and the world.

CHAPTER 3

Surveying the State
of Vocabulary Assessment

Any type of assessment depends on the underlying concept that you are trying to test, why this concept is important, and whether you can trust the results to give you the answers you need. These criteria correspond to foundational concepts in psychometric theory (the theory of testing):

- The *construct* is what we are trying to test.
- A test's *validity* depends on the relationship between the construct and the information provided by the test. How confident are we that a student's performance on the test reflects the skills we are trying to test? It is important to recognize that validity is contextual. To claim that a test is valid is to claim that it is valid for a specific population, for a specific purpose, under specific testing conditions. If we administer a test under different conditions, use it on a different population, or use test results for a different purpose than that for which it was designed, the results may no longer be valid.
- A test's *reliability* tells us how much we should trust the test scores. How consistent are test results? How precise is the information they provide?

Expectations about test design and validity are defined by the American Educational Research Association, the American Psychological Association, and the National Council on Measurement in Education (2014) Standards for Educational and Psychological Testing. As these standards point out, "tests are designed, developed, and used in a wide variety of ways" (p. 3). This is as true of vocabulary assessment as it is with any other form of testing and so, as we review the state of the art in vocabulary assessment, it is important to be sensitive to the following questions:

- What is the construct of interest?
- How is it assessed?
- How will the information provided by the test be used?
- Is the tested construct assessed comprehensively and appropriately for the information we wish to gain about student performance?

MULTIPLE PURPOSES FOR ASSESSING VOCABULARY

There are a variety of reasons for assessing students' knowledge of words and a variety of uses for assessment results. Some of these uses are summative—they focus on testing what students have already learned at the conclusion of an instructional unit or course. For instance, researchers trying to improve classroom practice often look at vocabulary acquisition to test what students know and don't know. Other uses are formative—they provide developmental information about students that help teachers make decisions about what to teach (or how to teach) week to week, day to day, or even during the course of a single lesson. For example, a teacher may assess student vocabulary knowledge on the fly during lessons to get a sense of whether her students will understand the upcoming vocabulary in a reading assignment.

Vocabulary is also used to assess quite different constructs. In some cases, a test may be intended to determine whether students know specific words. For instance, teachers who want to know whether their students understand disciplinary concepts such as the terms used in science lessons (e.g., *photosynthesis, cytoplasm, osmosis*) may give them an end-of-unit vocabulary test. In other cases, knowledge of the specific words on a test may not be the construct of interest. Instead, the tested words may be intended to represent words that students at a particular level are expected to know, with a goal of indirectly measuring the relative size of a student's vocabulary. Tests with this goal include commonly used standardized tests of vocabulary, such as the Peabody Picture Vocabulary Test (PPVT; Dunn & Dunn, 2007), the vocabulary section of the Gates–MacGinitie Reading Tests (MacGinitie, MacGinitie, Maria, Dreyer, & Hughes, 2000), or the reading vocabulary section of the Woodcock–Johnson Test of Student Achievement (Woodcock, 1998).

The focus of interest in assessment is not always vocabulary size. Vocabulary items may be used to assess general language achievement or reading comprehension. Because there is a strong connection between vocabulary knowledge and reading comprehension, vocabulary items are usually included in reading comprehension tests. Policymakers increasingly use standardized test scores with vocabulary components to categorize students, teachers, schools, and districts to make high-stakes educational decisions. For instance, district administrators who want to place English learners into appropriate classes may use a test such as the California English Language Development Test (CELDT; California Department of Education, 2005), an annual test of listening, speaking, reading, and writing for those students in the process of learning English. In this case, the assessment of vocabulary is embedded in the reading, writing, and speaking sections of the assessment, and the results are used to classify English learners by their level of English language proficiency.

Since the 1980s, we have entered an "accountability era" in which the assessment of student learning has been codified as part of our national educational blueprint (Booher-Jennings, 2006) and which has influenced literacy policy, research, and practice more than in the previous history of American education (Afflerbach, 2005; Wixson & Pearson, 1998). Large-scale assessments of reading, in particular, have become prominent tools for making important educational decisions, often overshadowing other sources of information such as teacher judgments and student work (Afflerbach, 2005; International Reading Association, 1999). We have increasingly relied on such assessments, sometimes seeming to ascribe them almost magical properties by expecting that they tell us with precision whether students have learned what they have encountered in school and thinking that learning is complete and mastery is permanent. Vocabulary assessment plays an important, though subsidiary, role in this larger conversation, but decisions made about vocabulary assessment in large-scale, high-stakes tests can have a significant impact on how teachers conceptualize vocabulary knowledge and, therefore, their teaching practice.

ISSUES ASSOCIATED WITH ASSESSMENTS

Because testing in general, and vocabulary assessment as a segment of overall testing, has been given such a prominent role in the policy decisions and everyday decisions that affect students, it is imperative to examine what these tests are and are not capable of contributing to any educational conversation. Current assessments suffer from severe limitations, and our interpretation and use of test scores only magnify those limitations. For instance, in discussing the limitations of reading assessments, the RAND Reading Study Group report (2002) points out that unless measures of assessment reflect and are consistent with existing, underlying theories of reading comprehension, researchers "will be severely hampered in our capacities to engage in excellent research" (p. 129). Unfortunately, the assessment measures used in many research studies and in classrooms are neither sensitive to nor consistent with underlying theories of reading comprehension and vocabulary acquisition. We know quite a bit about vocabulary acquisition, and yet this knowledge is only beginning to be addressed in assessments of vocabulary knowledge and assessments of reading comprehension beyond the idea of adding context (Pearson, Hiebert, & Kamil, 2007, 2012). Given that there are different kinds of vocabulary knowledge, different kinds of assessment, and different purposes for assessment, it is essential to understand the limitations and constraints inherent in current testing practices.

What we know about vocabulary acquisition (as outlined in Chapter 2) is that vocabulary is multidimensional, incremental, and a relatively open-ended domain. The words in a person's lexicon are known to various degrees, and each person has unique sets of words that they know vaguely, words that they are comfortable with and know reasonably well when they encounter them in print, and words that they are willing and able to use in oral language. For example, many people may recognize the word *zephyr* in a story as a type of wind, but not really understand how a *zephyr* is different from a *gust,* and they may be uncomfortable using it orally or in writing. Other people may have richer understandings of the same word and may draw a variety of specific inferences when it is used in a literary context but neither form of knowledge is likely to be as rich or as complete as the knowledge most people have of a word like *cat,* which is commonly part of oral vocabulary. Such words are deeply embedded in a network of semantic relationships and background knowledge, involving such things as the knowledge of cat-like behavior and taxonomic knowledge about how cats are similar to and different from other kinds of felines, such as mountain lions and tigers.

The most obvious implications of the facts we have just reviewed are linked to the concepts of breadth and depth of word knowledge (Nagy & Herman, 1987; Pearson et al., 2007). Breadth of vocabulary indicates the overall size of one's vocabulary—the number of words that a learner knows something about. Depth of vocabulary knowledge taps into the rich interconnected network of knowledge about individual words. The notion of depth is that word knowledge is multifaceted and that multiple dimensions contribute to the quality of knowledge about each word in a person's lexicon. However, in examining past vocabulary research, Scott, Lubliner, and Hiebert (2006) found that neither the selection of words for testing nor the constructs used for designing assessments reflect current notions of vocabulary as a multidimensional construct. The extent of knowledge students have about each word is not measured. In addition, test developers do not pay attention to the types of tacit knowledge we discussed in Chapter 2, and, as such, conventional vocabulary assessments do not tap students' understanding of generative patterns of language and word meaning. By virtue of what they omit, conventional assessments are, in essence, assessments of breadth.

TRADITIONAL VOCABULARY ASSESSMENT

Traditional standardized vocabulary assessments typically share two design features. They include a range of words, from common to rare, to differentiate students who know a lot of words from students who know fewer words. They also use a limited number of types of test items that usually focus on knowledge of definitions. These design constraints suggest a much narrower construct of vocabulary knowledge than defined by recent research and may have negative effects on how teachers approach the problem of teaching vocabulary.

Sampling Words by Difficulty

The conventional method for selecting words in a vocabulary assessment is based on two assumptions: that words can be placed on a scale of difficulty from easy to hard and that students' ability can be placed on a corresponding scale from which we can safely infer that someone who knows a hard word is likely to know all the easier words. From this perspective, the exact identity of the words does not matter; only their position on the scale. This is because these tests are based on the assumption that knowledge of the words sampled in a test reflects knowledge of a greater number of words.

The total test score—where on the scale an individual is placed—is assumed to reflect the overall size of a person's lexicon. Scores on these types of tests are strongly related to both reading comprehension scores and the background of students and thus provide an efficient method of distinguishing lower- from higher-performing students. However, as Pearson et al. (2007, 2012) point out, the words tested on these types of assessments tend to be chosen arbitrarily, with no theoretically grounded principles, theories, or frameworks to guide their selection. The purpose of such tests is to produce a range of scores that demonstrates differences in student achievement, and so words are chosen based on the extent to which they can sort students into categories of higher or lower proficiency. No consideration is given to whether the words are frequently encountered by students or are important for conceptual understanding at a particular grade level. The result is that the selected words are unrelated to students' opportunities to learn words or to the topics they study. A conventional standardized vocabulary test doesn't tell us whether students have learned the words they are exposed to in school, the rate at which such words are learned, or the amount of knowledge they might have about a word. Instead, it compares each student to all other students taking the test in terms of whether this particular set of words is known or not known.

Grade-Level Word Lists

The degree of arbitrariness in word selection can be problematic if one wishes to make even slightly more specific inferences—such as whether a student's vocabulary knowledge is grade-level appropriate—which has led to various attempts to define grade-level vocabularies and to align the scores of vocabulary tests to grade-level expectations (Educational Developmental Laboratories, 1989; Fry, Kress, & Fountoukidis, 2004; Marzano, 2004; Zeno, Ivens, Millard, & Duvvuri, 1995). Yet grade-level designations of words are not without problems (Flinspach, Scott, & Vevea, 2012). The words considered for a grade-level vocabulary assessment generally come from sources such as grade-level word lists, publisher-identified vocabulary in textbooks, grade-specific curriculum standards, or words identified by researchers or educators. Authoritative sources that identify grade-level vocabulary do not necessarily agree with one another, however, and no source is comprehensive (Flinspach et al., 2012). This is because there are no agreed-upon principles for words that students can or should know at various grade levels. Grade-level lists are based on the words that appear in some specific set of grade-level materials. They do not represent what students know at various levels, nor do they indicate whether students easily understood or learned concepts at a particular grade level.

In fact, assigning words to grade levels can be problematic in several ways. For example, grade-level assignments usually depend on the words themselves, rather than on their meanings. Consequently, students may fail to understand what they read, not because they are unfamiliar with a word, but because they are unfamiliar with a specific sense of that word that only appears in a particular context. For instance, a person who knows what a *base* is in a baseball game may not know that a *base* is the chemical opposite of an acid in science.

Only one large-scale resource for grade-level vocabulary takes word meanings into account—the Living Word Vocabulary (LWV; Dale &

O'Rourke, 1976). The LWV assigned distinct grade levels to multiple senses of approximately 7,500 words based on the results of testing word meanings with students at various levels. Yet we do not know how these meaning distinctions were selected or the specific test questions that were used to assign each sense of a word to a grade level. In addition, this resource was based on work done more than 50 years ago, when student demographics were very different from today. Although the LWV is out of print, Biemiller (2009) created a revised and adapted version of the list that is accessible today.

Another issue that calls into question the meaningfulness of grade-level designations is that the grade level of words is influenced by opportunities to learn those words. Opportunities can differ by curriculum—that is, the curriculum in use in a school influences, to a great extent, the words that students will or will not learn. For example, in some third-grade math curricula, students are taught that a *rhombus* is an example of a *quadrilateral*. Students not exposed to such a curriculum are unlikely to understand these words and their relationship to each other. That does not mean these students are not up to grade level or even that they lack math vocabulary—merely that the math curriculum they studied did not choose to include these words in third grade. Opportunities can also differ across individuals. For instance, words for different types of dinosaurs, such as *triceratops* and *brontosaurus*, would seem to be hard words, yet they are well known by quite a few students in the early elementary grades because these students were interested in the topic and engaged in this learning.

Words have no inherent grade level at which they become meaningful or learnable. A word acquires a grade-level designation because it starts to appear with some level of frequency in materials developed for a particular grade. That does not mean, however, that the word never appears before that or that students at that grade need to know it.

The fundamental problem is that grade-level lists are too often treated as prescriptive, rather than as samples from a descriptive spectrum of words from higher to lower frequency. It is completely appropriate to teach and assess words that are labeled above or below students' grade level, if that facilitates their understanding. In fact, going beyond grade-level designations may be necessary, as the exact mix of words within specific texts tends to be driven more by subject matter or register—such as informative or literary, formal or informal—than by grade level. It is an open question about which sets of words will provide "the biggest bang for the buck" and which alternatives will best serve to exemplify patterns of morphology, semantics, syntax, and pragmatics. We discuss this issue further in Chapters 4 and 5.

THE RECEPTIVE ASSESSMENT
OF DEFINITIONAL KNOWLEDGE

The other typical feature of traditional vocabulary assessments is the use of items that assess definitional knowledge. The most common item type presents a word along with four choices, one of which represents a definition or a synonym of the word (Scott et al., 2006). Although presented in various formats, the items in Figure 3.1 exemplify assessment tasks that require definitional knowledge (including categorical knowledge and recognition of synonyms). These kinds of items appeal to teachers because they align directly with commonsense understandings that equate word meanings with definitions.

Of course, a definition can be a great shorthand for what a word means; however, let us consider the concept of a definition a bit more deeply. Those who study vocabulary development describe the knowledge of a word as a mental representation based on features of the word, including how it sounds, its spelling, and meaning. Learners build the meaning part of a mental representation based on encounters with the word in contexts from which they extract information about the word's

---

I think the word *commercial* is closest in meaning to:
- ☐ A sad poem usually about or for someone who has died.
- ☐ Making someone very mad.
- ☐ Very active and full of energy.
- ☐ Relating to business or the selling of a product.

A _____ is a type of bird.
- ☐ chimpanzee
- ☐ pheasant
- ☐ gecko
- ☐ beagle

To *search* is to:
- ☐ sob
- ☐ race
- ☐ look
- ☐ pour

FIGURE 3.1. Examples of assessment tasks that require definitional knowledge.

meaning and use. After learners have enough experiences with a word, they begin to abstract its features—put together the ones that are common across contexts—and produce a generalized representation of meaning. This representation may be very much like a definition; however, much mental effort has gone into producing it, and the learner truly owns it. It is part of the learner's mental network of word knowledge, and it entails rich and varied connections to other words and concepts. Contrast that kind of development with reading a definition of a word in the dictionary, which takes minimal mental effort but is not likely to activate connections to related words or relevant contexts. Even if the definition is remembered, it may have little utility as far as allowing the learner to use the word correctly. Therefore, the value of knowing a definition depends, to a great extent, on how one arrived at that definition.

On the flip side, correctly identifying a word's definition on a test carries different implications, depending on the relationship of the definition to the learner's network of vocabulary knowledge. Is the definition an integral part of that network such that it includes a variety of features of the word and is connected to words with similar meanings or words that may be used in similar contexts? Or is the definition an isolated unit of memorized information? Those two possibilities cannot be distinguished by a test of definitions. Thus, restricting vocabulary assessment to definitions makes it difficult to determine the quality, depth, or utility of the learner's knowledge of the tested words.

The fundamental issue is that vocabulary knowledge integrates many different kinds of information—information about broad conceptual categories; background knowledge associated with individual concepts; information about finer meaning distinctions and connotations; information about semantic relationships between words; information about usage and grammar; information about word families; and information about how words take on different shades of meaning in context, and so forth. The use of a single type of test item can limit the construct and may have the undesirable effect of encouraging teachers to focus on inappropriate teaching strategies, such as requiring students to memorize definitions.

WHAT TRADITIONAL ASSESSMENTS MISS
(AND THE PURPOSES FOR WHICH IT MATTERS)

It should be clear at this point that traditional vocabulary assessments work well if they are interpreted as measuring overall vocabulary size, which is the specific purpose of their design. Although the tests achieve this goal efficiently, in so doing, they limit the range of inferences that can be drawn. As Pearson et al. (2012) describe it, "All we know [from these tests] is that a given student performed better or worse than the average student on the set of words that happened to be on the test. We know nothing about what the scores say about a student's vocabulary knowledge of any identifiable domain or corpus of words" (p. 238). For other purposes, we need other kinds of assessments that will capture the right kinds of information. In particular, if we want richer information about student learning, we need to take an entirely different approach.

Tests of general vocabulary knowledge are poor measures of short-term growth and cannot measure specific word learning, but they are often used that way, in both research and practice. For example, a standardized vocabulary test such as the Gates–MacGinitie (MacGinitie et al., 2000) is often used by researchers at the end of an instructional intervention to evaluate whether an intervention has promoted general vocabulary learning beyond the specific words that were taught. Similarly, teachers who have introduced vocabulary instruction into their curriculum are often tempted to examine standardized vocabulary results as a sign of the effectiveness of their efforts in vocabulary. But results of a general knowledge test are unlikely to address the question of how well students learned over a short period of time. Getting unexpected growth on the test would certainly be a good sign, but even positive results on a general measure may not be due to the instruction of specific words.

What we can learn from assessment results is complicated even further by the incremental nature of learning a word. In initial encounters with a word, a learner usually comes away with an incomplete knowledge of its meaning. Knowledge then grows incrementally with repeated exposures, becoming richer and more robust as more contexts are encountered (Nagy & Scott, 2000; Paribakht & Wesche, 1999; Shore & Durso, 1990; Stahl, 2003). Before fully mastering a word, for example, a student may know it sufficiently well to recognize it when it is used correctly in a sentence but not be able to define it. Or he or she may be able to understand the word when used in supportive contexts but not when the context of its use is less transparent.

The assessment problems that result can be illustrated by considering the following sentences that use the word *insist*: *Mom insisted that Bella finish her homework before she went out to play* versus *Mom had to insist that Bella ride her new bike*. The first use is strongly contextualized, with a highly congruent word meaning and context. It is typical for a parent to insist that a child finish homework before play. The second use requires a more decontextualized understanding of the word; the reader needs to accommodate the meaning of *insist* within the context because it is less obvious why a mother would need to insist that a child ride a new bike (McKeown & Beck, 2014). If we restrict our attention to definitional knowledge, we will never detect the difference between (1) shallow word knowledge that allows students to understand only contexts that strongly support the correct interpretation and (2) rich word knowledge that allows students to understand even poorly supported contexts.

Because word learning is incremental, an all-or-nothing measurement strategy is going to produce a distorted picture. As described in Chapter 2, Swanborn and de Glopper's (1999) meta-analysis of studies focusing on learning word meanings from context concluded that readers learn an average of about 15% of the unfamiliar words they encounter.

Interestingly, some of the studies examined in this meta-analysis included measures of partial word knowledge, and those studies showed higher word-learning gains. This result demonstrates that what students learned from context was not "all or nothing," yet that knowledge would not have been captured on most traditional types of assessments.

Similar concerns apply to vocabulary assessment in the classroom. Failure to capture partial word knowledge can lead to misinterpretation and confusion about students' knowledge. Consider, for example, a student who scores poorly on a test of recently taught words. The teacher may conclude that instruction was ineffective, but it could be that the student has learned aspects of the words other than those tapped on the test. Alternatively, consider that if the student performed well on a test, the teacher might assume that the words have been mastered and then provide no further instructional attention.

WHAT'S ON THE HORIZON IN ASSESSMENT

New large-scale vocabulary assessments are reflecting changes in practices that go beyond traditional vocabulary assessment in two ways. First, they are beginning to target particular types of vocabulary for assessment, although the categories are usually defined in broad ways, such as general vocabulary (Tier One in Beck et al., 2002), academic vocabulary (Tier Two in Beck et al.), or domain-specific vocabulary (Tier Three in Beck et al.). Second, they are increasingly testing vocabulary knowledge in passage or sentence contexts rather than in isolation.

Targeted Word Lists and Explicit Selection Principles

The focus on high-utility words can be traced to efforts in the vocabulary literature to identify general-purpose academic vocabulary, either for the purpose of second-language teaching (Coxhead, 1998, 2000; Schmitt,

Schmitt, & Mann, 2011) or to support selection of high-priority vocabulary for K–12 instruction (Beck et al., 2002). Several modern high-stakes tests are informed by these efforts and offer a degree of justification for the words they test. A recent development in high-stakes testing is the explicit commitment to assessing general-purpose academic (Tier Two) vocabulary, as required by the Common Core State Standards Initiative (CCSS; 2010).

The specific criteria vary from one high-stakes test to the next, but almost all of them have frameworks that include principles that govern the selection of words for testing. For instance, the vocabulary section of the National Assessment of Educational Progress (NAEP) Reading Test (National Assessment Governing Board, 2008) prefers to assess words that: (1) are characteristic of written language rather than oral communication; (2) are broadly distributed across a wide range of text genres; (3) label reasonably familiar concepts that do not require any form of technical knowledge; (4) are necessary to understanding the text in which they appear; and (5) are found in appropriate, grade-level reading materials.

Thus far, the basis for word selection tends to be fairly broad, and it is often driven by passage difficulty. Once a reading passage has been selected that is appropriate to the population and grade level to be assessed, common practice is likely to treat all but the most obscure or difficult words that appear in such a passage as appropriate targets for assessment. We discuss selection principles for testing vocabulary in greater depth in Chapter 4.

Testing Vocabulary Knowledge in Context

The most common type of vocabulary item in modern, large-scale assessments tests vocabulary knowledge in passage or, minimally, sentence contexts. The use of context represents an advance on purely definitional approaches to vocabulary assessment, since it requires the test taker to understand a particular use of a word in a specific, meaningful context. In most cases, contextual vocabulary items are embedded in a test of reading comprehension, in which using both lexical and meta-cognitive knowledge to build the correct interpretation in context is a critical part of the construct.

Passage Reading with Cloze Items

The trend of testing vocabulary in sentence or passage contexts initially emerged in a relatively simple form with such formats as cloze items. The term *cloze* refers to a specific method of testing vocabulary knowledge in context (Bachman, 1982; Bormuth 1967, 1968, 1969; Rankin & Culhane, 1969; Taylor, 1953, 1956). Originally proposed as a measure of passage readability, the cloze technique presents a passage in which words are "blanked out" at regular intervals. The test taker's task is to infer what word originally appeared in each blanked-out location, either directly (as an open-response task) or by selecting an option from a multiple-choice item. Cloze items can have a strong predictive relationship with reading comprehension scores (Greene, 2001), although some scholars (e.g., Levenston, Nir, & Blum-Kulka, 1984; Shanahan, Kamil, & Tobin, 1982) have argued that cloze items primarily measure local, sentence-level comprehension. Variations on the cloze technique attempt to control the location of blanks, such as by controlling for the part of speech, word frequency, and other linguistic features. Assessments with cloze items are particularly prominent for testing language proficiency.

A test with cloze items is clearly not a pure vocabulary assessment. Identifying which words should go in the blanks may draw on a range of comprehension processes that are not related to the specific word that appears in the blank—if a target word is not supplied as a multiple-choice option, a cloze item cannot be said to assess knowledge of any specific word. However, cloze items represent a fairly pure example of a contextual language task in which the reader is forced to consider which word best fits in a specific context. The nature of that task can be manipulated in a variety of ways—for example, by choosing sentence contexts that can plausibly be filled only by a very small number of words or by manipulating features of the larger discourse context to make certain concepts particularly salient. These kinds of manipulations form the basis of more focused vocabulary item types that require the test taker to select the correct word in context.

Vocabulary Items That Include Sentence or Passage Context

Tasks that require the reader to respond to a particular word that appears in a context have been commonly used in tests designed to assess reading comprehension. Typically, within a set of items designed to tap comprehension of a passage, one or two of the items will focus on words from the passage. Thus these are not vocabulary items per se, but they sample vocabulary knowledge as part of comprehension. Although words targeted in such tests appear within a context, the items themselves tend to be of the traditional format that requires choosing a definition or synonym from among several choices. No context appears in the item itself. For example, the TOEFL® test of English language proficiency uses an item format in which students are asked to read a passage and then answer questions of the following kind (Educational Testing Service, 2016a).

> The word "excavating" on line 25 [of the text] is closest in meaning to:
>
>   (a) digging out
>   (b) extending
>   (c) destroying
>   (d) covering up

In this example, the sentence that contained the target word is *This impact released an enormous amount of energy, excavating a crater about twice as large as the lunar crater Tycho.* Here, definitional knowledge by itself is sufficient to determine the correct answer (*digging out*), as long as the reader understands what a crater is. However, testing words that appear in a larger passage can be accomplished using much more sophisticated items that require careful reasoning about the interaction between words and context. In the sections that follow, we illustrate many of the considerations that go into the design of these more sophisticated context-driven items by examining sentence- and passage-context items for the GRE® and NAEP assessments.

One vocabulary item type deployed in the revised GRE Verbal Reasoning section is the text-completion item type, which can be viewed as a carefully controlled form of a cloze item. The student is provided with a passage with a small number of blanks. For each blank, three choices are provided and the student must choose the best answer for each blank. Consider the following example (Educational Testing Service, 2016b):

> The Parisian École des Beaux-Arts (School of Fine Arts) was (i) _____ many nineteenth- and twentieth-century artists, so that by 1930 the associated term "academic art" had become a (ii) _____.
>
> | Blank (i) | Blank (ii) |
> | --- | --- |
> | Influential among | pejorative |
> | ridiculed by | conundrum |
> | attended by | misnomer |

Note that in this item, the words or phrases that fill in the blanks are all syntactically appropriate. Eliminating choices requires the reader to be sensitive to fine details of meaning that interact with the overall intent of the passage and to ignore surface cues that might mislead them.

Another type of item employed in the GRE Verbal Reasoning section is called a sentence-equivalence item. It requires the student to select two words that are synonyms of one another, either of which could fit meaningfully and appropriately into the sentence context provided. Consider the following example (Educational Testing Service, 2016c):

It was her view that the country's problems had been _____ by foreign technocrats, so that to ask for such assistance again would be counterproductive.

    (a) ameliorated
    (b) ascertained
    (c) diagnosed
    (d) exacerbated
    (e) overlooked
    (f) worsened

Notice several considerations that have affected the design of this item. To begin with, all six choices are syntactically appropriate and reasonable in terms of English usage. Any of them could be substituted into the blank to produce a grammatical and fairly plausible sentence. A simpler type of vocabulary item might require the student to discriminate between grammatical and ungrammatical sentences or between normal and aberrant usage. Second, this item calls on a sophisticated knowledge of the word choices and their relationships. The correct choices are synonyms—*exacerbated* and *worsened*—but there are other rough synonyms in the set (*ascertained* and *diagnosed*) and other words that are closely related to the synonyms but contrast in meaning (*ameliorated* vs. *exacerbated*, *overlooked* vs. *ascertained*). To identify the correct answer, the test taker must be able to access this kind of semantic information.

But knowledge of the words themselves is not enough. The student must be able to integrate the words chosen with the sentence context to determine which choices produce the most coherent interpretation. In this case, *exacerbated/worsened* is the best choice since it provides the most coherent explanation for why it would be counterproductive to ask for assistance from foreign technocrats a second time. This GRE item is pitched to a high level of vocabulary knowledge. Getting the right answer requires knowledge of a relatively difficult academic vocabulary and fine discrimination among closely related words, without access to surface cues that would make it easy to eliminate the incorrect choices.

Vocabulary items developed for the 2009 NAEP Reading Assessment also emphasize understanding how a word is used within a context rather than focusing on definitions (U.S. Department of Education, 2013). The rationale for the new direction of this assessment is that it involves the kind of knowledge that students need to have about words in order to understand what they read—that is, readers need to integrate meanings of words into the context.

The NAEP items are based on text passages. Each item describes a sentence from the text that contains a targeted vocabulary word and offers four choices for the meaning of that sentence. The items are designed to assess whether the student knows the targeted word well enough to use it to understand the context in which the word appears. For instance, the following item is presented as a sample question for eighth graders (U.S. Department of Education, 2013, pp. 14–15):

> . . . the author says that her mother "thought that she could replicate" the great-grandfather's mint syrup. This means the author's mother thought she could:
>
> (a) buy back the mint syrup recipe
> (b) make mint syrup that tasted like this
> (c) remember how the mint syrup tasted
> (d) make a better mint syrup than this

It may appear that the correct answer can be inferred from reading the passage that describes the mother's attempts to create a mint syrup like the great-grandfather's. However, the item choices are designed to include plausible alternative meanings of the context—ones that could be true, but do not represent what the targeted word means, which diminishes the ease of figuring out the correct response from context.

This careful control of distractors is a fairly distinctive feature of NAEP vocabulary questions. Incorrect options may (1) paraphrase a common meaning of the target word that is not the meaning the word has in context, (2) repeat correct information from the text that does not match the actual meaning of the word, (3) provide an alternative interpretation of the context in which the word appears, (4) paraphrase a meaning of a word that is similar to the target word in spelling or pronunciation, or (5) present an associate of the target word that is not correct in context.

The kinds of items we have just reviewed require the student to integrate vocabulary knowledge with passage reading in order to comprehend the context. These items thus provide the kinds of tasks that resemble how students use their vocabulary knowledge during reading.

THE IMPACT OF RECENT EDUCATIONAL REFORMS

The Common Core State Standards: Major Shifts in Emphasis

A recent trend in educational reform has been to try to write standards that more closely reflect recent research. An example of this is the CCSS (NGA & CCSSO, 2010), which represent a major effort to reform instruction and assessment in the United States and embody a distinctive and highly nuanced understanding of the role of vocabulary in education. In particular, they emphasize the idea that college- and career-ready readers and writers control effective strategies for inferring word meanings in context and apply that knowledge to interpret texts and choose effective language in writing. We can get a quick sense of CCSS priorities by reviewing the following relevant standards*:

Language Standard 4. Determine or clarify the meaning of unknown and multiple-meaning words and phrases by using context clues, analyzing mean-ingful word parts, and consulting general and specialized reference materials, as appropriate.

Language Standard 5. Demonstrate understanding of figurative language, word relationships, and nuances in word meanings.

Language Standard 6. Acquire and use accurately a range of general aca-demic and domain-specific words and phrases sufficient for reading, writing, speaking, and listening at the college and career readiness level; demonstrate independence in gathering vocabulary knowledge when considering a word or phrase important to comprehension or expression.

Reading Standard 4. Interpret words and phrases as they are used in a text, including determining technical, connotative, and figurative meanings, and analyze how specific word choices shape meaning or tone.

In addition, the grade-level specifications for Writing Standard 2 include additional, specific expectations for vocabulary use in writing, such as the following:

Grades 4–8: Use precise language and domain-specific vocabulary to inform about or explain the topic.

Grades 9–10: Use precise language and domain-specific vocabulary to manage the complexity of the topic

Grades 11–12: Use precise language, domain-specific vocabulary, and tech-niques such as metaphor, simile, and analogy to manage the complexity of the topic.

Vocabulary also plays a key role in the CCSS definition of text readability because it focuses on the acquisition of what Beck et al.

---

*These and all other CCSS excerpts are from the Common Core State Standards Ini-tiative. Copyright ©2010 National Governors Association Center for Best Practices and Council of Chief State School Officers. All rights reserved.

(2002) term Tier Two words—in other words, the CCSS emphasize mastery of common academic vocabulary in a variety of written contexts. These emphases represent significant shifts in how vocabulary is approached in high-stakes testing. To recap, there are four related shifts: an emphasis on Tier Two academic vocabulary; an emphasis on word-learning strategies; an emphasis on the ability to use word meanings flexibly, as influenced by context; and an emphasis on the application of vocabulary knowledge to support literary interpretation and effective word choice.

1. *Common academic vocabulary.* Because the standards emphasize common academic vocabulary, vocabulary size has been de-emphasized. Instead of using knowledge of obscure words to identify higher-performing students, tests aligned with the new standards are more likely to test whether students understand use of Tier Two academic vocabulary across a range of scientific, historical, and literary contexts.

2. *Word-learning strategies.* Current thinking places much more emphasis on students' ability to infer word meanings in context than traditional vocabulary assessments. In particular, Language Standard 4 focuses attention on whether students can use context clues and the morphological structure of words, not just dictionary definitions, to determine what words mean in context.

3. *Word-meaning flexibility.* Because of their emphasis on common academic vocabulary and word-learning strategies, new assessments also place much more emphasis on the ability to interpret words flexibly in context. The same word can have very different meanings, depending on the context of use; thus, to master academic vocabulary is to learn how to interpret words differently from one context to the next. For instance, a broad academic word like *generate* can refer to very different things: *generating* electricity; *generating* support for a policy; *generating* a password; or *generating* new organs during fetal development. There may be a common, abstract, or figurative meaning running through a series of related meanings, but the kind of knowledge being tested cannot be acquired by memorizing definitions. It requires a deep engagement with word meanings in context.

4. *Application to higher-order literacy skills.* There is also increased emphasis on close reading and contextualized vocabulary knowledge as a key contributor to students' ability to analyze word choices and build text-based interpretations. The goal is a flexible, nuanced understanding of language that may result in a larger vocabulary, but cannot be reduced to vocabulary size.

Innovative Items Types Associated with Recent Educational Reforms

The shifts in emphasis we have just described play out in a series of innovative formats for vocabulary assessment, including innovations in computer use described in Chapter 7. Some newer vocabulary items require students to link decisions about what words mean in context to show evidence that supports specific interpretive decisions about the text. A striking change in vocabulary assessment is that tests often contain items that assess students' ability to identify clues from context that help them infer word meanings. The Smarter Balanced Assessment (Sireci, 2012), for instance, contains items for which the student needs to identify words or phrases in the passage that provide evidence of what *scarred* means, such as *bite marks, scuffs, fraying, smudged,* or *faded*. The following is an example:

Read the sentences from the passage. Then answer the question.
My grandma pulled the ball out, unwrapped it, and held it out for us to see. The ball was *scarred* almost beyond recognition. It had dog bite marks, dirt scuffs, and fraying seams. Right in the middle was a big signature in black ink that I had somehow overlooked. It was smudged now and faded, but it still clearly said "Babe Ruth." I began to shake inside.
Click on two phrases from the paragraph that help you understand the meaning of *scarred*.

Similarly, on the fourth-grade, publicly released Partnership for Assessment of Readiness for College and Careers (PARCC; 2016) assessment, we encounter the following item:

Which sentence from the story helps the reader understand the meaning of *disputing* as it is used in paragraph 1?
(a) "'Heyday, sirs!' said His Majesty, going up to them, 'let me know the cause of your quarrel.'" (paragraph 5)
(b) "Upon hearing this, off they started." (paragraph 10)
(c) "The latter, seeing at a glance how matters stood, extended his long trunk, and reached the helmet quite easily." (paragraph 11)
(d) "'And you,' said the Lion, turning to the Crocodile, 'although unable to reach the helmet, were able to dive for it and save it.'" (paragraph 13)
Which word has the opposite meaning of *disputing*?
(a) confessing
(b) discussing
(c) questioning
(d) agreeing

To answer this question, students are expected to read the passage shown in Figure 3.2. The intent of this item seems to be to test the ability to infer word meaning from context. In this case, the key feature of the passage is that the meaning of *disputing* can be inferred from the passage, specifically, from the lion's response in the fifth paragraph. If, however, a student already knows what *disputing* means, he or she may be able to determine the correct answer to either part of the question

---

1 An Elephant and a Crocodile were once standing beside a river. They were disputing as to which was the better animal.

2 "Look at my strength," said the Elephant. "I can tear up a tree, roots and all, with my trunk."

3 "Ah! but quantity is not quality, and your skin is not nearly so tough as mine," replied the Crocodile, "for neither spear, arrow, nor sword can pierce it."

4 Just as they were coming to blows, a Lion happened to pass.

5 "Heyday, sirs!" said His Majesty, going up to them, "Let me know the cause of your quarrel."

6 "Will you kindly tell us which is the better animal?" cried both at once.

7 "Certainly," said the Lion. "Do you see that soldier's steel helmet on yonder wall?" pointing at the same time across the river.

8 "Yes!" replied the beasts.

9 "Well, then," continued the Lion, "go and fetch it, and bring it to me, and I shall be able then to decide between you."

10 Upon hearing this, off they started. The Crocodile, being used to the water, reached the opposite bank of the river first, and was not long in standing beside the wall.

11 Here he waited till the Elephant came up. The latter, seeing at a glance how matters stood, extended his long trunk, and reached the helmet quite easily.

12 They then made their way together back again across the river. The Elephant, anxious to keep up with the Crocodile in the water, forgot that he was carrying the helmet on his back, and a sudden lurch caused the prize to slip off and sink to the bottom. The Crocodile noticed the accident, so down he dived, and brought it up in his capacious mouth. They then returned, and the Crocodile laid the helmet at the Lion's feet. His Majesty took up the helmet, and addressing the Elephant, said:

13 "You, on account of your size and trunk, were able to reach the prize on the wall but, having lost it, you were unable to recover it. And you," said the Lion, turning to the Crocodile, "although unable to reach the helmet, were able to dive for it and save it. You are both wise and clever in your respective ways. Neither is better than the other."

The Elephant and the Crocodile by H. Berkeley Score—public domain (1905).

FIGURE 3.2. Passage from the PARCC fourth-grade assessment.

without reading the full passage, by finding the term *quarrel* in the first item and finding its opposite (agreeing) in the second item. Although this does not fulfill the goal of learning if a student can infer unfamiliar word meaning from context, the item still requires more mental processing than simply selecting the correct definition choice among presented options.

WHAT WE DO NOT YET SEE IN RECENTLY DEVELOPED VOCABULARY ASSESSMENTS

Recently developed vocabulary assessments have made improvements over traditional vocabulary assessments, in part by including passage context and paying attention to word learning. Yet there are several ways in which the large-scale vocabulary assessment tools currently in use do not yet appear to address what we know about vocabulary learning. In particular, they do not fully address the depth of vocabulary knowledge or the incremental status of vocabulary learning. An equally distressing note is that very little of the information presented so far regarding depth of knowledge has made it into classrooms in either assessment or instruction. Teachers typically depend on "off-the-shelf" vocabulary assessments found in textbooks and English language development curriculum materials, or use spelling assessments as tests of vocabulary knowledge. Alternatively, they create lists of words they will be covering in a particular unit of study and assess whether students recognize their definitions.

Deep vocabulary knowledge involves mastery of many different aspects of words, including their morphology and syntax, usage, semantic relationships, and connotations, among other things. There are very few assessments that seek to systematically (and separately) measure multiple aspects of vocabulary knowledge. One exception is the Vocabulary Assessment Study in Education (Flinspach, Castaneda, Vevea, & Scott, 2014; Scott, Flinspach, Vevea, & Castaneda, 2015; Vevea, Flinspach, & Scott, 2013), which is discussed in more detail in Chapter 5. Assessments reflecting the incremental nature of word learning would tap more deeply into students' depth of vocabulary knowledge and provide a fuller picture of the extent to which students had developed rich representations of the words they had acquired in school. A test that captures partial, expanding word knowledge would require multiple measures of word knowledge over time, although this may be an ambitious goal to accomplish for any significant number of words.

Similarly, existing forms of assessment do not yet directly measure word-learning ability. It can be hard to do, as the examples we have reviewed suggest. We may not know which words students do not know until we assess them, and thus, if we try to test word-learning ability, some students will answer based on prior knowledge, while others will have to infer the correct meaning from context. It would be useful if we could acquire better information about how students infer the meanings of unknown words, and even better to measure how they proceed when they have to assemble information from multiple sources to interpret and use an unfamiliar word sense. In particular, it would be useful to know whether students are able to use tacit understanding of language patterns, as described in Chapter 2.

Assessing depth of vocabulary knowledge and examining incremental word-learning processes could provide useful information in a classroom context. Tests designed with these characteristics in mind could help teachers determine how well words are known, how easily specific students are able to learn them, and whether students have sufficient understanding to be able to use a word on their own. More importantly, it would allow teachers to know how students are approaching unknown words, what strategies they have available to assist in this process, and whether they are able to use either metacognitive or tacit understanding to unlock the meaning of unfamiliar words. This is particularly important for underserved students, who may lack sufficient English language exposure to develop strong vocabulary skills.

FINAL THOUGHTS

Because issues of vocabulary learning are intertwined with conceptual and cultural knowledge, instructional opportunities, and the slippery nature of words, assessing vocabulary is not an easy subject to tackle (Scott, Nagy, & Flinspach, 2008). However, in their review of vocabulary assessment, Pearson et al. (2007) suggest that it is feasible to do a better job than is currently done, for only when we have more sensitive and valid assessments can we figure out the effects of different ways of acquiring vocabulary and understand the relationship between vocabulary knowledge and other aspects of literacy.

CHAPTER 4

Which Words and Word Meanings Should We Teach and Assess?

At this point, the complexities of vocabulary assessment should be very clear. Vocabulary knowledge involves much more than definitions; the size of the vocabulary makes it impossible to sample more than a small subset of the words in the language, either for explicit, focused teaching or for assessment. We are afloat on a sea of words and can cast only a small net into that sea. How, then, can we trust what our net brings back? How can we know whether we are teaching and assessing the right targets?

Selecting words for teaching and selecting words for assessment are related but not identical issues. The teacher has limited time to make a difference in students' learning, so he or she must select instructional targets that will make the largest difference for the largest number of students. The assessment designer has limited time to measure differences among students and so must select assessment targets that most reliably differentiate between students at different levels of performance. When selecting words for teaching, for instance, many authors focus on root words, assuming that morphologically derived words will be easily learned (Bauer & Nation, 1993). Someone who knows the word *sleep* should have little trouble inferring the meaning of *sleepless* and *sleeplessness*. If someone knows the word *generate*, we might equally assume he or she should have little trouble inferring the meanings of *generation, generative, regenerate, regeneration,* and so forth, but there is a danger in that assumption. *Regenerate* does not normally mean "generate again," but something more specific—to grow back something that has been lost. *Generation* can mean the process of "generating something," but it can also refer to groups of individuals born at about the same time. Almost any process can be *generative,* but no one would refer to a power plant as "generative," no matter how efficiently it functions to generate electricity. Every word has its idiosyncrasies, even if it is derived transparently from a known root word, and learning about such idiosyncrasies is central to vocabulary acquisition. As a result, it would be a mistake to focus assessment on root words alone, no matter how appropriate it may be for teachers to adopt root-word-based pedagogical strategies.

The literature thus far has focused primarily on pedagogical motivations for word selection and so that is where we start. We return to the issue of word selection specifically for assessment later in this chapter, when we will be better placed to evaluate differences among priorities.

SELECTING WORDS, WORD PATTERNS, AND CONTEXTS FOR INSTRUCTION

Because adequate vocabulary knowledge is such a strong prerequisite for comprehension, a major principle for selecting words to teach and test is text coverage; that is, teaching words that account for a large proportion of the language in the texts students read will minimize the amount of unfamiliar words that students encounter, but how many words do students need to know to understand the texts they have to read in school? Conversely, how much should students' reading expose them to words they do not know? Some estimates suggest that students need to know at least 95% of the words in a passage in order to read it with full comprehension, although the exact conditions under which vocabulary knowledge is necessary for comprehension have not been investigated in depth (Nation, 2001).

Prioritizing Words by Frequency and Age of Acquisition

Word frequency and age of acquisition are two measures that are commonly used to identify when words are appropriate for students to encounter or to know. A word's frequency is an estimate of how common it is in the language, as measured by how often it appears in some large corpus of text. The age of acquisition is the estimated age when a learner acquires specific words. When we explore the selection of words to teach based on word frequency and the age of acquisition, we are confronted almost immediately with the much-skewed nature of word frequency distributions (Zipf, 1935, 1945). What that means is that a small set of highly frequent words appears everywhere, while most words are much rarer. In fact, just over 100 English words account for nearly 50% of any text (Adams, 1990). However, there are many much rarer words that do most of the heavy lifting because they carry most of the semantic load of the sentences in which they appear. For example, in the previous sentence, the words *rarer, semantic,* and *sentence* are by far the least-frequent words, but without them, the sentence means almost nothing. Many of the most frequent words are referred to as *closed-class* words because there is a limited number in each grammatical category. Closed-class words include articles (*the, an*), conjunctions (*and, or, but*), and prepositions (*in, of, for, with*). These words are akin to the mortar that holds bricks—the more semantically informative words—together.

Word frequency can be taken as a fairly good proxy for the number of opportunities people have to acquire a word because the more often a word appears, the more chances people have to learn it. As a result, much of the work on selecting words for instruction has focused on word frequency. This effort can be traced back to the pioneering work of Edward Thorndike (1921) to quantify vocabulary and prioritize words for education. Thorndike identified the 10,000 words that appeared most frequently in a collection of children's books and classic literature. Later, with the help of Irving Lorge, the list was expanded to approximately 30,000 words (Thorndike & Lorge, 1944). Kučera and Francis (1967) produced word frequencies from a corpus selected from largely adult, academic texts that contained about one million words of running text. The expanding availability of ever-larger electronic text collections (corpora) has led to more precise word frequency estimates. The CELEX corpus (Baayen, Piepenbrock, & van Rijn, 1993) and TASA corpus (Zeno et al., 1995) were based on corpora containing between 17 and 18 million words. The British National Corpus was based on a corpus of 88 million words, while the HAL Corpus (Burgess & Livesay, 1998) contained about 130 million words. More recent corpora, such as the English Gigaword corpus, derived from newspaper text (Parker, Graff, Kong, Chen, & Maeda, 2011), are based on much larger corpora, containing more than 4 billion words.

Frequency is most often used to identify words that should be a priority for instruction. For instance, Hiebert (2011) classifies words into eight frequency-based zones, based on their frequency in the TASA corpus (Zeno et al., 1995). Zones 0–2 cover words that appear 100 or more times per million words of text and correspond roughly to words that should be known by students in kindergarten through second grade. Zones 3 and 4 cover words that appear from 10 to 99 times per million words and are associated with third and fourth grade. Zones 0–4 contain approximately 80% of the words in the TASA corpus. Zones 5 and beyond are not tied to any particular grade, but occur less frequently than 10 times per million words of text and include specialized vocabulary in content areas. Zone 5 covers words that appear two to nine times per million words; Zone 6, words that appear once per million words; and Zones 7 and 8, words that appear less than once per million. Words in Zones 6–8 are least likely to be known, as they appear very infrequently in grade-level texts. Hiebert argues that because these words are so infrequent, focusing instruction on them is less effective than one might desire. We need to be judicious in the words we select from this group.

An issue to consider in using frequency to guide word selection is that words with the same frequency can play very different roles in the language. For example, the words *respected* and *ski* have similar frequencies (Gardner & Davies, 2014), yet the frequency of *respected* reflects its use across a broad variety of contexts, while the frequency of *ski* reflects its role in contexts particular to sports and recreation. To account for these differences, the field has developed measures of dispersion—the extent to which words appear in a variety of contexts across a wide range of subject matter (Carroll, 1970, 1972). Measures of dispersion are related to ideas about balance and representativeness. Dispersion helps to identify words that may be more important than their frequency suggests. Dispersion is reported along with frequency in contemporary guides to word frequency.

Several approaches to word selection consider both frequency and dispersion to sort words into categories that have different educational priorities. We have already discussed one such system in previous chapters: Beck et al.'s (2002) distinction between Tier One words (high-frequency, high-dispersion words that form part of the core English oral vocabulary), Tier Two words (somewhat lower-frequency words with high dispersion, typically found in academic texts), and Tier Three words (rarer words with low dispersion, typically domain-specific in nature). Nation (2001) makes similar distinctions among types of words, although he divides the vocabulary into four sections: high-frequency general-purpose words, academic vocabulary, low-frequency general-purpose vocabulary, and technical vocabulary. Specific word lists reviewed in earlier chapters, such as the General Service List (West, 1953), the Academic Word List (Coxhead, 2000), and the Academic Vocabulary List (Gardner & Davies, 2014) focus on one or another of these subsets.

High-frequency general words such as those on the General Service List are of particular importance in second-language teaching since they provide the foundation upon which the knowledge of rarer words must build. Developing knowledge of academic vocabulary—mid-frequency, high-dispersion words preferentially appearing in academic written texts—is particularly important for K–12 vocabulary development and for advanced language learners. Tier Three technical vocabulary is often treated as a lower priority for vocabulary instruction since it is closely linked with specific domain knowledge and is typically taught explicitly when domain-specific content is introduced.

Many approaches to vocabulary instruction focus on targeted words selected from academic vocabulary lists as the most productive target for focused instruction (e.g., Lesaux, Kieffer, Faller, & Kelley, 2010; McKeown, Crosson, Beck, Sandora, & Artz, 2012; Snow, Lawrence, & White, 2009). Lists such as the Academic Word List (Coxhead, 2000) and the Academic Vocabulary List (Gardner & Davies, 2014) are compiled from expository text corpora. Thus an important category of words is often left out of these discussions: sophisticated words that are typically found in novels and literary texts. These words, such as *grim* or *desolate*, are not typically introduced in academic subjects such as science or mathematics. Although there is a great deal of overlap between literary and expository academic texts, the set of words most frequently encountered in narrative reading is quite distinct (Gardner, 2004; Hiebert & Cervetti, 2011). Vocabulary from the literary dimension of academic language emphasizes common human experiences and situations and tends to be descriptive or colorful. Literary words are often more imageable (e.g., *remorse, solace, surreptitious*) than words that typify expository discourse (e.g., *coordinate, variable, attribute,* and *duration*). Literary words occur on a gradation of meaning that emphasizes particular elements of a concept. For example, word pairs such as *grim/unpleasant, desolate/lonely,* and *sweltering/warm* are associated in meaning but not really synonyms. Gardner (2004) found that literary words are less likely to represent complex concepts than words typical of expository text. This characteristic is similar to Graves and Prenn's (1986) differentiation between words for which students already possess a general concept (*indigenous, embroiled, ubiquitous*) and those that require building new conceptual knowledge (*photosynthesis, circumference, government*). This is another important distinction that can be useful for selecting words for both teaching and testing vocabulary.

Frequency is closely related to another concept that is used to identify appropriate words to teach and assess: the age of acquisition. The majority of age-of-acquisition studies have focused on subjective adult estimates of the age at which they acquired a word—that is, simply asking adults when they thought they learned specific words. Empirical studies of the age of acquisition have also been conducted by ascertaining whether children of various ages had knowledge of specific words. Such studies yielded results comparable to the subjective adult studies; however, they either examined only very young children or included only a very small set of words (Dale & Fenson, 1996; Goodman, Dale, & Li, 2008; Morrison & Ellis, 2000; Morrison, Chappell, & Ellis, 1997).

Carroll and White (1973) proposed a subjective measure for estimating the age of acquisition and demonstrated that age-of-acquisition estimates predicted how quickly people could access the right word to name what was shown in a picture; these estimates were more accurate at predicting reaction time than were the predictions based on word frequency. Since then, a variety of studies have indicated that age of acquisition is an important predictor of reading comprehension and other language-related skills, although frequency remains an important predictor as well (Gilhooly & Gilhooly, 1979, 1980; Gilhooly & Logie, 1980; Kuperman, Stadthagen-Gonzalez, & Brysbaert, 2012; Morrison & Ellis, 1995; Morrison, Ellis, & Quinlan, 1992; Zevin & Seidenberg, 2002). More recently, estimates of the age of acquisition have been developed from collections of school-age text using advanced statistical techniques such as latent semantic analysis ("word maturity"; cf. Landaur, Kireyev, & Panaccione, 2011).

To a significant extent, age-of-acquisition estimates overlap efforts to estimate the grade level at which words are learned. The Living Word Vocabulary (LWV; Dale & O'Rourke, 1976) provides the largest single study of the grades at which English word meanings are acquired. More than 30,000 word meanings are assigned to a grade level in the LWV, although grade-level estimates are provided only for every other grade from fourth grade through the end of college. The LWV reflects a series of studies in which items testing vocabulary knowledge were given to multiple grades. The grade-level estimate associated with each word was calculated by identifying the first grade level at which two thirds of the students gave the correct answer for the item used to test the targeted word. Biemiller and Slonim (2001), following up on LWV grade-level estimates for the lower grades, argue that vocabulary tends to be acquired in the same sequence, whether students are at the high end of achievement (acquiring a large vocabulary early), or at the low end of achievement. However, the reason that words may seem to be learned in a certain order may be an artifact of children's exposure to the words. At least in the early grades, students tend to read similar texts within a grade level and thus are likely to learn the same words in roughly the same order.

The variability of student vocabulary size presents the greatest challenge for instruction. After second grade, when most students have mastered decoding skills, many students can read words that they do not know and therefore do not understand, at which point vocabulary size can become a critical limiting factor in reading comprehension (Biemiller, 2005, 2006; Scarborough, 2005). The point is simple. In the early grades, students know more words than they can decode, and decoding is the barrier; once they master decoding and start encountering more complex texts, they may be able to decode words, but knowledge of their meanings becomes the barrier.

Because many students enter school with much smaller English vocabularies than their peers, a critical issue for vocabulary instruction is to determine what words need to be taught to bring lower-performing students up to grade level (Biemiller, 2015; Hart & Risley, 1995; Hoff, 2003; Rowe, Raudenbush, & Goldin-Meadow, 2012). The relative difference in vocabulary size tends to increase progressively as students move to higher grades in part because of a positive feedback loop: large vocabularies facilitate reading, which in turn facilitates vocabulary growth (Duff, Tomblin, & Catts, 2015; Stanovich, 1986, 2000). Biemiller thus recommends selecting words for direct instruction that are known to higher-performing students at a given grade level but not known to lower-performing students. This is because these are likely to be the next words that most students would learn anyway (making them more susceptible to instruction) and because learning those words will help bring lower-performing students up to the level of their peers.

Frequency, especially when combined with dispersion, provides very useful data about words. However, there are a number of both technical and conceptual issues with frequency that limit its usefulness and that should provide caution about what it tells us about a particular word.

Problems with Measures of Frequency and Age of Acquisition

We all know, for instance, that *the* is the most frequent word in English. What word is in second place? The answer is, surprisingly, corpus-specific. Frequency is typically measured using a large text corpus, but frequency calculations may differ, depending on which corpus is used to calculate frequency. Each corpus has a bias, based on the selection criterion that was used to decide which texts would be included (or excluded). This can have significant effects on the relative frequency rankings of words. For instance, the words *of, and,* and *to* are all candidates for second place, and their corpus frequencies are relatively similar. The words are ranked in that order for the Wikipedia and Project Gutenberg (literary text) corpora, but *to* moves to second place for the GigaWord corpus (newspaper text) and a corpus of essays written for the GRE assessments. The shifting of rankings becomes even greater for words that are less frequent. As the variety and size of corpora increase, the stability of a word's frequency across a range of corpora may become a significant indicator of its usefulness. The fact that a word appears in a wide variety of corpora suggests it is generally useful across a variety of contexts. Words that are consistently ranked high in frequency can be considered to be more generally useful than words that are less consistently frequent across corpora.

Somewhat different issues arise with measures of the age of acquisition. There are online systems that can inexpensively gather large amounts of information from people. This crowdsourcing technology has made it much easier to create large databases of subjective age-of-acquisition ratings, such as those produced by Kuperman et al. (2012). However, these subjective ratings are far more reliable as a relative measure of word difficulty than as actual estimates of when words were mastered by most of a target population, and it remains very difficult to collect objective measures from students for age of acquisition for a large number of word meanings. By now, the LWV is well out of date, since the demographics of the U.S. school-age population, and for that matter aspects of English vocabulary, have changed significantly since LWV estimates were collected. For example, *microwave* is defined in the LWV as a *high-frequency wave,* but it is typically understood by contemporary students as a type of oven. *Internet* and *iPod* are among the most frequently used words in modern student essays, but they do not occur in LWV. Updating the LWV remains an extremely challenging proposition, and thus far, no one has undertaken it. Moreover, except for the LWV, no other resources provide estimates of the age of acquisition for word meanings rather than for undifferentiated words.

As useful as frequency is as an indicator of word difficulty, there are some inherent problems with frequency calculations that conceptually limit its utility. The chief issue is that frequency is calculated from strings of letters and thus it does not make distinctions between words' senses or homophones. For example, the frequency for *game* reflects both its meaning of *playing a game* as well as *hunting game,* even though the latter meaning is much less frequent. More subtly but just as important for selecting words to teach or test, the frequency of a word does not tell you how often the sense of a word appears. For example, the frequency of the word *transfer* does not reflect how often that word was used to mean concrete senses, such as *transferring* groceries from the car to the kitchen or a more abstract sense of *transferring* power or authority. Frequency can also be affected by a word's appearance in multiword expressions. The frequency of *hot* includes expressions like *hot dog, hot line, hot rod,* and *in hot pursuit.*

Another issue with the reliance on frequency is that frequency cannot provide information about the role or importance of a word, either in the language as a whole or in a particular context. For example, the following pairs of words have nearly identical frequencies, according to the Corpus of Contemporary American English database (Davies, 2009): *piglet* and *metacognitive; entitled* and *lip; confirmed* and *eighteen;* and *dismissed* and *helicopters.* A cautionary note to heed when interpreting labels such as "high-frequency words" and "rare words" is that frequency is relative, since nearly every scholar has set different thresholds for defining words as high or low frequency and there is no agreed-upon set of "high-frequency words." For example, Nation (2001) notes that the words he categorizes as low frequency include those that a reader will rarely encounter, in addition to words very close to the threshold for high-frequency words. In general, no matter how the category of low-frequency words is defined, it will contain a huge number of words because most words in the language are not used frequently. Frequencies vary across corpora and scholars vary in the thresholds they assign, so the same word may be classified as high frequency in one analysis and lower frequency in another. As a result, the categorization of words based on frequency is flexible, although the overall trends are likely to remain the same.

Alternative Approaches to Word Selection

In light of the limitations of frequency as a guide to word selection, a number of strategies have been suggested that prioritize words for instruction, based on additional kinds of selection criteria. One approach is to group together words belonging to the same morphological word family (Bauer & Nation, 1993; Nagy, Anderson, Schommer, Scott, & Stallman, 1989; Nagy & Hiebert, 2010). In particular, instruction focused on common root words has generally proven more useful than instruction focused on affixes. For example, teaching *organize* and its family members such as *disorganized, organization, reorganize* allows students to learn other forms that can be taken with this root. Teaching specific prefixes and suffixes in isolation is less effective, as not all affixes can be combined with all roots (e.g., adding *bi-* or *-ful* to *organize* does not work). A focus on word families allows a teacher to address the relationships between the family members (as we discussed with *interpret* in Chapter 2) and can help with decisions about which words to assess and teach. The larger word families provide a rich set of relationships between the variant forms and can act as exemplars for how the semantics of the morphemes combine.

Another kind of word relationship that has been used to group words is based on categories or topics, including communication; emotions and attitudes; character traits; social relationships; social categories to which people can belong; actions people can perform; comparisons/values; the body and bodily health; places/dwellings; physical attributes; descriptions of nature, of machines, and of aspects of social systems. Hiebert and Cervetti (2011) advocate this approach and call the groupings *vocabulary mega-clusters*. They suggest that teachers identify such clusters and use them to teach students how to relate words with common meaning elements across texts. This approach is especially useful when considering that individual words will appear relatively rarely. For instance, a teacher might have students analyze multiple stories that focus on a specific cluster of emotion words, such as words related to *fear.* This might cover a broad range of words from different parts of speech, such as *caution, fright, fear, shock, terror* (nouns); *scare, frighten, petrify, wince, flinch, tremble* (verbs); or *afraid, frantic, desperate* (adjectives). Developing graphic organizers that link vocabulary into clusters, Hiebert argues, would help to develop a deep understanding of vocabulary that focuses around critical concepts in narratives.

The approach of teaching semantically related words together is not uncommon in the vocabulary literature; however, it is not without its problems. Nagy and Hiebert (2010), reviewing the literature on semantically driven approaches to vocabulary teaching, warn of a risk in teaching semantically related words together: the words may be confused in memory and therefore learned less well than if they had been taught in isolation (Tinkham, 1997). Nagy and Hiebert suggest that it may be better to teach topically related vocabulary together (i.e., words like *law/police* or *learn/school*) than to teach categorically related vocabulary together (i.e., words like *peach* and *apricot*), which may be more susceptible to confusion.

Graves et al. (2014) advocate a system for selecting words for instruction from the texts that students are reading using multiple criteria. They distinguish four categories of unfamiliar words:

1. *Accessible words*—"more common or higher-frequency words that are not likely to be understood by students who have limited vocabulary knowledge" (p. 336). These words correspond roughly to the words that Biemiller recommends for direct instruction in order to help students who need to catch up with their peers.

2. *Valuable words*—words that "have broad, general utility for students' reading and writing and thus have enduring importance" (p. 336). This group of words corresponds roughly to Beck and McKeown's Tier Two words, although what counts as a valuable word is determined in relation to both the text and the sophistication of students' vocabulary.

3. *Essential words*—words that may or may not be "valuable" in general, but are crucial for comprehending a specific text that students are reading.

4. *Imported words*—words that "help students analyze and extend what they learn in a text" (p. 336). These words capture key elements but may not actually occur in the text. Rather, they have morphological and semantic connections to the texts that students are reading and

could thus help by creating stronger connections among sets of related words.

Efforts to develop alternative word selection procedures have been chiefly motivated by a desire to help students see relationships among words and present words that are optimally useful for students' future comprehension.

Subjective Judgment

Each approach to word selection that we have reviewed ultimately relies on subjective judgment. This is particularly the case when trying to select words that will play important roles in students' literacy futures. Biemiller and Boote (2005) acknowledge this state of affairs in two ways. First, they discuss the lack of clear criteria for distinguishing teachable words and defining words that may be considered too difficult, saying that teachers are "left with testing and some uses of intuition for identifying word meanings for instruction" (p. 4). Second, they mention in their study the need to evaluate "word importance" to distinguish words that are the most useful to learn. Similarly, Hiebert (2005) acknowledges the judgment component in discussing implications for teachers like pointing out the relative utility of words that appear in the same text, for example, *checkpoint* and *cautiously* (pp. 260–261).

Using the judgments of experienced teachers to capture the words that students are likely to find difficult is time-consuming but yields a rich picture of vocabulary demands from the words that students are typically exposed to over the course of a year. Scott and her colleagues (Flinspach et al., 2012; Scott, Flinspach, & Vevea, 2011) created a word bank that reflects widely used classroom materials as source materials for determining grade-level vocabulary, based on 19 commonly adopted fourth- and fifth-grade math, science, English language arts, and social studies textbooks and 21 Newbery Award–winning novels. A team of eight experienced elementary teachers, used to working in classrooms with large percentages of English learners, combed through these materials to find words that they considered "unfamiliar" or "conceptually new" for typical students in each grade. The resulting list yielded more than 39,000 individual word forms. Winnowing this list down to words that occurred more than once, with attention to morphological patterns and polysemy, allowed them to create a teacher-tested pool of challenging vocabulary from across the curriculum. One benefit of this exercise is that it exposed the vast array of words that we expect students to be able to understand in grade-level materials and how traditional techniques may be underestimating the task. The teachers identified words used in unfamiliar ways (*board* as in *board a train*) and as different parts of speech (*respect* as both a noun and a verb), as well as infrequent words in various subject areas (*latitude, luxurious, yucca, vaporize*). An analysis of the almost 3,000 words that occurred at least twice from the math and science textbooks revealed that 75% were beyond the 2,000 most frequent words in English—the Academic Word List only captured 13% of the words identified by the teachers. The agreement rate between teachers was 72%, but the overlap between teacher judgments and publisher-identified words was only 31%.

Selecting words for instruction is inherently a fuzzy problem space. This presents difficulties in decision making, but the positive side is that, to some extent, it does not matter which words are taught. That is, although we can identify sets of words that students will need and will likely encounter frequently, there is no perfect set of words that students must know. The set of requisite words depends on the students, their conceptual understanding, the texts they will read, and the evolving use of language.

The impossibility of identifying the perfect set of words means that teachers have and should take liberty in making selections, using a combination of informed judgment based on information about word frequency and other approaches for selection, and then develop a sense of their students' language needs. Astute word selection means attention to how words are used, which words seem to turn up repeatedly in classroom materials, and which words students seem to trip over or find difficult.

The other side of this decision making is that decisions must be made! As we have noted before, there are far too many words in the language to teach them all. There may also be far too many unfamiliar words in a text to teach them all, and attempts to do so may simply make the learning task so overwhelming that students may not learn the words they need the most. As a quick exercise in developing such word sensitivity, consider the following set of words from Harper Lee's *To Kill a Mockingbird*, as identified on *vocabulary.com*: *abide, evasion, kin, sound* (as in *sound mind*), *resentment, pauper, sweltering, trudge*, and *apprehensive*. Which are best to teach? We would suggest that a teacher might choose to prioritize some of these words over others, as follows:

Teach	Possibly teach	Don't teach
evasion	*abide*	*kin*
resentment	*sound* (as in *sound mind*)	*trudge*
apprehensive		*sweltering*
		pauper

Evasion, resentment, and *apprehensive* are good, general words that can turn up in many contexts. They are also complex words containing multiple morphemes that will support future discussions of word families and affixes. *Apprehensive* also provides the potential for a discussion of multiple word senses, especially physical and abstract mental senses, with one sense of its root, *apprehend,* meaning literally to capture someone. The words in the "Teach" column are prioritized because they are useful for multiple reasons, such as both exhibiting morphological complexity and secondary senses.

The words in the "Don't teach" column (*kin, trudge, sweltering,* and *pauper*) are rarer and more specialized than the words in the "Teach" column, and also less morphologically productive, which means that they are less likely to be useful when students encounter a new text. They are the kind of words that may be briefly explained during class discussions, and which students should be encouraged to look up on their own, but are probably not worth sustained class time. Not teaching them, however, does not mean that they are useless or that students will never encounter them again; they are more concrete in meaning and thus students are much more likely to learn these words on their own. The "Possibly teach" words fall somewhere in the middle—they are not concrete, but not as morphologically rich. Both words have multiple senses, so this might be a reason to include them; yet they seem simpler in meaning than the recommended group.

Another way to treat words like *kin, trudge, sweltering, pauper, sound,* and *abide* is to recognize them as representing concepts that students will mostly know and discuss them in ways that help students recognize relationships to other words. Having students collect words in their own reading related to known concepts such as *hot,* ways of *walking,* and terms that describe *wealth* and *poverty,* provides a set of words from books that students are interested in knowing and using. Teaching then becomes less about selecting particular words and more about recognizing relationships among words and building on what students already know. Words such as *sound* and *abide* can engender a discussion about polysemy, drawing on information about nouns and verbs and how one might be able to infer which sense is being used in a passage.

Multiword Expressions

In addition to individual words, multiword expressions (MWEs) also should be considered in decisions about vocabulary instruction. These expressions vary along a continuum from idiomatic expressions to phrases composed of two or more words that have entirely predictable meanings. The extent to which an expression is idiomatic determines whether it must be learned individually, as a whole phrase, or whether it can be inferred from the words that it comprises (Ellis, 2003). Academic English, in particular, requires learners to acquire a large inventory of idioms, collocations, and lexical bundles (Coxhead & Byrd, 2007). For English learners, mastering academic vocabulary is part of the transition from intermediate to higher levels of academic English proficiency (Eskildsen, 2008; Yorio, 1989).

As mentioned in Chapter 2, we know very little about how MWEs are learned developmentally. We do not have an exhaustive inventory, since standard dictionaries only contain a fraction of the MWEs in common use and are inconsistent about which expressions are included. There are no resources that a teacher can use to provide guidance about what should be taught and assessed. Nevertheless, such expressions make up at least half of our vocabulary—they are a source of student errors, and they are crucial for fluency. Some factors to consider when deciding which MWEs to teach might be their relationship to a particular discipline or to academic learning, their dispersion or frequency in English, and whether they can be used to point out particular patterns of interest.

Words with a Latinate origin are associated with academic vocabulary and with a higher degree of linguistic competence (see Corson's [1985] *The Lexical Bar*). For example, *vice versa, status quo, bona fide, carpe diem, ad hoc, ipso facto, Homo sapiens, prima facie, habeas corpus, cum laude, pro bono,* and *modus operandi* are among the most frequent expressions found in a variety of corpora. Many of these words are highly associated with the legal profession and many of them are a part of Tier Three vocabulary. In studying a particular subject, such as social studies, it might be worth drawing students' attention to these MWEs and their origins.

MWEs often use restricted secondary senses of commonly known words, creating an issue for students who know only the primary meanings of words. For example, *real estate* does not use *real* in the sense of *reality* or *real number*. Because students are often unaware that words can be used with secondary senses, MWEs can be confusing, as they exhibit a variety of senses. For example, *Milky Way* has two completely different senses, as a candy bar and as a galaxy; *garbage collector* has both the literal meaning of collecting garbage and a figurative meaning in computer science as a form of memory management; and some MWEs can have systematic secondary senses such as *New York,* which can refer to both a location and an entity (as in "New York passed a law").

MWEs can also have idiomatic meanings that cannot be understood by understanding their component words. We can understand *gravity of the offense* if we understand the secondary sense of the word *gravity* as extreme seriousness. However, this differs from expressions like *across the board, clear the air,* and *red herring,* where an understanding of the component words does not allow the reader to understand the meaning of the expression. The *red* in *red herring* is not a secondary sense, just as we do not think of *hot* in *hot dog* as a secondary sense.

Identifying patterns associated with MWEs would promote a metalinguistic understanding of how English works. One such pattern is that phrasal verbs and idioms can be broken up into nonadjacent parts in a sentence. For example, the phrasal verb *look up* can occur as *We looked up the word* or *We looked the word up.* Similarly, idioms can be broken up into nonadjacent parts in a sentence, such as *calling someone to account* or *letting something slide.* Like variations within morphology, MWEs can be organized into families of patterns, such as the subset of phrasal verbs that expresses the concept of completion (e.g., *eat up, drink up, grow up*).

Morphology is useful in understanding restricted contexts of meaning for MWEs. The words *preoccupy* and *preoccupation* are highly related because they refer not to occupying in general, but having one's time occupied with an activity or interest. We do not talk about preoccupying a seat in the theater or say that an army sent in advance forces to set up a preoccupation. In other words, a prefix can be applied to a single sense of the base word, just as an MWE can create a restricted context in which only one secondary sense of a component word is relevant (Krovetz, 1993).

Earlier in the chapter, we divided individual words into three categories: "Teach," "Possibly teach," and "Don't teach." A similar division can illustrate some of the principles for selecting specific MWEs for attention.

Teach	Possibly teach	Don't teach
vice versa	*miles per hour*	*good morning*
ad hoc	*life expectancy*	*blue sweater*
bona fide		*car door*
eat up		
soup up		
carbon monoxide		
Civil War		
standard deviation		
scuba diving		
Herculean effort		

The first three expressions, *vice versa, ad hoc,* and *bona fide,* were selected because they have Latinate origins and because they have high dispersion. The next two, *eat up* and *soup up,* were chosen to illustrate a pattern and exceptions to that pattern. With many verbs, the particle *up* implies that the action described by the verb has been completely accomplished (*drink up/drink, finish up/finish, grow up/grow,* and so forth). There are exceptions to the pattern, which do not have the same relationships with the verb, such as *soup up, beef up, gear up.* It is useful both to help students recognize general patterns, but also recognize that there are limitations and exceptions where the patterns do not apply.

Words in subject areas, such as science or social studies, offer opportunities to talk about MWEs, for example, expressions such as *carbon monoxide* or *Civil War. Carbon monoxide* is proposed because of the morphemes *mono* and *oxi.* Such decomposition is especially important to decoding the vocabulary of science and technology. *Civil war* is proposed because the Civil War was not *civil* in the sense of a civil discussion. *Standard deviation,* a term in statistics, illustrates the same point; there is a different sense associated with a component word.

We propose the next item on the "Teach" list, *scuba diving,* because it provides an opportunity to describe the concept of acronyms and how acronyms can evolve to become words themselves. The word *scuba* is an acronym for *self-contained underwater breathing apparatus.* The same is true for *radar* (radio detection and ranging) and *laser* (light amplification by stimulated emission of radiation). *Herculean effort* is suggested because of a connection with Greek myths, which is an often-recommended aspect of literature study. It is a particularly useful choice because it has a family of terms associated with it (*Herculean task, Herculean accomplishment,* and *Herculean feat*) and because it provides an opportunity to mention other expressions in which names are included (e.g., *Socratic dialogue, Platonic ideal,* and *Euclidean geometry*). We exclude expressions that can be easily understood by understanding the component words.

Beyond Words: Attending to Contexts and Word Patterns in Instruction

A possible consequence of thinking in terms of which specific words to select for instruction is that it may reinforce the idea that a person's vocabulary is a list. A major focus in this book, however, has been to offer a different conception of vocabulary, based on patterns of language use. This conception, taken from modern linguistic theory, implies that we should attend not only to selecting important words to teach, but also to the kinds of contexts that surround words in vocabulary instruction (Goldberg, 1995a, 1995b, 2006, 2016; Tomasello & Tomasello, 2009).

In usage-based theories, learning is driven by the words that serve as prototypical cases around which language learning can coalesce.

Consider the word *asylum*, which is representative of one of the major patterns we have discussed and exhibits multiple senses (polysemy). The sentence *The refugees sought asylum in a foreign country* allows a learner to generalize to the meaning that *asylum* has in typical social studies contexts. The example places the word in a typical syntactic construction (*seek asylum*), which implies that *asylum* is something that one looks for or obtains; indicates who typically seeks *asylum* (*refugees*); and indicates the typical location in which *asylum* may be obtained (a foreign country). The syntactic pattern of the context also suggests what synonyms of *asylum* might be—*seek refuge, seek safety.*

Including generative patterns as part of instruction essentially switches the focus of instruction from words that play an important role in the language to linguistic patterns that underlie effective vocabulary knowledge, but that may or may not include specifically targeted words. Including generative patterns in instruction does not necessarily imply direct, explicit instruction of patterns. Usage-based approaches suggest that effective vocabulary development can be encouraged by exposing students to informative contexts and enabling them to engage with those contexts in meaningful ways, for example, by talking about what a context means and what they notice about how the words fit together within the context. Noticing contexts and how they work encourages students to internalize the linguistic patterns that such contexts exemplify.

SELECTING WORDS, WORD PATTERNS, AND CONTEXTS FOR ASSESSMENT

Moving now from selections for instruction to selections for assessment, we acknowledge that one of the fundamental issues in assessment is the problem of generalization—given the sample of words tested, what conclusions can be justified about vocabulary knowledge that is broader than simply knowledge of those particular words? In Chapter 3, one of our main critiques of traditional vocabulary assessment was that the word selection principles and item types effectively limited the set of justifiable inferences about relative vocabulary size. If we want to support a broader set of inferences, we need to select words, word meanings, and contexts that will provide the relevant evidence. The question, then, is what other kinds of information do we want to capture about students' knowledge?

In this section, we first consider a perspective on selecting words that might yield broader information. We then suggest three additional aspects of vocabulary knowledge to consider for assessment design. Two of these are drawn from our conception of generative patterns, morphological knowledge, and polysemy, and the third is a category we have discussed as a key part of the structure of our vocabulary: MWEs.

Words can be selected for assessment either in a passage context (if we obtain specific supporting texts that are appropriate for a population) or, more generally, outside any specific passage context. If we select words in a passage context, it is important to consider the purpose for which a word is being assessed, which, in turn, is related to why a teacher might choose to teach it. The categories developed by Graves et al. (2014) for selecting words for instruction might thus be usefully adapted to consider selections for assessment. For example, words that may be important for assessing students with limited vocabulary knowledge, such as English language learners, correspond to Graves et al.'s *accessible* words.

Other words might be selected because they are challenging for most students and important for reading a variety of texts in the future, which would correspond to *valuable* words. Other words may provide important information about students' reading comprehension because students may misunderstand a text solely because they have failed to understand an *essential* word. Moreover, there may be words that do not appear in the text, but which relate to the text, and which might be useful to assess to evaluate students' knowledge of the topic or theme more broadly; such words would correspond to *imported* words. These categories of words comprise four distinct reasons to prioritize words for assessment. If we do not test *accessible* words, we may miss a significant source of difficulty for struggling students. If we do not test *valuable* words, we may not know how well students' performance will generalize across texts. If we do not test *essential* words, we may not know how well students will be able to deal with the key content the text presents. In addition, if we do not test *imported* words, we cannot determine how well students will perform when they are asked to discuss or analyze text content. Depending on the purpose of a vocabulary assessment, we might choose to assess different mixes of *accessible, essential, valuable,* and *imported* words for inclusion in a vocabulary assessment.

Note that these distinctions are best treated in relation to targeted texts. If we select texts that exemplify the reading demands that we expect students in a particular population to be able to handle, it should be possible to develop effective methods to identify words from each of these categories. During assessment design, an analysis of a corpus of such exemplary texts can be used to develop lists of targeted words that could be used to support stand-alone assessments that do not make direct use of passage reading. This was the approach taken by Scott and her colleagues in developing the VASE assessment (Flinspach et al., 2012; Scott et al., 2011). However, for many purposes, it may be most appropriate to select rich contexts and base the words to include in an assessment of those words' presence in those texts. It seems especially important to select contexts that can be used to determine whether students have generalized from instruction. It is crucial to assess vocabulary that has not been explicitly taught. In the discussion that follows, we suggest three additional aspects of vocabulary knowledge that we believe should be considered during word selection for assessment design drawn from our conception of generative language patterns. Each has implications for the choice of words, word meanings, and contexts for assessment.

Tacit Morphological Knowledge

As discussed in Chapter 2, a key source of vocabulary growth between third grade and the end of high school is the ability to combine known words and morphemes to acquire new, morphologically complex words. Success with this learning depends on morphological awareness, the ability to recognize how a new word is related to words that have already been learned. Thus, knowing the word *bribe* and the meanings of the affixes *un-* and *-able* would allow a student to infer that the word *unbribable* means someone who cannot be bribed (Anglin, 1970).

Because strong morphological awareness predicts strong vocabulary knowledge and reading comprehension, it is important to include words with various morphological patterns in a vocabulary assessment. This will allow us to assess not only tacit morphological knowledge, but to obtain information about students' conscious knowledge of morphological patterns. The type of word forms that we choose to test will allow us to gather information on the level of students' implicit awareness of morphological patterns. If we test a rare word like *sleeplessness* and discover that students know it is a noun, we have evidence they understand the implications of the *-ness* suffix. If they understand what the word means, we may have evidence that they understand not only the base word *sleep* but also the semantic implications of *-less* and *-ness*. Since the base word and the prefix are part of the core Anglo-Saxon vocabulary and since the suffixes represent highly productive syntactic patterns, a failure to understand them would represent a far lower level of vocabulary development than a failure to understand a word like *irreversibility*, which draws on opaque Latinate morphology. Latinate morphology is more complex than Germanic, and it is typically acquired later.

If learners have a grasp of tacit morphological patterns, they will be well equipped to make sense of unfamiliar words that have transparent, productive morphological patterns. Even very rare words like *irreversibility* are accessible if a learner first knows the word *reverse*, understands the tricky nature of the *in-/ir-* prefix, how *-ble* can be added to a verb to create an adjective, and how that can then change to *-bility* to indicate a noun form. However, the successful use of morphology relies on already knowing the root—either a base word such as *reverse* or a bound root within a word such as *-nov* in *innovative*. Without that key knowledge, morphology is not an effective tool. If we do not obtain a clear sense about the range of morphological patterns with which students are able to deal with effectively, we are unlikely to have a clear sense of how well prepared they are to address the ever-increasing variety of derived words they will encounter in more advanced texts.

We have been talking about knowledge of morphological patterns as tacit—learners have the knowledge and can apply it to understand language, even though they may not be able to explain either the patterns or what they know about them. However, there is strong evidence that learners who are consciously aware of such patterns and can manipulate them are more effective at reading and word learning (Anglin et al., 1993; Carlisle, 2000; Carlisle & Feldman, 1995; Kirby et al., 2012).

Polysemy

We have introduced polysemy, multiple but related meanings of a word, as a generative mechanism that underlies much of the expansion in vocabulary knowledge that happens during the school years. Polysemous words, therefore, are prime candidates for inclusion on assessments, as the ability to understand polysemous senses and extend their meanings to novel contexts is key to successful reading comprehension. When selecting words for assessment, we cannot assume that students will know one meaning (especially secondary, less common meanings) even if they know other meanings of the word. Thus selecting words for assessment is really a matter of selecting word senses, and secondary meanings should not be ignored.

Students with strong word-learning skills may have the semantic flexibility to infer what a word means in context. For example, the sentence *She felt a lot of pressure to join the group* favors a different meaning than the dominant sense of the word, as in *He put pressure on the wound to stop the bleeding.* To understand the first sentence, people must recognize the abstract, metaphorical meaning of *pressure* as social pressure and infer that is the intended meaning. But we cannot assume that all students will be able to make this kind of inference. Many students may not be aware that this second meaning exists or they may fail to retrieve it in context.

There is significant evidence that primary senses are more easily accessed than secondary senses; that individuals can vary in semantic flexibility; and that students, at least in the primary grades, tend to recognize secondary senses of words less accurately, even when the words appear in compatible, supportive contexts. There is also evidence that the dominant senses of word meanings come to mind readily, as the default, whereas if a context uses a secondary sense, understanding it requires more effort to integrate the meaning with the context (Foraker & Murphy, 2012; Giora, 2012; Graves, 1980; Titone & Salisbury, 2004). For example, third and fourth graders are much more likely to ignore the context of the sentence *The workers are going to strike tomorrow,* relying on their knowledge of the primary meaning to choose *hit* as the meaning of the word *strike* (Mason, Kniseley, & Kendall, 1979). Mason et al. conclude that when words were assigned their primary (most frequent, prototypical) sense in context, students remembered the words accurately and assigned them the correct meaning, but that when words were assigned secondary senses, they frequently misremembered the context and assigned the word to its primary rather than its secondary sense. This tendency was significantly correlated with reading ability, such that higher-ability students performed more accurately on secondary senses, without any significant difference across grade levels.

Sullivan (2006) had a similar finding about the relationship between ability and word senses. She found that higher-ability students were able to provide explanations of relationships between senses compared with less proficient students, regardless of the grade. Her work also demonstrates that the acquisition of secondary senses accounts for much of the growth in vocabulary knowledge between third and 12th grades. This body of research makes strong arguments in favor of selecting secondary as well as primary senses of words for both instruction and vocabulary assessment and in selecting contexts that provide evidence to support word-sense disambiguation, since the context in which students read a word may provide stronger or weaker support for the inferences they need to make. If we do not design assessments to gauge semantic flexibility, we may miss critical differences among stronger and weaker students.

Multiword Expressions

Choosing to assess MWEs can help teachers determine whether the students can recognize systematic patterns, such as the notion of completion that is a part of *eat up, finish up,* and *grow up,* and can provide information about whether students have the correct understanding of the expressions. For instance, we can ask students to paraphrase *soup up* as *modify and improve* and *beef up* as *strengthen*. We can also ask them to create "idiom books" by creating illustrations that show both the literal and the actual meaning of common idioms. Some good candidates would be *kick the bucket, red herring, raining cats and dogs, face the music,* and *hold your horses.*

FINAL THOUGHTS

So let us return to the core question of this chapter: how many words should be selected and how should those words be taught? It should now be clear that the criteria for selecting words are multiple and complex. A one-size-fits-all approach to word selection may not best serve the learners. In the classroom, much depends on a teacher's judgment and where students are in their mastery of English. However, we have identified several principles that can help teachers make effective choices.

1. Focus explicit instruction on useful, general-purpose words that will help students acquire academic English. Resources like Biemiller's Words Worth Teaching (Biemiller, 2009), Beck et al.'s (2002) Tier Two words, the Coxhead (2000) Academic Word List, and Hiebert's (2011) Word Zones may prove to be useful for this purpose.

2. Emphasize words at or slightly above grade level, which will usually be understood by the stronger students in a class. These are the critical words weaker students need to learn.

3. Pay attention to words in context in the texts students are reading. Look for teachable moments when students encounter unfamiliar or difficult vocabulary—and be alert for challenging features, such as polysemy (multiple meanings) and MWEs. Encourage students to actively identify words they need to know in the texts they are reading and teach them how to make effective use of language resources (dictionaries, thesauruses) as tools, not crutches.

4. Encourage students to think about and analyze words as a normal practice as they read, and encourage them to recognize patterns in how words are used. This includes explicitly analyzing morphology, focusing on common root words. It includes identifying lists of related words that describe the same categories and topics. It includes paying attention to the reasons for choosing one word over another and identifying important or repeated words that can help them better understand the texts they are reading.

These suggestions provide a framework for selecting words, word patterns, and contexts for instruction and assessment that can help teachers and students to navigate the sea of words. In the end, the teacher plays a critical role. Teaching vocabulary is not merely teaching lists of words, but also choosing words that extend students' understanding for multiple contexts so they can take charge and become able to expand their own vocabulary.

CHAPTER 5

How Should We Assess Vocabulary?

At this point, we are ready to take a deep dive into the mechanics of vocabulary assessment. In previous chapters, we emphasized the following ideas:

- Vocabulary knowledge includes the skills that enable students to learn new word meanings efficiently.
- Vocabulary knowledge is rich, involving several different kinds of knowledge.
- Vocabulary knowledge can develop incrementally. Students can have shallow or partial knowledge of words they have not yet wholly mastered.
- Rich vocabulary knowledge derives from multiple experiences with words in a variety of contexts.
- Vocabulary knowledge, when combined with metalinguistic awareness, enables students to apply word knowledge in more complex literacy tasks.

We have also argued that we should conceptualize vocabulary assessment formatively, and not just summatively. Rich forms of vocabulary assessment should make it possible to identify patterns of student strength or weakness. Ideally, a rich vocabulary assessment might suggest ways to improve instruction and model useful classroom practices. We will explore these issues at length. In so doing, we will consider how to conceptualize depth of vocabulary knowledge, although it may be useful to conceptualize vocabulary depth as vocabulary richness—the idea that as vocabulary knowledge develops, multiple forms of knowledge about words are woven together to form an integrated whole.

In this chapter, we discuss word-learning skill, that is, the use of all kinds of lexical knowledge to derive the meaning of words either from morphological or contextual clues. Through the use of examples, we demonstrate ways to assess specific kinds of vocabulary knowledge to help teachers pinpoint where their students may struggle. Instead of merely creating assessments comprising lists of words and primary word definitions, we seek to exemplify students' depth of vocabulary knowledge, covering specifics such as syntax, connotations, collocations, and partial word knowledge. While we acknowledge the role that background knowledge of a domain plays in understanding words and comprehending entire sections of texts (McNamara, Kintsch, Songer, & Kintsch, 1996; Nagy & Herman, 1987), the focus of this chapter lies in assessing word learning from the context of presented texts or learning that can be inferred from the words themselves through deduction and a deeper understanding not of texts, but of words.

In the sections that immediately follow, we consider a variety of formats for assessing vocabulary, many of which have primarily been deployed in studies of second-language vocabulary knowledge. Since our primary concern is with how different parts of the vocabulary construct can be assessed, we will not highlight the L1/L2 distinction in sections where we are focusing on possible methods of vocabulary assessment. Yet the issue of how native speakers versus English learners differ in vocabulary knowledge will come into focus in some sections of this chapter, when we consider the extent to which we may expect different kinds of vocabulary assessments to yield different results within and across individuals and populations.

WORD-LEARNING SKILL

Theoretical Considerations

Kieffer and Lesaux (2012) draw a distinction between *general* vocabulary knowledge and *word-specific* vocabulary knowledge. General vocabulary knowledge is derived from a broader grasp of the system of the language, such as morphological awareness and sensitivity to syntactic context, and can be applied to making inferences about unknown or partially known words. Word-specific knowledge is tied to specific lexical items: it is the knowledge of the orthographic, morphological, syntactic, or semantic properties of a word (Perfetti & Hart, 2002). Kieffer and Lesaux found both word-specific and general word knowledge were needed in order to account for the kinds of language skills that predicted higher student achievement for the sixth graders they tested. This distinction is much the same as the distinction between generative mechanisms and word-specific knowledge that we discussed in earlier chapters. We argued that general forms of vocabulary knowledge, such as morphology and the ability to infer new word meanings in context, are critical aspects of word-learning skill and support students' ability to learn word meanings during reading, either incidentally or by the conscious application of strategies.

In the case of morphology, morphological awareness—the ability to use morphological structure to infer word meanings—has been shown to have a significant impact on the ability to read as early as first grade (Carlisle & Feldman, 1995) and to have a significant impact on the ability to infer the meaning of morphologically complex words as early as third grade (Carlisle, 2000). If anything, the effect of morphological awareness strengthens in the upper grades, and in general, helps to better predict reading comprehension over measures of vocabulary size (Nagy, Berninger, & Abbott, 2006). There is thus considerable evidence that morphological awareness is worth assessing separately from knowledge of specific, already-known words.

In the case of inferring word meanings from context, there is a rich history of investigating that ability, presumably because of its critical role in acquiring vocabulary. Studies spanning several decades from the 1950s to the 1980s (McKeown, 1985; van Daalen-Kapteijns & Elshout-Mohr, 1981; Werner & Kaplan, 1952) examined how the process of inferring word meaning from context unfolded for students of different abilities. All of these studies examined how learners used sentence contexts to assign meaning to a word. The targeted words used were pseudowords to ensure that the learners did not already know them. The studies presented multiple examples to students to explore how they used additional information from successive contexts and asked learners to discuss their thinking about what the word meant. The studies yielded insights about the process of inferring word meaning from context and about the different approaches used by successful and less successful students. Werner and Kaplan found a common error made by students ages 8–13 was to conflate context with word meaning and then carry some of that contextual meaning to the next context, which led students astray from the assigned word meaning. For example, when asked to derive the meaning of *bordick* from the sentence *People talk about the bordicks [faults] of others but don't like to talk about their own,* they were prone to restate the sentence as the meaning of *bordick,* saying that *bordick* means "People talk about other people but don't like to talk about themselves." Students then tried to use that meaning for all subsequent sentences, such as saying that *People with bordicks are unhappy* meant that "People who talk about other people are unhappy."

The task in McKeown's study of fifth graders included providing students with a series of sentences that provided clues to the meaning of a pseudoword and that eventually narrowed to one meaning that made sense in all of the presented contexts. At that point, students either inferred the correct meaning or the meaning was provided to them. An additional set of sentences was then presented, and students were asked which ones made sense with the word.

Results suggested that lower-performing students were prone to using unsuccessful strategies to evaluate the fit of the word to a context. Students sometimes carried over parts of the context from one sentence to another or ignored the meaning of the word and evaluated the sentence based on the rest of the context. For instance, students were given the pseudoword *narp* with the meaning of *ordinary,* then asked to evaluate whether the word *narp* was used appropriately in the following sentence: *People dress up and look narp on Halloween.* A student misevaluated the sentence as correct, explaining, "People do dress up on Halloween."

van Daalen-Kapteijns and Elshout-Mohr (1981), working with college students, sought to characterize the difference between more and less efficient word learners. Their study found that all students seemed to form a rough notion of a word's meaning from initially presented contexts, but the more successful students were able to maintain the same core understanding of the word while remaining flexible enough to revise their inferences with later contexts. Less successful students were more likely to abandon the core meaning when confronted with new contexts and to come up with an entirely new model of word meaning if their original one did not seem to fit.

More recently, Frishkoff, Perfetti, and Collins-Thompson (2011) used a related approach to explore word meaning from context. Their in-depth study of word learning in context provided students with multiple opportunities to guess what a word meant in the context of a sentence. They manipulated the quality of the contexts: some contexts were highly constrained, where only the target words or their synonyms were appropriate; other contexts were less constrained so that a variety of semantically unrelated words was also appropriate. They found that highly constrained contexts produced stronger word learning; that the quality of student-produced definitions increased incrementally over multiple exposures; that students were more likely to retain that knowledge a week later; and that students with stronger reading comprehension skill learned more from context than students with weaker reading comprehension skill.

The results of all the studies in this line of research suggest that the ability to infer word meanings from context is closely linked to what Perfetti, Yang, and Schmalhofer (2008) term *word-to-text integration,* the ability to fit the meaning of the word within the rest of the context to make sense of both the word and context. This ability is a key component process in reading comprehension and almost certainly underlies incidental word learning from reading, which is a critical driver of vocabulary gains (Cain & Oakhill, 2011).

There is likely to be a correlation between vocabulary size and word-learning ability. However, some students may enter school with smaller vocabularies because they have had fewer opportunities to learn words than their peers. This may be particularly true for second-language learners, who may have had only limited opportunities for incidental word learning prior to their arrival to school (Kapantzoglou, Restrepo, & Thompson, 2012). In such contexts, it is important to distinguish between students who will rapidly learn new word meanings as they are exposed to them from students who may need more intensive vocabulary intervention.

There is one important complication in designing tests that assess word-learning ability. We may not know in advance who knows which words, as each person possesses a unique set of known and unknown words. This can cause problems in assessment design. For example, in some of the assessments reviewed in Chapter 2, we observed that there were at least two ways to answer vocabulary items correctly: from memory, using preexisting word knowledge, or by inference from information presented in the reading passage. Research studies often get around this problem by using nonsense words as stimuli, which guarantees that all students will be forced to apply word-learning strategies. However, such strategies may not be appropriate in school assessments, suggesting that there may be a need for an adaptive approach to assessment: first identify words that a student does not know and then test that student's ability to infer what the word means in context. This suggests a place for technology-enhanced assessments that can yield this kind of diagnostic information.

Sample Tasks

To get a clearer sense of what the assessment of word-learning skill might look like, it will be useful to review some of the specific assessment methods that have been proposed. While the examples we review are exemplary, rather than exhaustive, they may help to pin down what it would mean to assess word-learning skill rather than existing vocabulary knowledge.

Morphological Inference

A relatively conventional approach to assessing morphological knowledge can be found in Sasao and Webb (2017), who focus on evaluating whether students can: (1) distinguish between English affixes and other letter sequences that appear in English words, (2) identify whether students can identify the meanings of English affixes, and (3) recognize the syntactic effects of attaching an affix to a word. This kind of general morphological knowledge is likely to indicate morphological awareness.

Larsen and Nippold (2007) provide an example of morphological word learning using the format of a dynamic assessment (Lidz, 1987), a highly interactive procedure in which an examiner takes a student through stages of a learning process in order to identify the student's skills and learning potential. The examiner deliberately supplies information at different stages in the task if the student does not respond correctly and then observes how the student uses the additional information to perform the next part of the task.

In Larsen and Nippold's procedure, the interviewer starts by asking students to explain what a morphologically complex word means, without providing any prompts or scaffolding. Students who respond correctly are asked to explain how they know the meaning, and if their answer references the word's component morphemes, they are credited with full knowledge of the word's morphological structure. Students who fail to provide a morphological analysis unprompted are then asked to identify any smaller parts within the word, and if necessary, they are told what the parts are. They are then given another chance to explain what the word means. Students who cannot explain what the word means from its component parts are then given the word in a sentence context and given another opportunity to explain what the word means. Finally, students who are consistently unable to produce an adequate explanation on their own are asked to choose which of three definitions best defines the word. The more scaffolding students require before they produce a correct answer, the less morphological knowledge they are assumed to possess.

Similar assessment tasks have been used by Anglin et al. (1993), Pacheco and Goodwin (2013), and Crosson and McKeown (2016) to investigate students' ability to figure out morphological components and how their meanings function to make sense of unfamiliar words. In Crosson and McKeown's task, the examiner asked sixth- and seventh-grade students a series of questions to elicit their morphological analysis of an unfamiliar word presented in a sentence. In contrast to the other studies cited here, their task focused on the role of Latin roots to explore whether students could recognize Latin roots within words, link the root with its meaning, and use that information to understand the meaning of an unfamiliar word within a sentence. A sample sentence from their task used the word *minutiae,* containing the root *min-,* also found in familiar words such as *minute*:

> *Most of their conversations were about the <u>minutiae</u> of daily life.*

The point of these types of assessments is to figure out what students know, with follow-up questions that provide additional scaffolding. While this is time-consuming for a typical classroom teacher, it is easy to envision similar (but automatically scored) questions in a formal assessment that uses such tasks as providing synonyms and identifying word parts. Something similar could be transferred to both formal and informal word-learning assessments in classrooms.

Word Learning from Sentence Context

Frishkoff, Collins-Thompson, Hodges, and Crossley (2016) used a tutoring tool that illustrates how to assess inferences of word meanings from context. Their approach starts by presenting a rare (but real) word in a sentence context and asking the respondent to provide a synonym. For example, the rare word *impavid* might be provided in a context like the following (Frishkoff et al., 2011):

> *The <u>impavid</u> firefighter ran into the burning house.*

If respondents provided correct synonyms like *fearless* or *brave* or related words like *courage,* they received feedback telling them they had answered correctly. Otherwise, they received feedback indicating that their answer was partially correct or incorrect, depending on how similar their answers were to a correct synonym (as judged through the use of natural language processing techniques). If their answer was incorrect, they were given another context, perhaps like the following:

> *Policemen must be <u>impavid</u> to fight crime every day.*

The exact nature of the support provided by subsequent sentences can be manipulated in various ways: by the degree to which the context cues the correct answer; by the nature of the context clue provided; or by the extent to which a student's answers provide evidence about knowledge of a network of related meanings. The cycle is repeated until the student converges on a correct answer, and a score can be provided that focuses on the speed with which the student's attempted synonyms converged on the intended meaning. This kind of dynamic assessment of lexical inferencing also measures changes in incremental knowledge about a word in real time, in which we can actually observe whether the student is narrowing in on an answer or floundering, and in which we can observe whether the respondent is more or less sensitive to particular kinds of contextual cues.

DEPTH (OR RICHNESS) OF LEXICAL KNOWLEDGE

The preceding sections focused on students' control of generative mechanisms, but when we speak of the breadth and depth of vocabulary knowledge, we are describing the types or extent of knowledge someone has about specific words. Breadth and depth of vocabulary knowledge are sometimes contrasted. Schmitt (2014) indicates that there is less separation at an early stage of development, but he found that depth lags behind breadth for lower-frequency words. However, an individual's breadth and depth can be hard to separate, since the people who know more words are also likely to know more about individual words (Nagy & Herman, 1987; Perfetti & Adlof, 2012).

The distinctions between breadth and depth of vocabulary take on greater meaning when we consider instruction as a vehicle for vocabulary growth. Different types of instruction can result in very different types of knowledge. If students are taught words by practicing definitions, their breadth of vocabulary may increase, as measured by tests that require recognition of definitions. But students are unlikely to gain the type of knowledge that will support their language comprehension or production (see the discussion in Chapter 2). It may also be the case that instruction may be more or less successful for specific students and for specific word meanings. To understand the success of instructional interventions we need to be able to characterize the kinds of knowledge that students acquire.

Initial efforts to examine depth of knowledge used self-assessment, such as asking students to evaluate the level of their own knowledge of individual words. For example, an assessment of this type might contain items that present the following choices for each word that is tested:

(a) I don't *remember* having seen this word before.
(b) I have *seen* this word before, but I don't know what it means.
(c) I have *seen* this word before, and I think it means _____ [synonym or translation].
(d) I know this word. It means _____ [synonym or translation].
(e) I can use this word in a sentence: _____.

Variations of this approach can be found in a range of vocabulary assessments (Meara & Buxton, 1987; Wesche & Paribakht, 1996), often in simplified form, such as lists of words in which students can check off the words that they know. Student self-assessments can provide reasonably accurate measures of vocabulary knowledge, particularly when students say that they do not know a word (Heilman & Eskenazi, 2008). Yet the assessments may be unreliable since they not only depend on depth of word knowledge but also on a degree of metalinguistic awareness that some students may not have obtained.

Depth of vocabulary knowledge is, however, a complex construct along the lines suggested in the lexical quality hypothesis (Perfetti, 2007). Depth involves having richer representations of words' meanings, pronunciation, and orthography and the ability to efficiently access these representations from each other. These go together so that words that are known richly are also accessed more efficiently. As a result, highly frequent words tend to be known more deeply by learners (Bybee, 2006). Repeated exposures to a word provide more opportunities for incremental learning and increased efficiency of processing (Joseph, Wonnacott, Forbes, & Nation, 2014; Juhasz & Rayner, 2006).

Psycholinguistic studies link this efficiency of processing to the concept of *lexical access* (activating all aspects of word knowledge when a word is retrieved). Efficiency of lexical access tends to increase not only for words that are more frequent in the language but also for words that are learned earlier, as measured by subjective judgments of age of acquisition (Brown & Watson, 1987; Keuleers, Lacey, Rastle, & Brysbaert, 2012; Morrison & Ellis, 1995).

As a result, efficiency of lexical access can be used as an indirect measure of depth of vocabulary knowledge by assessing how easily the meaning of a word (and its secondary senses) can be accessed from its phonological or orthographic form. Lexical access is usually assessed by asking an individual to make rapid decisions about words (Schmitt, 2014). In typical lexical access tasks, words are presented one at a time on a computer screen, and a student is asked to click a key to respond if the string of letters is a word or if the word has some feature, such as whether the word is a verb. Efficient lexical access indicates that the words are more readily available for comprehension processing when encountered in text (Perfetti & Adlof, 2012; Richter, Isberner, Naumann, & Neeb, 2013) and thus fluent access to word meaning is essential for comprehension.

Lexical access tasks are common in psycholinguistic studies but rarely found in school vocabulary assessments (although see Pellicer-Sánchez & Schmitt, 2012, for an evaluation of the use of reaction time data with a yes/no assessment of known vs. unknown words) in part due to the historic lack of appropriate computers and access available in school settings. It is becoming more feasible to collect such information and to use it to estimate fluency with targeted vocabulary due to improving and more reliable computer access.

Components of Depth of Knowledge

The critical point to recognize about depth (or richness) of vocabulary knowledge is that, given the multifaceted nature of word knowledge, word-specific knowledge comes in many forms, and each word in our lexicon has numerous links to other words. Some of these links are straightforward, such as membership in a word family—*happy, happiness, unhappy.* Others are much harder to explain clearly. Researchers continue to struggle with this complexity and in the process have created a variety of organizing devices to conceptualize the kinds of knowledge we have about words and multiword expressions (Schmitt, 2014).

In Chapter 2, we used morphology, grammatical constructions, and polysemy as a framework for organizing that knowledge. In this section, we extend that framework to structure our discussion of depth of knowledge. We can identify at least the following types of information that might be considered components of depth of vocabulary knowledge (Brown, Frishkoff, & Eskenazi, 2005; Christ, 2011; Henriksen, 1999; Nagy & Scott, 2000; Schmitt, 2010; Stahl, 2009):

- *Syntactic knowledge.* To what part of speech does this word belong? How is it grammatically used in a sentence?

- *Morphological relatedness.* Is this word part of a word family? How does it relate to other members of the same morphological series?

- *Connotations.* Does this word imply positive or negative sentiment? Is it associated with particular social attitudes or particular styles or registers? The word *register* refers to distinctions such as oral versus written context, formal versus informal, academic versus nonacademic, or informative versus literary.

- *Collocational knowledge.* A collocation is a word that typically occurs with a word sense, such as *blustery* co-occurring with *day* and *serious* co-occurring with the word *offense.* Questions include: In what usage patterns and characteristic collocations does this word normally appear? Does the word appear as a part of phrasal verbs, idioms, and other types of multiword expressions?

- *Semantic and topical association.* What other words are associated with this word or are used in connection with roughly the same meanings or topics? For example, the words *monarch, royal,* and *ruler* are all topically related.

    • *Semantic relations and attributes.* What other words mean roughly the same thing as this word (*synonyms*) or are directly opposite (*antonyms*) to it in meaning? What words name a broader category to which this word belongs (*hypernym*) or a smaller subcategory (*hyponym*)? Which words have some other (*metonymic*) relation to the word? Metonymy uses the name of an object or concept to refer to a related object, such as referring to a businessperson as a *suit* or referring to a nice car as *a nice ride.* Another aspect of semantic relations is differentiating one concept from other, closely related concepts—for example, the distinction between a *bicycle* and a *tricycle* or between *cars, trucks, vans,* and other types of vehicles. What functional properties, sensory attributes, or other characteristics distinguish one word meaning from another?

Syntactic Knowledge about Individual Words

Basic grammatical knowledge about a word is relatively easy to acquire since it can usually be inferred from the context of a single sentence. For instance, recall our discussion in Chapter 2 about Lewis Carroll's poem "Jabberwocky" from *Alice in Wonderland.* Even though the poem consists of almost nothing but nonsense words, the syntactic properties of the words are very clear from the way they combine with inflectional morphology and grammatical function words:

> 'Twas brillig, and the slithy toves
> Did gyre and gimble in the wabe;

    That is, *brillig* and *slithy* are adjectives; *tove* is a noun (plural *toves,* probably animate); *gyre* and *gimble* are verbs; *wabe* is a noun, probably naming a place. Understanding these syntactic categories requires metalinguistic knowledge—that is, the ability to label the parts of speech. Relatively few vocabulary tests measure this kind of knowledge directly, except for Scott, Hoover, Flinspach, and Vevea (2008) and Scott et al. (2015), which have vocabulary assessments that include part of speech identification as part of a larger battery of vocabulary items.

    Knowledge of syntactic categories and constraints can be tested indirectly, asking students to use tacit knowledge to distinguish between correct and incorrect uses. Assessments of this kind of knowledge are, by definition, both lexical and syntactic, and as a result, items that test implicit knowledge may be classified as assessments of either vocabulary knowledge or syntactic knowledge (Alderson & Kremmel, 2013; Shiotsu, 2010). Consider, for instance, a fairly straightforward item such as the following, which assesses the ability to fit words into a range of characteristic sentence patterns for different parts of speech.

In which of these blanks would it make sense to use the word *intend*?

    (a) I _____ to complete my book next month.
    (b) The _____ kitchen was easy to clean.
    (c) The _____ shone brightly.
    (d) The dog barked very _____.

Crosson and McKeown (2017) include items that assess syntax in an assessment designed to test several levels of knowledge of words taught in an instructional intervention. The assessment presented four cloze sentences for each word and asked students to decide whether the targeted word fit each one. Each item varied such that one or two of the sentences were correct. The syntax items used in this study were sentences in which any word that could correctly fit the sentence was a different part of speech from the target word, for example, *I hurried to _____ the contest* for the target word *integral*. These items were designed to assess a minimal level of word knowledge such that learners with enough familiarity with the target word could recognize the word's syntactic role and correctly reject these sentences. Crosson and McKeown indeed found that these items were the easiest for students.

Morphological Relatedness

Inferring the meanings of new words and the morphological awareness that supports the explicit analysis of word structure have already been discussed under the topic of word-learning skills. However, tacit knowledge of morphological relationships also supports memory for words already learned (Aitchison, 2012). For instance, linguistic theories generally assume that words like *worker* and *rework* are remembered at least in part by their relation to the base word *work*, but that morphologically unrelated words like *tailor* and *retail* are not mentally linked to what might appear to be their apparent base word *tail*. This assumption is supported in that the difficulty of recognizing multimorphemic words is predicted not only by the frequency of the word itself but also by the frequency of its component morphemes and the size and average frequency of its word family (Carlisle & Katz, 2006).

Tacit knowledge of these kinds of morphological relationships can be assessed by tasks that call on the knowledge of word relationships without requiring students to explicitly analyze word structure. For instance, knowledge of morphological relationships can be tested by requiring students to find the correct, related word to use in a sentence (Carlisle, 2000; Kieffer & Lesaux, 2012; Schmitt & Zimmerman, 2002) as in the following examples:

> Even though she doesn't care much about *popularity,* my friend keeps getting more _____.
>
> My cousin owns a *farm*: therefore, my cousin is a _____.

Connotations

The connotations of words may reflect positive or negative sentiment, or other social attitudes or evaluations, depending on the specific emotions called forth by the choice of one word or phrase over another (Allan, 2007; Wilson, Wiebe, & Hoffmann, 2009). The connotations of words can also include inferences about the attitude of the person who chooses to use a particular word (Biber & Finegan, 1989) or about the register and social situation in which the word is normally used (Biber, 1995). Sensitivity to connotation is particularly important to understanding word choice since the writer's selection of one synonym over another reflects a decision about what kinds of connotations the author wishes to convey (Crovitz & Miller, 2008). For instance, it makes a great difference whether an act of eating together is referred to as *dining, devouring, noshing,* or *pigging out.* Alternatively, to consider a rather different context, it makes a great deal of difference if a person who refuses to give up on a course of action is described as *pigheaded, stubborn,* or *persistent.*

For the most part, connotations have not been systematically assessed in vocabulary assessments, although Corrigan (2007) has created such an assessment in which probe sentences are presented and students are asked to provide adjectives that reflect particular types of connotations, such as weak or strong, positive or negative, evaluation, and potency. For example, a probe sentence might take the form *Ted defies John.* Participants were then asked to produce sentences in which the actors—in this case, Ted and John—are described using adjectives. Corrigan's results indicated that the meaning of the verb influenced the selection of adjectives to match the social implications of the verb's meaning; for instance, given the sentence *Ted defies John,* participants were more likely to use adjectives with negative connotations to describe Ted. Thus the word choices that participants applied to the sentence were seen as evidence of the impact of connotation.

Collocational Knowledge

The words in our vocabulary do not appear randomly with any and all other words in the language; rather, there are patterns in the ways words occur together. Collocation is the term for sequences of words that characteristically occur together inside the same phrase, such as *strong tea* or *painful memory*. There is a great variety of collocation types, ranging from idioms such as *in the ballpark* or *last straw*, to expressions that can be partially understood from the component words, such as *status quo*, to formulaic expressions whose meanings are obvious, such as *regular exercise*. An important category of collocation uses high-frequency verbs to express a variety of different shades of meaning, such as *make* in *make the bed, make a decision, make a difference, make do,* and so forth. Frequent words typically are associated with a large number of collocations, covering many different meanings so that, for instance, the word *common* is associated with such different collocations as *common man, common law,* and *common sense.* These kinds of common collocations also come under the umbrella of what we have been calling multiword expressions.

Common collocations are usually well understood by native speakers, even from a fairly young age. Difficulty can arise with understanding them, however, for students whose first language is not English. Some collocations reflect word combinations that may not be obvious or predictable solely from the meanings of their component words and, as such, may not have a direct translation. For example, native Spanish speakers may not be aware that the Spanish collocation *dia violento* would not be literally translated as *violent day,* as it expresses the same meaning as the English collocation, *blustery day.* Similarly, they may not be aware that one <u>makes</u> the bed (in Spanish: *hacer la cama,* literally *do the bed*) but also <u>makes</u> a decision (in Spanish: *toma una decision,* literally *take a decision*).

Rarer words, in particular academic words, also form collocations. Here is where the variety of meanings that can appear in different collocations can cause problems even for native speakers. Consider, for example, *resolve,* as in *resolve a conflict, resolve doubts,* and *resolve to quit smoking.* Learners will need multiple encounters with each of these different phrases in order to fully understand and use the different expressions. Thus knowledge of collocations reflects one's exposure to the patterns of language. Assessments of collocations can provide some insight about how familiar students are with typical expressions and how flexible they can be in inferring meanings of expressions that represent common language patterns. The literature contains both productive and receptive methods for assessing collocational knowledge.

Productive Methods

Crossley, Salsbury, and McNamara (2015) created a productive assessment of collocational knowledge that asks students to produce a short text, which is then scored for the presence of collocations. This approach places no constraints on what the student writes, but uses a general resource of collocational knowledge to distinguish between accurate and inaccurate collocation usage. Schmitt (1998b) uses a somewhat more constrained method, in which students are given a word and its meaning and asked to produce a sentence containing that word. The sentences students produced were then scored by their presence or absence from a list of allowable collocates compiled from corpus data. Another common method is to use cloze-style tasks, where the stimulus consists of a sentence in which a key collocate has been deleted from a context where no other words are likely (Bonk, 2003; Voss, 2012). For instance, Voss (2012) provides the following examples of cloze-like items used to assess collocational knowledge:

Example Item 1: *It is difficult to _____a decision when you have two good choices.* [Key: *make*]

Example Item 2: *A distinction can be _____ between planned and unplanned decentralization.* [Key: *made*]

Receptive Methods

There is a similar range in receptive methods to assess collocational knowledge. A common method is to ask students to respond to a phrase by deciding whether it is a valid collocation. For instance, Gyllstad (2007) asks students to check off "yes" or "no" for a list of 100 possible collocations, indicating which of them are valid, commonly used phrases. Barfield (2003) asks students to rate potential collocations with regard to their relative frequency.

Other types of items include the more standard multiple-choice formats. For instance, a collocation can be provided in the form of a partial phrase, as in the following item from Gyllstad (2007):

Choose the word sequence that is a normal, commonly occurring English phrase:

(a) do damage
(b) make damage
(c) run damage

On the other hand, the valid collocation (and alternate, invalid collocations) can be embedded in a larger context, as in the following example from Bonk (2003):

Find the error:

    (a) Are the Johnsons throwing another party?
    (b) She threw him the advertising concept to see if he liked it.
    (c) The team from New Jersey was accused of throwing the game.
    (d) The new information from the Singapore office threw the meeting into confusion.

Using vocabulary without collocational knowledge is likely to be a challenge for second-language learners. The use of collocations is a stereotypical distinction between native and non-native speakers. Assessment of collocational language gives an indication of whether language users are gaining facility with everyday English.

Semantic and Topical Association

Both this topic and the next one (semantic relations and attributes) embody the knowledge of how single words relate to other words in the language. Schmitt (2014) refers to this as lexical organization, that is, the degree to which any word is integrated into the rest of the mental lexicon.

Word associations have a long history in psychology (Osgood, Suci, & Tannenbaum, 1957), particularly as tests in which a person is given a series of words and asked to respond with the first word that comes to mind. The results from a wide range of studies (e.g., Postman & Keppel, 1970) have demonstrated that the associations that people produce capture important information about the pattern and structure of conceptual relationships in long-term memory (Steyvers, Shiffrin, & Nelson, 2004; Steyvers & Tenenbaum, 2005). The associations produced by psychological tests are very similar to the results obtained by computational analysis of large corpora (Burgess 1998; Lund & Burgess, 1996). This has led to the hypothesis that learners internalize these associations as they encounter them in text and use them in subsequent encounters as clues to the word's meaning (Landauer & Dumais, 1997). Word associations are easy to collect for large numbers of words and thus are well suited to gathering information about word knowledge at a level of detail that is relatively hard to obtain with more difficult kinds of lexical judgments.

One of the most commonly used assessments of depth of word knowledge examines learners' ability to recognize different types of word associations. A well-known example is Read's Word Associates Test (Read, 1993, 1998). Variations of this idea have been applied in different contexts, primarily with second-language populations (Qian, 1999; Schmitt, 1998a). In the Word Associates Test, a target word is presented in conjunction with a list of eight word choices. The task is to choose four words that are associated with the target. In the following example, *common* is the target word; *ordinary* and *shared* have meanings similar to the target, and *boundary* and *name* appear in familiar collocations with the word (common boundary, common name).

> common
>
> - complete
> - light
> - ordinary
> - shared
> - boundary
> - circle
> - name
> - party

As this example indicates, word associations typically fall into two rather distinct types: those that reflect the fact that two words are typically used in a shared phrase and those that reflect a common meaning or topic. We covered the former in discussing collocational knowledge, so here we focus on semantic and topical associates.

One advantage of word associations is that they can be assessed very efficiently, making it relatively easy to collect data for large sets of words. An example can be provided by two recent studies that collected associative data for a large number of words (Feng et al., 2013; Halderman et al., 2013). In these studies, lists of topically related words were created for 101 biology topics and 166 history topics and validated by the judgment of domain experts. For instance, the biology topic of *biomes* included words like *Antarctic, arctic, fauna, flora, lowland, marine, temperate, terrestrial,* and *tropical.* Let us call these "prototypical topic words." These lists were supplemented by identifying words with a high-average association with topic words in a large text corpus that consisted primarily of magazine and journal articles (Sheehan, Kostin, & Futagi, 2007). Let us call these words "associated topic words." For example, words not on the *biome* topic list but associated with them included *atmospheric, biodiversity, climate, ecosystem, forests, habitat,* and *waters.* Prototypical and associated topic words were matched with foil words that had the same frequency in the language overall as the corresponding topic word but had little to no association with any of the topic words. Judgments of whether the words were related were then collected from domain experts in biology and history/social studies as well as from students in grades 7, 9, and 11.

The expert study assumed that all words were known to the experts and asked them to judge whether the words were "related," "somewhat related," or "unrelated" to the topic, identified by a short word or phrase, like *biome*. This task was easily performed by the experts: 86% of expert biology judgments and 88% of expert history/social studies judgments rated prototypical topic words as being related to the topic. Associated words were still largely judged as "related" (60% in biology, 62% in history/social studies) or "somewhat related" (27% in biology, 29% in history/social studies). Foil words were mostly judged as "unrelated" (77% in biology, 71% in history/social studies) or only "somewhat related" (24% in biology, 21% in history/social studies).

For the topic of *citizenship,* the majority of the words were known to seventh graders who mostly judged that they were related to the topic. Perhaps the most striking feature of this topic set is the fact that many students who knew the words *superpower* and *asylum* did not judge them as related to the topic probably because they based their judgments on the meanings of the primary senses of these words, which were irrelevant to the citizenship context.

Responses between the middle school and high school populations in these studies were compared, and some student responses changed significantly. For example, for the topic of *conservatism* and *capitalism,* there were increases both in the number of students who judged certain words as known and as relevant to the topic, including such words as *bourgeois, Marxism, partisan, neoconservative, individualism, imperialism,* and *progressive* (all relevant as part of the left-wing/right-wing political divide). There was a corresponding drop in judgments of relatedness for the foil words, which have no relation to the topic. As these examples illustrate, it is relatively easy to collect hundreds of association judgments from a single person in a very short time and thus to examine that person's vocabulary knowledge in tightly constrained areas, such as the vocabulary relevant to a domain or specific concept or topic.

To date, most assessments have focused on word associations in isolation, rather than the function of word associations in reading passages. However, word associations play a critical role in the analysis of textual coherence (Foltz, 2007; Foltz, Kintsch, & Landauer, 1998; McNamara, Louwerse, & Graesser, 2002). Within a text passage, there are groups of associated words that typically correspond to particular themes or topics that are being developed in the passage. Knowledge of these associated words, and knowledge that they do associate around a given text topic, support a reader's understanding of the text and learning of the content related to that topic or theme. Therefore, it should be possible to create assessments that assess word association knowledge in a passage context, allowing for richer assessments in which, for instance, it would be possible to determine whether students are sensitive to the lexical associations of the secondary senses of polysemous words. Knowledge of secondary senses can be difficult to evaluate outside of a passage context, given the tendency of students to use the primary sense of a polysemous word when it is used out of context. For example, given a developmental progression, as was seen with the words *superpower* and *asylum,* we can select passages in which those words occur and ask students to provide definitions for them. If the response indicates *invisibility* for the first word and a *place for mentally ill people* for the second, we know that the student misunderstood the meaning in context.

Semantic Relations and Attributes

There are a number of other types of relationships among words that reflect how word knowledge is organized and the extent to which specific learners can access that knowledge for understanding and producing language. These relationships might be useful as the basis of assessments that indicate the quality of learners' lexical organization.

Categorical Relations

Computerized lexical databases like WordNet (Miller, 1995) map out categorical relationships between word senses. WordNet, for instance, is organized around sets of synonyms, or *synsets*. Each synset exhibits a number of semantic relationships. For instance, the nouns *good* and *goodness* are opposites, or antonyms, of *evil*. They are members of the category, or hyponyms, of words that can label the quality of things. They can be labels of a category, or hypernyms, of words that mean a specific type of "goodness," such as *worthiness, desirability, benefit/ welfare,* or *wisdom.* Categorical relationships can cross parts of speech, such as the relationship between attributes (*weight*) and the corresponding adjectives (*light/heavy*).

Functional Relations

Another type of relationship among words can be described in terms of the function or role that an entity plays in an action or event. Most notably, these relationships define the roles that nouns play in sentences (cf. Dowty, 1991; Fillmore, 1966; Gruber, 1965; Jackendoff, 1972). For example, the noun *cook* is defined in linguistic terms as the doer, or agent, of the act of cooking. Similarly, the noun *food* is defined as the *theme*, or affected entity, in the act of eating. The specific roles are determined by the relationship between the verb and the category of the noun. For example, in the sentence pair *I ate spaghetti with my fork* versus *I ate spaghetti with my wife,* we assign a different relationship based on the noun. Other functional relationships include location (a *residence* is the place where people reside or live), manner of action (*sauntering* is a way people walk), or causal consequence (a *meal* results when someone *cooks*). Some of these types of relationships are captured in systems like WordNet, including part–whole relationships (*body/arm, house/porch*) and entailment or cause–effect relationships between verbs (such as *strike/shatter*). Many others are not captured in WordNet, although they are encoded in other digital lexical resources, such as PropBank (Kingsbury & Palmer, 2002) or FrameNet (Baker, Fillmore, & Lowe, 1998).

Prototypical Attributes

Many words are also associated with prototypical attributes—characteristics that are not logically necessary to define a word but that are associated with typical examples of the concept (Rosch, 1999). We envision a *cat* as having soft fur; we assume that a *teacup* has a handle; we take for granted that an *orange* is orange in color, even though we might well encounter a hairless cat, a teacup without a handle, or a green (and unripe) orange. This kind of information is central to the way people reason about concepts. We often reason in terms of prototypes, but apply concepts flexibly, extending them to cases where the prototypes do not fully apply.

Methods of Assessing Semantic Knowledge

A wide range of assessments test people's knowledge of semantic relations. This includes, of course, conventional assessments of definitions, which are based on semantic relationships. Classical definitions typically take the form of a statement about a word's categorical relationships, restricted by additional information usually stated as some kind of functional relation—for example: *a house is a building in which people live,* which expresses a categorical relation (a *house* is a kind of building) and a functional relation (people live in a *house*). There are several ways to assess definitional knowledge. People can be asked to assess the truth of a definitional statement *(Is a bachelor an unmarried man?)*. They can be given a list of definitions and asked which one is correct. They can

be asked to identify or produce a synonym or an antonym or to determine whether a word fits under a larger category (*Is a banana a fruit?*).
They can also be asked to generate a definition of their own. Since we
reviewed definitional items in an earlier chapter, we do not elaborate at
length on the possibilities here.

Analogies between words have been used as the basis of some
assessments. Analogy tasks present a pair of words that have a particular
semantic relationship and require the test-taker to identify a second pair
of words that have a similar relationship (Bejar, Chaffin, & Embretson,
1991; Carroll, 1979; Enright & Bejar, 1989; Whitely, 1977). In an analogy item, the relationship is not explicitly provided; the test-taker must
infer the relationship from the first pair and use it to solve the second.
The following is a typical verbal analogy item:

Hot is to Florida as _____ is to North Pole.
    (a) *explorer*
    (b) *snow*
    (c) *cold*
    (d) *Santa Claus*

Analogy tasks are designed to assess the verbal reasoning needed
to identify the initial relationship between the word pair and make sure
that the same relationship holds between each pair of words. Items that
make use of an analogy are also appropriate for testing an understanding of metaphor, which is an extension of a literal meaning based on
analogous properties.

Integrating Multiple Forms of Lexical Knowledge

Thus far, we have focused on assessments of specific types of vocabulary
knowledge, but true depth of knowledge requires the ability to access
and coordinate multiple aspects of a word simultaneously. A type of
item that requires this kind of integration is used in Laufer and Nation's
(1999) Productive Vocabulary Levels Test. In this assessment, test takers
are given a sentence with a blank in it. Usually, the blank is only part of
a missing word with one or more letters at the beginning of the blank
space providing a cue for the missing word. By providing this cue, the
solution is restricted to one possible answer. For example, one of the test
items for university-level vocabulary is the following sentence (where the
correct answer is *anomaly*): *The anom _____ of his position is
that he is the chairman of the committee, but isn't allowed to vote.*

The ability to recall a word, given a partial orthographic cue and a constraining sentence context, depends on having a high-quality lexical representation of that word that includes both a full orthographic representation and significant knowledge about the target word's characteristic collocations. This kind of item may be particularly useful to assess word and phrase pairs that are likely to be misunderstood, for example, *exceptional/exceptionable, persevere/perseverate, new age* and *modern age, at least* and *the least* (cf. Pinker, 2015). Such cases involve a difference of a few letters, common affixes, or frequent words, and it is predictable that they would cause confusion.

PARTIAL AND INCREMENTAL KNOWLEDGE OF WORDS

In previous chapters, we criticized traditional vocabulary assessments on the grounds that they only measured definitional knowledge and provided no way to measure incremental growth, and so far in this chapter, we have outlined a rich variety of ways to assess different aspects of vocabulary knowledge. But we have not yet addressed a key question: namely, does testing one of those aspects mean that others are present? This may be true in many cases depending on how word knowledge was acquired and the characteristics of the learner, but very often what we want to know is whether individual students have learned words differentially, and whether a certain kind of learning experience has produced vocabulary knowledge that will support literacy tasks, such as comprehending sophisticated texts and writing.

One aspect of acquiring vocabulary that we know for sure is that the process is incremental. What we learn from one experience with a new word, whether that experience is an incidental encounter in text or instruction, is usually insufficient to provide complete information. Multiple encounters are needed. Given that state of affairs, it seems that one of the things we want to do in instructional settings is to know how close students are getting to a complete understanding of a word from a sequence of experiences. We want to be able to gain insight into how well students are moving along in stages of knowledge for particular words. Likewise, we want to know the strength of students' metalinguistic knowledge and skills such as morphological knowledge and word-learning ability.

All of the above brings us to the proposition that we may need to assess multiple aspects of vocabulary knowledge. That is, it may be important to measure different aspects of vocabulary knowledge separately and we may need to collect multiple measures for each word.

To date, there have not been many studies that have purposely assessed multiple aspects of vocabulary knowledge for the same words, despite considerable evidence for partial or incremental development of vocabulary knowledge (Anderson & Nagy, 1991; Stahl, 2009). One line of research (Durso & Shore, 1991; Nagy & Scott, 1990; Schwanenfugel, Stahl, & McFalls, 1997) provides evidence that people can have knowledge about syntactic and semantic properties of words they do not believe that they know, and thus provides some evidence that familiarity judgments can be separated from other aspects of lexical knowledge. Another line of research (Chaffin, 1997; Whitmore, Shore, & Smith, 2004) suggests that semantic information such as category membership is more salient to learners when words are partly known, whereas finer-grained distinctions like functional relationships and prototypical attributes become more salient as words become more familiar. In addition, there are automated methods to generate items to assess different aspects of vocabulary knowledge (cf. Brown et al., 2005). Such methods are discussed in Chapter 7.

More direct evidence of partial or indirect knowledge can be obtained from two major lines of research. One line of research (Deane et al., 2014; Deane, Lawless, Sabatini, & Li, 2015) developed a battery of four distinct item types to measure different aspects of vocabulary knowledge for a large set of academic and domain-specific words. The following item types were developed:

- The *idiomatic associates* item type—intended to measure collocational knowledge.
- The *topical associates* item type—intended to measure knowledge of words that tend to appear together when people are discussing a particular subject.
- The *hypernym* item type—intended to measure knowledge of categorical semantic relations.
- The *differentiating definitions* item type—intended to measure deep knowledge of semantic relations and attributes.

Idiomatic Associates Items

Idiomatic associates items were designed to measure collocational knowledge without interference from definitional knowledge. They are a kind of sentence completion task with three options. The word to be tested is included in the sentence context. The item key is a strong collocate of the target word and frequently occurs in contexts with the target word. Incorrect answers have little or no association with the context provided. None of the answers is cued semantically or topically by the rest of the sentence in order to keep the task entirely focused on knowledge of collocations. In the following example, the key is *energy*, which frequently collocates with the target word *conserve*.

> We must conserve _____.
>
> (a) energy
> (b) gravity
> (c) insects

Topical Associates Items

Topical associates items present a set of three strongly associated words, and the learner is asked to choose a word that can be associated with the same topic as the other three. The answer choices contain the key, which is the word that is tested and is strongly associated with the stimulus words and two incorrect options, which must not have any strong associations or semantic relationships with the stimulus words. In the following example, the three associated words *preservation, restoring,* and *refuge* call up the general topic of conservation of natural resources; only the key, *conserve,* has a strong association with any member of the set.

> preservation, restoring, refuge
>
> (a) conserve
> (b) attract
> (c) restrain

Hypernym Items

Hypernym items contain words that represent members of a subset of words from a broader category. In these items, the sentence formed by the item key constitutes a true definitional statement. For instance, if we constructed an item in which *animal* named the hypernym and *dog* was the key, the resulting sentence would be *A dog is an animal.* The following example is a hypernym item for the verb *conserve.*

> To *conserve* a living thing is to _____ it.
>
> (a) copy
> (b) protect
> (c) describe

Differentiating Definitions Items

Differentiating definitions items present a word that is to be defined and several possible definitions for the word, including a correct definition and incorrect options that are definitions of semantically related words. In the following example, (b) is the correct definition for *conserve,* (a) is the definition of *restore,* (c) is the definition of *damage,* and (d) is the definition of *recycle.*

> *conserve*
>
> (a) to bring back to a former condition
> (b) to keep from being damaged or lost
> (c) to make unclean or impure
> (d) to reuse again

Deane et al. (2014) provided initial evidence that the item type that required the least semantic knowledge (e.g., idiomatic associates) was relatively easy, while that which required the most semantic knowledge (e.g., differentiating definitions) was the hardest. In a related study, Deane et al. (2015) directly address the issue of whether different item types provide distinct information that contributes to a richer characterization of partial vocabulary knowledge. The results of this study suggest that each item type contributes different kinds of information about vocabulary knowledge. In another study that used the same item types, Lawrence, Hwang, Deane, and Lawless (2015) examined data from 5,228 students from an urban school district, the majority of whom were second-language learners. The results suggest that using multiple item types to measure depth of vocabulary knowledge may reveal specific weaknesses for particular types of learners that might not be identified by a traditional vocabulary assessment.

Another line of research that utilizes multiple items for each word (Scott et al., 2015; Scott, Vevea, Castaneda, & Flinspach, 2017) addresses depth of vocabulary knowledge by measuring six dimensions for each word tested. For each word, six items are administered that draw on various dimensions of vocabulary knowledge found to be significant in research. These are illustrated in Figure 5.1.

The first item asks for students' metacognitive assessment of their own knowledge of the word. The second assesses their familiarity with semantically related words, that is, with words that either are synonyms or topically related, using a variety of syntactic categories (e.g., nouns, verbs, adjectives, or adverbs). The third measures their recognition of morphologically related words. The fourth, choosing

Fill in the small circle beside the correct answer (only one answer).

How well do you know the word *official*?

- ☐ I'm sure I know what this word means.
- ☐ I think I know what this word means.
- ☐ I am not sure what this word means.
- ☐ I don't know what this word means.

I think that these words are related to *official*:

- ☐ *slowly, inefficient, dragging on*
- ☐ *suggesting, guidance, informative*
- ☐ *jewelry, ornamental, wearing*
- ☐ *rightful, endorsed, permission*

Which word do you think is a correct word connected in meaning to *official*?

- ☐ *reofficial*
- ☐ *officialen*
- ☐ *unofficial*
- ☐ *officialest*

Choose the sentence that you think makes the most sense.

- ☐ *There is an official website for the new movie.*
- ☐ *Any outfit looks fancy when you put on a fine official.*
- ☐ *The teacher wanted to official the student about going to college.*
- ☐ *Jessica is so official that it takes her hours to do a simple job.*

I think the word *official* is closest in meaning to:

- ☐ Giving good advice to someone
- ☐ Unable to finish something in a reasonable amount of time
- ☐ Approved by someone in authority
- ☐ A large decorative pin or clasp

Some words have one part of speech, but some have more than one. Fill in the circle beside the correct answer or answers.

I think the word *official* may be:

- ☐ A noun
- ☐ A verb
- ☐ An adjective
- ☐ An adverb

FIGURE 5.1. Six items measuring dimensions of vocabulary knowledge for the word *official*.

which sentence makes the most sense, mines both their understanding of the meaning and how the word can be used in context. The definition item assesses prototypical knowledge, and the last item taps into an understanding of syntactic labels as well as recognition of alternative meanings with different parts of speech (e.g., *official* as both a noun and an adjective).

On each test, the six questions were asked about 24 words chosen from materials students typically encounter in school from grade-level novels as well as science, social studies, and math textbooks and English language arts textbooks. Words were selected to represent the approximate distribution of class time throughout the day in fourth and fifth grades—40% English, 20% math, 20% science, and 20% social studies. All the tests shared four words that allowed analysts to equate the instruments and measure student growth across one or both years. Fourth and fifth graders took one of two timed tests for their grade.

Results from 5,269 fourth and fifth graders (50% native English speakers; 30% English learners; 20% either initially or reclassified English proficient) suggest that conceptualizing word knowledge as the six different types of understanding tested provides a more accurate picture of students' vocabulary knowledge than the traditional view of vocabulary as a single construct. The results indicate that word awareness, semantic networks, morphological knowledge, the syntactic context of words, definitions, and parts of speech all tap related but unique aspects of vocabulary (Scott et al., 2015). In addition, results demonstrated that this kind of assessment was effective for both English learners and those proficient in English. Other analyses of the VASE tests indicate that the combined use of all six item types provide information about breadth of knowledge overall, capture what each student understands about the various aspects of word knowledge, and, with the linking words in different forms of the test, allows the tracking of student growth over time (Thissen, Steinberg, & Mooney, 1989). Scott et al.'s (2015) assessment demonstrates that it is possible to evaluate growth in vocabulary knowledge and identify students' strengths and weaknesses on specific dimensions of vocabulary knowledge.

Another assessment that was designed to test multiple aspects of vocabulary knowledge is the Cloze Evaluation test, or Cloe (Crosson & McKeown, 2017). The assessment was developed to test 196 words from the Academic Word List (AWL; Coxhead, 2000), and thus development began with recognition of the need to address the nature of academic words as abstract and polysemous. Additional considerations were what a learner might know about a word at different stages of familiarity, including its part of speech and relationship to other words in a lexical network. The assessment presents four cloze sentences per target word, and students must make a decision about each sentence, asking themselves, "Does this sentence make sense with [target word] in the blank?" One or two of the choices may represent semantically and syntactically accurate uses of the word. The number of correct matches depends on whether the word typically has several senses or distinct usages that would be included in a high-quality mental representation of the word. For example, *confine* has both a physical sense of restricting someone's movement and a mental sense of confining one's thoughts or creativity. Thus the item for *confine* contains a sentence in which the target word makes sense for each of these senses.

Incorrect choices were designed to vary in difficulty, with performance on different choice types intended to indicate different aspects of word knowledge. One of these types was mentioned in the section of this chapter on syntactic knowledge. These syntax choices are contexts in which the word that could plausibly fit the cloze sentence is a different part of speech from the target word. Unrelated choices are contexts that contain no association with the target word, but the word that could plausibly fit the sentence is the same part of speech as the target word—for example, *I read an _____ fairytale* for the word *empirical*. Thus learners with enough word knowledge to recognize the word's syntactic role, but who are unaware of the word's semantic properties, may think this sentence is correct. Semantic choices are contexts that contain a strong association to the target word's meaning and exhibit typical patterns of construction around the word, but do not use the word in a meaningful way. For example, a semantic choice for *criteria* is *When Chris had to choose a college, he met many _____ to help him make a decision*, based on criteria being something that one uses in the process of making a decision, and the phrase *met criteria* being a common construction for the word. Choosing semantic association items as correct indicates that the learner has enough familiarity with a word to know the situations in which the word is used, but not enough knowledge to understand that the specific sentence represents an incorrect use. Sample sentences and synsets from WordNet were consulted to generate the associations that were used.

Data collected from about 200 students in sixth and seventh grades over 2 years showed, first of all, that the assessment was sensitive to growth in knowledge from an instructional intervention. Results also suggested that, in general, the incorrect choice sentences behaved in the predicted way. That is, syntactic choices were the easiest for students to reject. Unrelated choices were the next easiest, and it was easier to recognize the correct contexts for the words than it was to reject the semantically related false choices.

ASSESSING THE IMPACT OF VOCABULARY ON HIGHER-LEVEL LITERACY

Most of the examples that we have provided have been discrete items in which words are tested with a minimum of context, typically no more than a sentence. We also need ways to more directly assess the impact of vocabulary on text comprehension, since improving comprehension is a major goal of vocabulary instruction. One obvious approach to exploring that influence is to present text passages and assess students' comprehension in a way that taps their use of the words in reading the text. However, many factors influence text comprehension beyond vocabulary knowledge, such as ability to sequence ideas, knowledge of text structure, knowledge of syntax, short-term memory limits, and referential understanding. Needing to attend to these multiple aspects of comprehension may overwhelm the benefits of a reader's knowledge of the text's vocabulary. Thus the role of vocabulary in comprehending a text can be difficult to measure.

Researchers have approached development of text comprehension tasks in two major ways. One is to ask students to read a text containing targeted words and then have them recall the passage (Beck, Perfetti, & McKeown, 1982; Coyne et al., 2010). The amount and accuracy of what is recalled determine the students' scores. Successful use of such tasks depends on how readers use the words in the text. That is, if the targeted words do not play important roles, then they may have little effect on a reader's comprehension of the text.

Another approach to assessing text comprehension is to develop questions that are keyed to the use of targeted words in a text. This approach was used by Apthorp et al. (2012) and McKeown et al. (2012). Apthorp et al. used the assessment with students in kindergarten, first, third, and fourth grades. The kindergarten and first-grade versions presented texts read aloud to students with answer choices provided as pictures. McKeown et al. used the assessment with seventh graders. In all cases, except for the third graders in Apthorp et al., students who had been taught the targeted words demonstrated better performance on the assessments.

In both studies, several short texts were presented to students, and for each text, students answered a series of multiple-choice questions. Each question required an inference about the role of a target word in the passage. For example, in a text about the development of a personal robot, one sentence read, *They spent 20 years on the project, working to minimize technical problems, until finally they had a reliable model.* A question geared to the target word *reliable* read, *What were the scientists able to achieve?* and the correct choice was *They built a robot that can be counted on to perform well.* Incorrect choices represented alternative interpretations of the context, such as *They built an inexpensive robot.* Because questions focus on the target words, this type of assessment seems like a more direct measure of the effect of target words on comprehension than having readers recall an entire text.

Another way to explore comprehension effects is to probe students' ability to integrate word meaning within a context. As we mentioned earlier, the ability to integrate words within context is characteristic of successful comprehenders. Beck et al. (1982) used an assessment to measure this ability with fourth graders, and McKeown and Beck (2014) used one with kindergartners. The assessment consisted of sentences that contained an instructed word, each followed by a question that asked students to make an inference about the context. An example is *Sam was stunned when he looked into the doghouse. What do you think Sam saw?* For this item, students needed to use their understanding that *stunned* meant "very surprised" and then connect that to something about a doghouse that might cause that reaction, such as "his dog and four new puppies."

The sentences used in the assessments were designed to be neutral, or even to invite interpretations that seemed to contrast with the meaning conveyed by the vocabulary word alone. The item about Sam being stunned seemed neutral, as someone might have any number of reactions to looking into a doghouse; the specific reaction is governed by accommodating *stunned* into one's interpretation. An item whose context might suggest an interpretation that contrasted with the word's meaning was *Jim had to insist that Freddy go on the merry-go-round. What did Freddy think about the merry-go-round?* It is likely that most young students would respond positively to a carnival ride, and thus being able to use the concept of *insisting* to interpret the context was critical to correctly responding to the question.

In both the Beck et al. and McKeown et al. studies, students who had experienced rich, interactive vocabulary instruction were more able to make correct interpretations compared to students who had experienced narrow, definition-based instruction. For example, students experiencing interactive instruction provided responses to the merry-go-round item such as, "Maybe he got sick to his stomach" and "It was scary—it went too fast." Responses from students experiencing narrow instruction were more likely to provide conventional reactions to going on a merry-go-round, such as, "It was fun."

FINAL THOUGHTS

In this chapter, we examined many different ways to assess vocabulary knowledge. This might almost seem an embarrassment of riches. There are so many words—and so many different kinds of knowledge about the same word—that the sheer variety of possibilities may seem overwhelming. And yet there is a reason we have explored so many possibilities. Vocabulary is a rich and varied form of knowledge. Teaching and assessing vocabulary knowledge depends upon having a clear understanding of that richness and variety. If vocabulary is assessed in just a few ways, the result will be a simplified picture of vocabulary knowledge, all too easily misinterpreted. The best outcomes depend on teachers having a rich understanding of how vocabulary works and providing students with the rich experiences of language that help them to develop their vocabularies organically and naturally. But the best outcomes also depend on sophisticated assessment practices that will keep teachers informed about student strengths and weaknesses. Teachers need to know when students need to develop key skills, such as the ability to understand morphologically complex words. They will not have that information unless we target a much richer vocabulary construct than we see in contemporary assessment practice.

CHAPTER 6

Classroom Practices
for Vocabulary Instruction

We have thus far emphasized how important it is for teachers to move beyond the traditional approach of teaching vocabulary, which emphasizes dictionary definitions and tends to ignore the rich tacit knowledge and high levels of metalinguistic awareness that students need to develop. We have also emphasized how important it is for students to develop enough breadth and depth of vocabulary knowledge to understand what they read, express their own ideas effectively, and think critically about what they are learning. Finally, we have discussed how often classroom practice fails to support the development of rich, complex, connected understandings of the words that students encounter. All too often, teachers recognize that vocabulary can be an obstacle for underprepared students, yet they fail to implement the kinds of instructional practices that will help them, but it is also understandable. A conscientious teacher might fully intend to attend to students' vocabulary needs, yet be puzzled about how to proceed when traditional definitional methods fail (Blachowicz et al., 2006).

In this chapter, we discuss how teachers can provide effective instruction that will support vocabulary growth for all students, so that we can achieve our ultimate goal—to become a nation of word learners. Ultimately, effective vocabulary instruction is effective literacy instruction, which cultivates a sensitivity to language and creates in students an enthusiasm for finding the right word and an appreciation for language used well. Within this context, teachers can help students acquire critical vocabulary while building the skills that students need to become independent word learners, including knowledge of structural regularities and generative mechanisms for word learning. As students gain experience with a broad variety of texts, develop metalinguistic awareness, and acquire the metacognitive knowledge they need to support reading, writing, and critical thinking, they will learn how to coordinate different forms of word knowledge to infer meanings in context. Instruction and assessment need to work together so that we are teaching and testing the knowledge that matters most for developing students' facility with language—knowledge that will most benefit their academic development. This means, chiefly, their ability to understand and learn from what they read and express themselves in effective ways.

We contend that effective vocabulary instruction has three critical characteristics that constitute the major sections of this chapter:

- The teacher establishes a *word-conscious classroom* in which learning about words is integrated with the curriculum and students are encouraged to engage actively in developing their own vocabularies. This kind of environment makes it much more likely that students will benefit from targeted vocabulary instruction. In this section, we discuss how to initiate a word-conscious attitude and how to keep it going through interactions with books and by responding to students in ways that engage their thinking about words.

- The teacher engages in *systematic, focused vocabulary instruction* designed to help students build rich representations of word meaning and usage for selected high-priority words. Here we demonstrate how to introduce words effectively and the kind of additional, follow-up activities that will deepen students' knowledge of the words. We also include ideas about how to attend to multiword expressions in instruction.

- The teacher builds students' *metalinguistic awareness of the generative patterns* that will help them acquire unfamiliar words when they encounter them. Our discussion in this section is structured around the frame from earlier chapters of grammatical constructions, polysemy, and morphology.

Beyond the characteristics of instruction, we also focus on characteristics of learners, in particular by considering linguistic differences that teachers may face. Here we discuss variant forms of English and second-language learners. A final section turns to discussion of aligning instruction and assessment.

ESTABLISHING A WORD-CONSCIOUS CLASSROOM

There is an obvious reason why teachers may find it difficult to teach vocabulary: it may seem overwhelming. When we survey the sheer number of words that students must acquire to be ready for college—and consider, in turn, how much information students must learn about each word they acquire—one may ask, quite reasonably, how a teacher who focuses on broadening students' vocabulary can teach anything else! But to think like this is to conceive of vocabulary instruction as something *separate* from teaching students to read, write, and think. Isolated lessons that focus on vocabulary will never be enough, no matter how effective they are in their own right. Gaining tacit understanding of structural regularities and generative mechanisms for word learning requires extensive exposure to vocabulary in multiple settings and contexts. Students who read well, who have encountered a wide variety of English vocabulary words, and who have been regularly exposed to patterns of word usage are much more likely to internalize these patterns and use them to infer the meanings of new words. Students who are learning English in addition to their home language, who struggle with reading English, and who have less exposure to word patterns are less likely to pick up such tacit word knowledge. This is often referred to as the "Matthew effect" in reading, where the rich get richer—that is, able to maximize benefits from language exposure based on prior experiences—but the poor get poorer (Stanovich, 1986). If some students must learn all their words from explicit classroom lessons, they are unlikely to catch up with their peers.

The problem for teachers is creating an environment that provides a rich exposure to language for all students that helps them build the tacit knowledge, metalinguistic awareness, and metacognitive knowledge that some students may develop without explicit instruction. Students in vocabulary-effective classrooms are immersed in a safe, collaborative, cognitively complex environment where teachers combine explicit instruction with exposure and with metacognitive and metalinguistic awareness to help students understand and use the power of words. As teachers, we need to create classroom environments that will foster metacognitive understanding of structural regularities and generative mechanisms for word learning so that all students can use this to their advantage. This entails both explicit and implicit opportunities to learn through all modes (reading, writing, speaking, listening, and technology) in all subject areas throughout the day.

Instigating Word Consciousness

The approach to vocabulary instruction known as "word consciousness" (Scott & Nagy, 2004) begins with a teacher developing alertness to language use and word encounters, followed by infusing classroom activities with opportunities to model awareness of language and enticing students to do the same. If students understand that learning words is an important part of their education—if they understand that it emerges naturally out of other learning experiences and supports all of their learning goals—then it will be much easier for teachers to engage students in examining and reflecting on language, and students will be much more likely to engage with word learning as a normal part of life inside and outside of the classroom.

Scott, Miller, and Flinspach (2012) describe cultivating an explicit focus on word-conscious instruction and how it led to accelerated word learning in fourth- and fifth-grade classes. The word-conscious focus encouraged growth in metacognitive, metalinguistic, and affective domains of word knowledge. To facilitate metacognitive awareness, teachers held classroom discussions on why word learning is important, how people learn new words, and different levels of word knowledge. They compared collecting other objects (e.g., Pokémon cards, rocks) to collecting words, using books such as *Donovan's Word Jar* (DeGross & Hanna, 1998) and *Max's Words* (Banks & Kulikov, 2006) as touchstone texts for this discussion.

Collecting words and phrases from the work of published authors provides the grist for *word banks,* which are not meant to be static decorations but active classroom resources. Word banks are particularly valuable as a springboard into effective vocabulary use in writing, where students try to emulate the language used in the books they hear or read. For instance, a gift of words from *Tuck Everlasting* (Babbitt, 1975), in which the character May is called "a great potato of a woman" resulted in a description of a character as "a long string bean of a man" in one fifth-grader's story. The bank of words collected by the class can be derived from materials used across the curriculum, with words and phrases that students can then withdraw from the bank to use in their essay descriptions, ranging from chemical experiments to character traits in narratives.

Organizing collected words and phrases with attention to language patterns can be particularly useful, as words that cluster around a semantic network of meaning, such as words that describe degrees of heat (*blistering, warm, searing,* and *tepid*), manner of speaking (*yelling, whispering, shouting,* and *muttering*), or other common phenomena provide aspiring writers with a toolbox of descriptive words. These "shades of meaning" words represent less frequent words for known concepts and can help students see the value of precision in word choice. When students write or are asked to use more precise spoken language, they move from receptive knowledge to productive ownership of vocabulary. Writing also provides a window into students' experimentation with new words and allows teachers opportunities to point out idiosyncratic language conventions, such as when students create phrases like "linger to a playground" or "loiter quickly home."

The active use of a word bank as an expectation for students' writing creates a classroom climate in which students challenge each other to produce more descriptive and precise language. Scott et al. (2012) document reports of students engaged in peer-editing discussions in which they ask each other, "What's a better word choice for that?" and praise each other for using words like *superfluous* in their writing. Scott et al.'s work also showcases a sense of excitement about word learning, in which students use their free time after school to look for cognates to add to the classroom chart and engage in word game challenges as they line up after recess. Such games include adaptations, such as playing " I spy with my little eye" with uncommon words (e.g., "something that is circular" or "something that is inscribed on a rigid surface") or games in which students guess each other's concepts, given a set of clues.

Word consciousness leads naturally to wordplay, and wordplay to greater word consciousness. Building a classroom environment that encourages word learning will happen most fruitfully when the teacher not only allows but also encourages students to play with the resources that the language gives them. Fostering this kind of environment is as much a matter of attitude as anything else, and with the right attitude, spontaneous comments become teaching opportunities.

It may be as simple as noticing a student's "*cumbersome* backpack" or being alert to opportunities to use recently encountered words. Perhaps the teacher will make a point of noticing that a student is *hesitating* before turning in an assignment or will remind a student who is asking a question to make his request *explicit*. Or perhaps the teacher will make a practice of posting favorite sentences on the bulletin board that students have found or written that display interesting, thoughtful, or even puzzling word use. A teacher may challenge students to caption funny pictures using words that had been encountered in the classroom; for example, a picture of a large cat sprawled on top of a suitcase might be captioned, "My _definitive_ answer is—you're not going anywhere!" If the teacher enjoys playing with words and shows it, her attitude can be infectious, whether it involves the teacher spontaneously starting an "I Spy" game as students wait for dismissal or accepting and expanding upon students' jokes and wordplay. It can be effective to push these spontaneous encounters even further and ask students to be aware of words outside of school and to bring them in and share them. This can include uses of words that have been studied in the classroom or simply uses of language that strike them. Two studies have found that extending vocabulary awareness outside the classroom has measurable effects on students' learning (McKeown et al., 1985; McKeown, Crosson, Artz, Sandora, & Beck, 2013).

Finally, teachers can include wordplay in the curriculum as part of the lesson. Jokes and puns are an excellent way to make students aware of some of the eccentricities of language. Helping students become aware of how puns and jokes often use ambiguous words to create humor can increase metalinguistic awareness and help them see the different types of ambiguity that are involved. Here are a few of our favorites that showcase the fun of lexical ambiguity organized by the type of ambiguity. The following three examples illustrate the concept of homophones:

- No matter how much you push the envelope, it will still be stationery.
- When an actress saw her first strands of gray hair, she thought she would dye.
- A three-legged dog walks into a saloon in the Old West. He slides up to the bar and announces, "I'm looking for the man who shot my paw."

These homophone pairs—*stationery/stationary, die/dye,* and *paw/pa*—all depend on similar-sounding words with meanings that twist the meaning of common phrases. Another type of pun draws on multiword expressions with sound similarities and different parts of speech:

- Two boll weevils grew up in South Carolina. One went to Hollywood and became a famous actor. The other stayed behind in the cotton fields and never amounted to much. The second one, naturally, became known as the lesser of two weevils [the lesser of two evils].
- Time flies like an arrow. Fruit flies like a banana [*flies* as a tensed verb and a plural noun].

The next four are intended to point out the difference between unrelated meanings of the same word (*tie* as in a *necktie* vs. *result of a race; curing* as a process of treating food vs. *curing* as a way to treat disease) and literal/figurative differences (*it hit me; it was riveting*). Note how the words that were chosen, *race/hospital/welding,* act to prime a particular meaning. This relates to our discussion in Chapter 4 about work in psychology and the mental lexicon.

- Two silk worms had a race. They ended up in a tie.
- A ham walked out of the hospital and said, "I'm cured!"
- I wondered why the baseball kept getting bigger. Then it hit me.
- He was fascinated by his new welding job. It was riveting.

Playing with ambiguous word meanings can occur at all grade levels, as long as students understand both meanings of the word. The *Amelia*

Bedelia books by Peggy Parish (1963) written for first and second graders have them laughing when she puts dust on the furniture and prunes on the hedge. Older students can develop their own jokes with different meanings of words like *trains, badgers, books, defects,* and *sandwiches.* Adding humor to lessons creates an affective component to learning that helps create memorable experiences and helps students enjoy learning about words (see Banas, Dunbar, Rodriguez, & Liu, 2011, for a review of research on humor and education).

The teacher's role in creating a word-conscious classroom is one of both facilitation and leadership. In a study by Scott et al. (2012), teachers reported that their own enthusiasm for word learning and wordplay was "contagious," spilling over in multiple ways in their classrooms. One teacher saw a student using *tenacious* as a hangman word, and two others using *plethora* at science camp. Teachers who nurture students' interest in effective word choices help students understand generative vocabulary-learning strategies, teach them to recognize the differences between everyday language and the language of schooling, help them enjoy word learning, orchestrate opportunities to try out new words in a safe environment, and cultivate their ability to use words to communicate ideas. These teachers are creating the type of learning environments that will go far in helping students learn about the nuances of vocabulary, particularly those students who are traditionally underserved by schools.

Interactions around Books

An ideal, if obvious, setting for promoting students' consciousness of words and word use is reading. Most of the words we know were learned from reading, and for those students who do not read widely and do not read the type of texts that bolster sophisticated vocabulary learning, that is precisely the problem. As we discussed in Chapter 2, learning words from context is an inefficient process since readers may need to encounter a word a dozen or more times before they fully integrate it into their vocabulary knowledge. The other part of that problem is that words that appear mostly in texts are much less frequent than those that occur in everyday conversation, which means that there may be long time lags between encounters, stretching out the learning process. These problems can be addressed in the classroom to a great extent by creating and taking opportunities during shared book reading to talk about words and about the word-learning process.

First, a word about the major precondition here—*shared reading.* This most frequently occurs in the form of reading aloud to children in early grades. We strongly recommend that this practice extend at least into middle school. We have observed classrooms in upper elementary and middle school where there is always a shared book in progress. Exposure to a variety of contexts that contain a word is important in developing a tacit understanding of word patterns, as well as knowledge of individual words; different types of texts create opportunities for exposure to different types of words.

Shared reading can be particularly beneficial if teachers are alert to the possibilities for helping students make connections with words that are particularly important in the text they are reading. For instance, a text about butterflies is likely to explain what they are, how they differ from moths, and use words like *caterpillar, antennae, wings, metamorphosis, cocoon,* and *chrysalis* repeatedly throughout the text, and the teacher can and should be prepared to help students learn these words and make connections between them in discussion. However, when a novel such as *Esperanza Rising* by Pam Ryan (2000) uses the word *caterpillar* along with words like *draped, tendril, incline,* and *resounding* on the first two pages, these words are unlikely to be repeated elsewhere in the book. Therefore the teacher will most likely find other words to focus on—words that are more central to understanding the characters and their motivations. Regardless of the type of text being read, shared reading provides a valuable opportunity for the discussion of word meanings.

Shared reading does not only have to be a traditional read-aloud. It is good practice to do some of the reading in the classroom together, where all students have the text and it is read aloud by the teacher or a student volunteer. Shared reading with the goal of comprehension is most effective if done in an interspersed way, where the teacher stops regularly to pose questions for consideration and discussion (Sandora, Beck, & McKeown, 1999). Some of these stops can provide a focus on vocabulary. The examples in Figure 6.1 present possible interactions during book reading and suggest what the interactions might add to students' growing understanding of language.

Example 1: *The Magician's Nephew*

In the first chapter of *The Magician's Nephew* (the first book of *Chronicles of Narnia*; Lewis, 1955), a strange boy shows up in Polly's neighborhood in London in the days of Sherlock Holmes. They introduce themselves to each other, and the boy tells her that he has lived in the country all his life and is unhappy to now be in a *beastly Hole like this*. *"London isn't a hole,"* said Polly *indignantly*. The use of *indignantly* provides a great opportunity to explore several facets of language using questions

(continued)

FIGURE 6.1. Two examples of possible interactions during book reading.

such as "How do you think Polly felt about his calling London 'a Hole'? So what do you think *indignantly* means? Let's take it apart—what parts can we take off that might help us?" This line of questioning might lead to *dignant*. Further questions might create a morphology moment: "Does that remind anyone of a word you know [*dignity*]? So if she spoke *indignantly,* what do you think that means?" Note here that the meaning of *indignantly* does not relate to *dignity* in a completely transparent way; it is not simply lack of dignity. But it is a part of what is being communicated in interactions like these—that you often reach the ballpark of a word's meaning using a combination of morphological and contextual clues. Students might take from this that *dignity* means acting properly, and *indignantly* means Polly thought what the boy said was not very proper. That is quite a sufficient amount of learning for such interactions.

Example 2: *The BFG*

A simpler example that focuses on context comes from The BFG by Roald Dahl (1982), which opens with Sophie, the main character, awakening early in her dormitory room. She is not supposed to get out of bed or disturb others, but she gets up and moves to the window. *When she reached the curtains, Sophie hesitated.* Here the teacher might pause and just repeat—"She hesitated"—then continue reading: *She longed to duck underneath them and lean out of the window to see what the world looked like. . . . The longing became so strong she couldn't resist. She ducked under the curtain and leaned out the window* (p. 10).

Stopping here, the teacher could initiate an interaction, saying, "She hesitated—what do you think that means? Did she open the curtains right away? Why not?" This interaction can lead students to see that Sophie stopped herself because she was a little nervous before she eventually opened the curtain. Thus students acquire information about the meaning and use of the word *hesitate* as well as get a glimpse of how context can help to figure out word meaning.

Productive opportunities during book reading can focus on multiword expressions as well as single words. In *The BFG*, Sophie sees the giant and watches him as he peers in a window: *Sophie could see now what it was up to* (p. 12). The teacher might stop and ask, "What it was up to—what does the author mean by that?" If this expression is somewhat familiar, students may respond that the giant was doing something bad or that it was up to no good. The teacher might respond, "Has your mother ever asked you, 'What are you up to'? So she's saying, 'What are you doing? I'm not sure I like it!'"

On page 13, the giant was bent over a suitcase he was carrying, and then Sophie watches the giant straighten up. Here the teacher might stop and ask, "What did the giant do—straighten up?" and lead students to see that the giant stood up straight and tall. The teacher might conclude by noting the connection with the other *up* phrase by saying something like, "Hmm, so there we have that word *up* again." The teacher might keep this in mind and then find an opportunity to point out the use of *straighten up* meaning "to make things neat and orderly." To move students toward understanding this more metaphorical use, she might comment, "So the room wasn't crooked; it was messy and we made it neat."

FIGURE 6.1. *(continued)*

The room is *straighter* in a metaphorical sense, but that does not need to be an explicit part of this conversation. The principle here is to seek opportunities for continuing conversations about words, meanings, and patterns. The *"straighten up"* conversation could lead to future interactions about people *straightening up* in a moral sense or *straightening out* problems or disagreements. All of this acts to awaken and extend students' awareness of how language works and simultaneously supports their building mental tools to help them figure out new encounters with word meanings.

Examining the Author's Craft

Shared reading also provides a platform for looking at the craft of writing and how authors use particular words and phrases to create images and enhance descriptions. Reflection on an author's choice of words and multiword expressions is a valuable way to begin to notice patterns of language. When an author chooses a particular phrase, he or she gives readers a "gift of words" that allows the readers to paint a picture in their minds of the scenario being described (Scott, Skobel, & Wells, 2008). Phrases like the following add both texture and tone to a book, making it come alive to readers:

- *With skin like parchment. (Bridge to Terabithia;* Paterson, 1977)
- *The house felt as lifeless as a tomb. (The Half-a-Moon-Inn;* Fleishman, 1980)
- *His long chin faded into an apologetic beard. (Tuck Everlasting;* Babbitt, 1975)

These gifts of words, with attention to metaphors, similes, and descriptive language create another entry point for discussions about word meaning and word use.

Attending to authors' word choices is particularly powerful when paired with writing instruction. In the act of becoming writers themselves, students are motivated to study authors' word choices. Finding interesting, unusual, or valuable words in shared books and the books students read independently helps them think about words differently (Miller, Gage-Serio, & Scott, 2010; Scott & Wells, 1998). Becoming "word hunters" creates a metalinguistic opportunity to reframe word choice as art form and helps young writers become artists who are learning to create their own stories while developing the command of words necessary to convey their meaning. Collecting interesting, useful, or "juicy" words from books that are shared or read independently creates a resource that they can draw on for their own writing (Scott, Skobel, & Wells, 2008; Scott, 2015; Scott et al., 2012).

Supportive Responses to Students

The kind of vocabulary knowledge that we have been promoting in this book is born of interactions. Substantial teacher–student and student–student interactions are required to build meaningful semantic representations. In classrooms, this involves modeling: back-and-forth discussions about what words mean; how they are used; how they compare; and the experiences and contexts that connect words. Yet it is not easy for teachers to prepare for the spontaneous interactions that will occur, or plan for how to intervene to expand students' understanding. Teachers need to acquire an eye toward opportunity and an ear toward what students are saying and how it might reveal struggle or a developing insight.

Every text that teachers discuss, every lesson that they teach, no matter what subject it addresses, may provide them with opportunities for modeling effective ways of thinking about words. For instance, it is very important to help students move beyond narrow uses or meanings for a word and develop semantic flexibility. A tuned-in teacher will be alert to situations in which students are attached to a single use. We have seen teachers handle this in a variety of adept ways. Consider, for example, a second-grade teacher introducing the word *aid* to her students. She suspected that they would immediately connect it to *first aid,* so she led with that acknowledgment and then used a student's response to establish a general meaning for *aid*:

> TEACHER: Now, most of you . . . yeah, I just . . . just heard it. Some of you have heard the term *first aid.* I heard you say it. What does that mean, *first aid*?
>
> STUDENT: That's like a little kit, like you stop to help put some Band-Aids and peroxide and stuff like that.
>
> TEACHER: Oooh, you said a very important word in that. You said it's a kit to help. That's the important word. *Aid* means to help. So, a *first-aid kit* would help someone if they get hurt.

Similarly, the tuned-in teacher recognizes when students' responses suggest they may be stuck in a narrow understanding and offers a way out. In this example, from a different second-grade class, the teacher picks up that students have been using the word *comfortable* in just one kind of context:

TEACHER: Who can remind us, what does *comfortable* mean?

STUDENT: It means like you're *comfortable* and it . . . it feels good on you.

TEACHER: Right. You feel good just as you are. Might not mean . . . doesn't always have to mean clothes. Like, it could mean other things. It could . . . you might be comfortable lounging on the couch.

Students also may need assistance when a word is introduced in a way that does not coincide with their prior understanding. These are situations where polysemy or collocational use might seem to be working against you. Here is one of our favorite examples, in which a seventh-grade teacher is confronted with students' understanding of the word *explicit*. The teacher had just presented the word in a context about a school's absence policy and provided the definition: when you make something explicit, you make it perfectly clear so there is no doubt about it. Here is what happened next:

TEACHER: Yes, their absence policy. Did you get another one? Yes.

STUDENT 1: Okay, so . . . you know those albums that have like *explicit* content on them . . . or those movies? Um . . . does *explicit* mean *clear*?

TEACHER: Yeah . . . like there's . . . if . . . a lot of times it says like *explicit* lyrics . . .

STUDENT 1: Yeah, like it'll be like the dirty version of it.

TEACHER: Yes. Which means that like . . . it's out there . . . Like it's . . .

STUDENT 2: No bleeping.

(*Students talking at once.*)

TEACHER: The message is clear.

STUDENT 3: Uncensored.

TEACHER: It's uncensored. That's a good example. Yeah. Yeah . . . that there's no covering anything up.

Often in interactions around words, some student responses will indicate misunderstanding. Really hearing what students say in their responses is key to mediating such situations. That is the first step, but then comes the challenge of steering students' ideas in the right direction—in other words, when students give you lemons, how do you make lemonade? Again, we have been privileged to observe many teachers who do this with aplomb, while avoiding the traps of either saying "No, that's not it" or accepting a response that is not really on target.

In this next example, a third-grade teacher deftly refocuses a student's incorrect response to the word *ravenous*:

> TEACHER: How would you look if you felt *ravenous*?
> STUDENT: Happy.
> TEACHER: Happy? I don't know about that. It depends if you were looking at some food, huh? If you were *ravenous*. I have a pizza sitting on my desk and you're *ravenous*. How are you going to look at that pizza?

Here is how a similarly nimble teacher redirected a student's response to the word *mortified*:

> TEACHER: Give me a synonym for *mortified*.
> STUDENT: Embarrassed.
> TEACHER: Good, absolutely. What else?
> STUDENT: Shy.
> TEACHER: Um, you wouldn't necessarily be shy. You might be shy afterward. After you're *mortified* you might be shy. 'Cause if you just really got embarrassed.

Notice that teachers are not only providing accurate directions for word meaning, but also demonstrating how language is used and how we connect ideas through language. The final example presented below shows that kind of deftness still in development. Here the teacher is clearly caught off guard, unsure of how to reconcile the words *defend* and *protect*, and the interaction is not completely successful. But kudos to her for opening up and sharing her thinking rather than simply offering different definitions for the two words and moving on:

> TEACHER: What do you think *defend* means?
> STUDENT: *Protect*.
> TEACHER: *Protect*. Mmm . . . Not quite (*thinking aloud*). Sorta in a roundabout way. Defend means you keep it safe from harm. You *protect* something; you keep it safe from harm. *Protect* was a good word to use. A mother bird defends its babies. How would you defend a pet?

Our advice for when these situations develop is to learn to take a deep breath, so that students know you are gathering strength of thought. Giving the words *protect* and *defend* a moment's consideration might allow a teacher to come up with something like:

"Wow! That is really interesting. *Protect* and *defend* really do have a lot in common. Because both of them mean you want to keep someone or something from getting hurt. Let's see if we can think about how they are different. *Protect* is kind of quieter, so you might [gesture as if bending over something to shield it] protect something like this. But if something was coming after you, you might need to defend—to really fight against them to keep from getting hurt. To *defend* you need to be more active."

From here, it might be useful to get students involved by asking, "How might a mother lion protect her cubs? And how might she defend her cubs? Why might she have to *defend* her cubs? What are some things that animals . . . people . . . use to *defend* themselves?" These kinds of interactions can also help students to see that vocabulary is not an automatic matching of word to definition but that there is some messiness to figuring out relationships and applications of words. For the teacher, the complexity is that these kinds of opportunities to create rich discussions about words could come up at any moment, whether as a planned part of a shared reading or unexpectedly in the middle of a completely different lesson.

FOCUSED VOCABULARY INSTRUCTION

No matter how rich the language environment, students (especially lower-performing students) need the support that can be provided by systematic, focused vocabulary instruction that will help them learn high-priority words and develop rich and flexible representations of word meaning and usage.

Introducing Words

Let us, therefore, consider how new words might be introduced to students in ways that provide the grist for rich semantic representations. The following example is from the RAVE (Robust Academic Vocabulary Encounters) program developed for middle school students (McKeown et al., 2012). This example demonstrates several of the features that we have discussed as important to learning words. These include polysemy, multiple contexts, and integrating words meanings into context. RAVE deliberately introduced two different senses or uses of a word, thus directly addressing polysemy. As we have mentioned, it is not clear-cut as to where to divide different senses of a word. Whether we consider them different senses or uses, the goal is to provide a variety of contexts to support a richer representation of word meaning.

One of the words taught in the RAVE program is *integrate*. To introduce this word, two contexts are presented. One context offers a prototypical use of *integrate*: *integrating* people who differ by race, ethnicity, or in this case, gender. Consider the connotations that may be inferred, however, if this is the only use of the word that students encounter. Examples of integrating races or genders may connote that *integrate* means to enforce the coming together of groups that may not get along. The second context for *integrate* offers a very different use— one of artistically integrating design elements. Here are the contexts:

Context #1: Joy Bright Hancock served in the Navy during World War II. When the war was over, she wanted to stay in the Navy, but women weren't allowed to be in the military unless there was a war. Joy fought this rule and got Congress to pass a law to *integrate* women into all branches of the military, the Women's Armed Services *Integration* Act of 1948. Even though many women serve in the military today, they still have not won the right to *integrate* fully into all military careers because women are not allowed to serve in direct-combat units.

Context #2: Frank Lloyd Wright, America's most famous architect, designed a house called Fallingwater for the Kaufmann family in 1936. The Kaufmanns loved the beautiful waterfalls on their property, and they hoped Wright would build their home nearby. Instead, Wright decided to *integrate* the home and the beautiful landscape, and he built the house right on top of the falls. He wanted the Kaufmanns to live with the waterfalls and to make them part of their everyday life. Today, Fallingwater is a museum for people around the world.

After the first context was read, a definition written in student-friendly terms was presented. The definition for *integrate* was, "If things or people are *integrated*, they are brought together to become parts of the same thing." RAVE introductory lessons also included the teacher asking students to describe how the word fit into the context. This was meant to prompt integrating the meaning and context. Below is a typical teacher–student interaction in which the student first merely paraphrases the definition, which does not reflect its role in the context. After the teacher presses, the student is able to articulate how the concept of *integration* was instantiated in the context.

TEACHER: So, how does the meaning of *integrate* fit Context #1, Ally?

ALLY: Uh, it brought them together into one thing.

TEACHER: Who's *them* and what's the *thing*?

ALLY: The women and the men into one Army.

The RAVE program is typical of many instructional interventions in vocabulary that are based around a set of specific words (cf. Nagy & Townsend, 2012; Snow et al., 2009), but a more typical context for introducing words in the classroom is in conjunction with a text that students will read. To understand the most effective way to introduce words associated with a text, consider the goal. The immediate goal is comprehension of the text. So initially, it is best to introduce only those words that would likely disrupt comprehension if students did not know their meanings. The introduction should be brief, just a paraphrase of word meaning in the context in which the word is used—just enough to assist with comprehension of the context. Reading a text together provides an ideal format, as the teacher can merely stop and offer meaning information or rephrase the context. For example, the book *Molly Rides the School Bus* (Brillhart, 2002) is about a shy girl's first day riding the bus to kindergarten. Near the end of the ride, as a friendship begins to develop with another girl, the text says, *As the bus bounced along, Ruby admired all of Molly's new school supplies.* To clarify the word *admired,* a teacher might stop momentarily and say, "That means Ruby told Molly how much she liked all of her new school supplies." The appropriate time for richer vocabulary work, such as supplying a longer, more explanatory definition and giving other examples of admiration would be after the story is finished.

If students are reading a text on their own, a small number of key-words can be introduced briefly before reading. It is best not to introduce sample contexts before the reading because the elements of those could interfere with the context of the text. Although our stance in this book has been to caution against providing students with narrow information about words, this is a case in which narrow, focused information is best. But again, it is best only when the goal is comprehension of a particular text. After that, focus can then turn to the vocabulary with the goal of supporting rich representations of word meaning.

Providing Additional Encounters

The foregoing examples of introducing word meanings, one based on a systematic program and the other on introducing words for a specific text, are quite different in the level of information provided and the expectation for student engagement. Yet neither of them is likely to provide rich, sustained knowledge of the word. That requires meeting the word again in additional contexts and reflecting on how to apply it. This kind of follow-up work is key to effective vocabulary instruction. However, that does not mean that it needs to be done with every word that enters the classroom. A good approach is to select some words that meet the criteria we discussed in Chapter 4 and return to those in follow-up work. We now present several examples of the kinds of activities that can deepen knowledge of individual words and draw attention to patterns of word meaning and how words work. These are drawn from the RAVE program.

One goal for follow-up activities is to help students develop the semantic flexibility that underlies understanding of uses of words in varied contexts. In one such activity, called "What's the Sense of It?", students are given pairs of questions for each of their target words. The pair can require accessing different senses of the word or dealing with different connotations:

---

valid

> If your zoo membership is *valid*, what does that mean?
> If your point about why zoos are good for animals is *valid*, what does that mean?

definitive

> If you reach a *definitive* agreement with your friend about the price of his used iPod, what does that mean?
> If you get *definitive* evidence that iPods are bad for your eardrums, what does that mean?

explicit

> If there is an *explicit* policy for everyone to stop using lead paint, what does that mean?
> If you give *explicit* consent to have your house tested for lead paint, what does that mean?

imply

> If you *imply* that your friend wouldn't like the *Twilight* series (Meyer, 2005), what does that mean?
> If you *imply* you've read the entire *Twilight* series, what does that mean?

Activities can also be structured to help students to see the different implications that words carry for the contexts in which they appear. This can be particularly useful when two targeted words are distinct, but share some meaning elements. The following examples are from an activity that asks students to think about differences in meaning between words and are part of the RAVE program. The activity presents a brief scenario, followed by a question containing the targeted words, and then asks students to develop a response to each question.

You love to eat ice cream.

What's the difference between your mother *monitoring* how much ice cream you eat and your mother *regulating* how much ice cream you eat?

You really want to join the soccer team.

What's the difference between feeling *inhibited* about joining the soccer team and feeling *excluded* from the soccer team?

A terrible storm swept through the city.

What's the difference between the storm *coinciding* with a tornado and the storm being *analogous* to a tornado?

Resources such as WordNet and the Corpus of Contemporary American English (explained further in Chapter 8) allow teachers to easily find words that are close cousins in meaning that might be worthy of this type of attention as well as additional contexts.

Teaching Multiword Expressions

Focusing instruction on multiword expressions (MWEs), as well as individual words, is beneficial for vocabulary growth. One of the key challenges to dealing with compound words and other MWEs is that they need to be learned, even if their meanings are mostly predictable from their parts. Imagine, for example, going to the store in a foreign country, looking for *dishwasher detergent*. This is a specific concept, "naming a specific kind of product," but there is no way of knowing in advance whether the product will be named with a single word or a compound or whether the compound will be formed in exactly the same way. For instance, in German the concept is named with the term *geschirrspül-mittel*, which roughly translates to "dish-washing liquid," whereas a *dishwasher* is a *geschirrspülmaschine*, a *dishwashing machine*, following somewhat different patterns than English, although both the English and the German compounds are completely transparent. The learner must learn how to name the concept (even if the name is a completely transparent compound). In fact, even if the compound is transparent in meaning, parts of its meaning can be unpredictable. Who would know, without having learned it, that in English a *washing machine* is only for washing clothing and not for washing dishes? As a result, teachers will need to include compounds and other MWEs in focused vocabulary instruction for two very different reasons.

On the one hand, there is a large inventory of MWEs that need to be learned as words in their own right. Teachers should be alert to the possibility that students may not know the meaning of common expressions and idioms, which may lead to serious failures in reading comprehension. Teaching specific MWEs can help students process expressions as a whole when they meet them in text, which can increase reading fluency and efficiency. For these reasons, teachers should cultivate their own awareness of MWEs in texts so that they can bring them to their students' attention.

On the other hand, MWEs are often idiosyncratic in their meaning even though they follow what are (on the whole) fairly predictable grammatical patterns. The complexities that arise can provide useful opportunities to cultivate word consciousness. Prompting students to analyze component parts of MWEs can build metalinguistic skill. MWEs can also be a vehicle for prompting discussion on how language works to help students see where patterns of language make sense and where the ways we use language are still a puzzle. In presenting and discussing these kinds of language patterns and eccentricities, we want students to come to consider themselves scientists on the one hand—raising questions and forming hypotheses—and artists on the other hand—using vocabulary to be creative.

For example, the Latinate layer of English draws on a systematic pattern using *ad* _____ (*ad hoc, ad infinitum, ad lib, ad nauseum*). The word *ad* means *to*. Figuring out the meanings of the individual expressions can involve using surrounding context, such as the description of an *ad hoc* meeting or someone going on *ad nauseum*. Figuring out the meanings can also call on morphological problem solving by having students notice familiar word parts such as the relationship of *ad infinitum* to *infinity*. A classroom conversation could help students become aware of the existence of phrases borrowed from other languages such as Latin and point out strategies they can use to figure out the meaning of foreign phrases in context.

Here we offer several other examples that could prompt conversations around useful MWE exemplars that not only can help students understand common expressions, but can also bring attention to specific patterns of language use and to how language works more broadly.

Phrasal verbs, such as *turn on* (as in *turn on the light*) are a common type of MWE. They consist of a verb combined with another word, often a preposition, which is called the particle. Phrasal verbs might be presented by asking students to notice that we *turn on* a light, and that *turn on* is the opposite of *turn off*. Exploring the uses of particles with different phrasal verbs reveals regular patterns (*on/off* frequently changes a verb's meaning to indicate that the action begins or ends), and *up* is associated with a pattern of completion: *eat up, drink up, grow up*. Nevertheless, there is also a great deal of apparent arbitrariness, and the particle can change the meaning radically (e.g., *give up* is not the same as *give away*; *cut up* is not the opposite of *cut down*). Phrasal verbs also offer opportunities to discuss the nature of English as a language with Germanic origins as well as roots in Latin. For example, we could use Latinate verbs such as *calculate, comprise, discharge,* and *exclude,* or choose their Germanic equivalents, *work out, make up, carry out,* and *leave out* instead. This contrast links to an ongoing debate about the use of vocabulary from the different layers of English. In particular, in writing, is it better to use the more academic Latinate terms, or should we aim for "pure" or "plain" English, most famously voiced by George Orwell, who argued against "pretentious, Latinized style" (Wild, 2011, p. 54)?

The expression *circumstantial evidence* illustrates additional complexities that arise in academic vocabulary, where words frequently have Latinate origins and multiple senses. The word *circumstantial* is an abstract, morphologically complex term with one sense that means the full details of a particular situation or event, such as providing a circumstantial account of a meeting, and a secondary sense that refers to information concerning a crime that suggests but does not prove guilt. Understanding the phrase *circumstantial evidence* requires students to know that we are talking about a specific type of legal evidence. Students who do not know the word *circumstantial* will encounter even greater difficulties, since guessing even the physical sense of the word requires a great deal of inference based on its morphology. Many other words that contain the prefix *circum-* are linked to the idea of the physical motion of going around (*circumference, circumnavigate*), but the meaning of *circumstantial* is based on a metaphor ("how things stand around") that is unlikely to be obvious to anyone who has not studied the word's Latin origins. This kind of pattern allows room for discussion of several different aspects of language, including polysemy, morphology, and the etymologies of words.

Another conversation might begin with a set of expressions with a word in common, such as *fire alarm, fire extinguisher, fire brigade,* and *fire hydrant.* All are common expressions in everyday language and likely known by many students. The first three expressions pair *fire* with a word that is either known or readily understood from its definition and used in other contexts, but what is a *hydrant*? A teacher can point out that its root, *hydr-*, appears in words like *hydrate, rehydrate, dehydrated,* and *hydroplane,* which may help students infer its connection to water. Extending this lesson further into morphology, the teacher could point out that *hydr-* is an instance of a combining form, and that other examples are *bio-* (life), *geo-* (earth), and *cardio-* (heart), all of which can combine with *-logy* (the study of). The first group of words (*hydrate, rehydrate, dehydrated*) illustrate a word family that shows how the addition of a prefix contributes to meaning. After presenting students with these examples, the teacher might ask, "What does *hydrology* mean?"

As these examples illustrate, effective vocabulary instruction does more than give students definitions to memorize. It exposes them to a variety of contexts in which a word can be used; it helps them build a conceptual representation that fits the ways that a word can be used, and it develops analytical skills that will help students to deal with unfamiliar words when they encounter them on their own.

BUILDING METALINGUISTIC AWARENESS OF GENERATIVE PATTERNS

A framework we have offered throughout the book involves the generative language patterns of morphology, polysemy, and grammatical constructions. Effective, word-conscious instruction builds knowledge of these generative patterns in part by training students to think flexibly in terms of underlying language patterns so that they have the tools they need to understand unfamiliar words when they encounter them. Here, we briefly discuss instructional considerations for grammatical constructions and polysemy before turning to a much more extensive discussion of morphology, which is particularly critical in developing students' ability to handle academic language.

Grammatical Constructions

As Firth (1957) famously stated, "You shall know a word by the company it keeps." Paying attention to grammatical constructions is a way to teach students to analyze the company that a word keeps—which includes, most importantly, words with similar meanings, and so it can be very useful to have students consider what words could replace each word in a construction. Consider a very straightforward sentence like the following: *The [student] touched [the teacher] on the [shoulder]*. Practically any animate noun could replace *student* or *teacher*; but only a small set of verbs could naturally replace *touch* (e.g., *tap* or *hit*), and the words that can naturally replace *shoulder* are mostly body part terms (*forehead, arm*) or terms for articles of clothing (*shirt, hat*). Recognizing such a pattern can be helpful in drawing the correct conclusion when students encounter a new word in a familiar context. For instance, if they encounter a sentence like *The doctor palpated the patient on one shoulder*, they will be more likely to see how the sentence context supports the inference that *palpate* means something like *touch*. If we then ask students to discuss a sentence like *That really hit him in the pocketbook*, it will become easier to reach the insight that the sentence provides a metaphor in which the pocketbook (what someone owns) is treated as if it were a part of the person's body.

If we want students to develop word consciousness, there can be a significant benefit in having them regularly stop and ask, "What other words could go here? Which of them are most like the word that is there already? What is the pattern of which words go together with which?" Many of the practices recommended in this chapter are aimed at fostering precisely this kind of sophistication, where students develop a tacit understanding of how words are used, but also develop metalinguistic awareness of their own knowledge, so that it becomes easier to generalize it to a new context.

Polysemy

Students with weak vocabulary skills are particularly likely to be unaware of polysemy and assume that a word has exactly one meaning (usually, the meaning they have already learned). The kinds of practices that develop word consciousness will, if carried through systematically, also help develop students' awareness of polysemy and increase their sensitivity to the fact that word meanings change in context, often following regular patterns. Students develop semantic flexibility when they begin to link meanings to contexts, observe how the same idea may generalize across contexts, or shift into a new (though possibly related) meaning in another context. As students become accustomed to making such observations, they begin to become comfortable with this process, and actively integrate their knowledge of word meanings with the contexts in which those words appear. However, it is also important to develop students' ability to distinguish multiple senses of the same word and to build their awareness of the regular patterns by which the same word may take on multiple, but related, senses.

Learning about Multiple Senses of the Same Word

Wordplay, as mentioned above, is helpful in drawing students' attention to multiple senses of words, and multiple senses are, as we have noted, a major characteristic of language. Another way teachers might help students deal with this aspect of language is to start a conversation about how word meanings develop and change over time. A starting point might be to draw students' attention to the use of *text* as a verb, as in *texting her friends*, which did not exist before the advent of mobile phones. Words can acquire new meanings in different ways. One method is via historical accident. For example, the word *race* can be used in the sense of a *horse race* or *human race*. This is because the first sense came into English from the Old Norse word *ras*, and the second from Middle French *race*, earlier *razza*, meaning "race, breed, lineage, family." Another method is via *semantic drift*, in which words gradually change meaning, coming to be applied more narrowly or more broadly. The word *hound* originally referred to any type of dog; it later became specialized to a particular kind. Similarly, *meat* originally meant any type of food. *Pudding* still means any type of dessert in many British households.

Sometimes words change over time in surprising ways. The word *stupid* originally meant "to be blessed by God," and the word *tell* originally meant "to count." While those meanings are now only encountered in historical documents, the original meaning can "leave a footprint" in our modern vocabulary. The word *teller* refers to a person who works in a bank (counting money) and *all told* means "everything counted." Such examples expose students to different ways that the meanings of words shift and give them insight into language as a living, growing phenomenon. Looking for similar patterns can promote further interest in words.

Teachers might also engage students' awareness of the polysemous nature of words through a phenomenon called *zeugma*. Zeugma describes a sentence in which a single word is used in two different parts of a sentence, but the word carries a different meaning in each part. Zeugma has been used in lexical semantics as a test that two senses of a word are dissimilar. For example, we can say, "The newspaper fired its senior editor" and we can say, "The newspaper fell off the table," but it would be confusing to say, "The newspaper fired its senior editor and fell off the table." Similarly, the sentence "The man and his license expired last week" does not work, although each could expire. To the best of our knowledge, zeugma has never been used for vocabulary instruction or assessment, but it provides an interesting possibility for increasing metalinguistic awareness and assessing whether a student understands the different senses of words that are used.

Noticing Patterns of Semantic Extension

As we discussed in Chapter 2, polysemy exhibits regular patterns that fall into three major categories: metonymy, metaphor, and specialization (or generalization). Drawing students' attention to these patterns and creating opportunities to explore such patterns provides students with generalizable knowledge that can be applied whenever they encounter similar words or MWEs.

Metonymy, in which one word or phrase is substituted for another word or phrase with which it has a close association (e.g., *suit* to denote *businessman*), comes in many forms. Helping students see that the producer of a product often becomes a name for that product (e.g., "I have a *Honda*"); that a part can refer to a whole (e.g., two *mouths* to feed); and that a place or a date can refer to a particular event (e.g., *the Alamo, 9/11*), allows students to recognize such patterns elsewhere in their lives.

Metaphor becomes increasingly important beyond the primary years, playing a key role in language (Gibbs, 2006; Lakoff & Johnson, 1980). With metaphorical extensions, concepts from one domain are applied to a different domain by analogy. In order to create these extensions, students need to understand which properties of an analogy are involved. If we say that someone is a *shrimp*, the property of size is used for the analogy. A teacher can point out the many ways that we can compare people with animals, and that the connotation is usually negative, such as in *snake, leech*, or *weasel*. In contrast, a woman might say that her husband is a *lamb*, and students need to recognize both the context and the properties of a lamb that make that a compliment. Part of our depth of knowledge of words is our understanding of the properties that are used as the basis for analogies.

Teachers can point out metaphors in shared books, such as the following found in *The Green Glass Sea* by Klages (2006) about nuclear testing: *green glass sea; a mushroom of dust; like geologic snowmen left to dry in the hot sun.* They can discuss the meanings of such phrases, including which aspects of a mushroom or a sea create effective metaphors, and why the author might choose to use metaphoric language to paint the images in the book. Discovering metaphors, such as *time is money*, can also occur when students explore how we talk about time as something that you can *waste, save, invest*, or *spend*. Sullivan (2006) showed that students between fourth and eighth grades learn metaphorical extensions of words at a rapid rate.

Patterns of specialization (or generalization) involve the use of a word more narrowly or loosely than is typical. For instance, the word *door* can refer to the physical door or the space a door occupies; verbs can be created from nouns that name tools (e.g., *comb, brush,* and *mop*); and colors often denote physical objects (e.g., *orange, lavender, gold, cream*). Using such patterns creatively, students can discuss new words such as *zorbing, wingsuiting,* or *hoverboarding,* and how new inventions or contexts can lead to new words and to the polysemy of known words.

Morphology

The number of morphological patterns is relatively small, and most of the value of explicit morphological instruction can be focused on a limited set of important prefixes, suffixes, and roots, where the relationship between these affixes and roots can serve as exemplars of word families. There is significant evidence that morphological instruction can be beneficial. Bowers et al. (2010) reviewed the evidence from 22 studies about the impact of instruction in morphology and provided a meta-analysis of its effects. They found that morphological instruction benefits learners and that a greater impact is seen for less proficient readers. The evidence was weak for the transfer of morphological information to understanding new words and to reading comprehension in many cases. Bowers et al. noted two characteristics that made such transfer more likely: when the instruction was integrated into other aspects of literacy instruction and when it included a problem-solving approach that, for example, asked students to apply what they were learning in order to deduce morphological patterns. Bowers et al. contend that a problem-solving approach prompts students to focus on the how words work and fosters deep processing.

Helping students see patterns and how words can be created using morphemes seems clearly useful, as more than half of the words in English can be analyzed morphologically. It is estimated that for every word a child learns, there are one to three additional words that should be understandable if the child is familiar with morphology, and we know that knowledge of morpheme structure contributes significantly to vocabulary growth (Anglin et al., 1993; Berninger, Abbott, Nagy, & Carlisle, 2010; Nagy & Anderson, 1984; Nagy et al., 2006). However, to hark back to one of our common themes, words are idiosyncratic and meaning is not always transparent, even if the parts of the word are known. Consider, for example, the most common prefix, *un-*, meaning *not.* If the prefix is applied to a known root word, new words such as *unafraid* or *unable* are readily understood, but if the prefix is applied to unfamiliar root words such as *unadulterated* or *unbridled*, understanding that *un-* means *not* does not lead to knowing the word. The situation can become more complicated if *un-* appears to be a word's prefix, but the morpheme is actually *under* as in *underpaid* or *underwent*, or if the morpheme is the Latinate *uni-* as in *unicycle* or *unity*. There are also cases where *un-* is not a prefix at all, as in *uncle*. Thus, the best approach is to help students to become morphological problem solvers who notice patterns in the meaning and structure of morpheme combinations and can interpret them flexibly.

When considering teaching morphological patterns, the first things to recognize about morphology are the different types of morphemes. As teachers, we usually break these down into roots, prefixes, and suffixes. However, in assessing the types of materials that would be most useful to students, a further breakdown into inflectional and derivational morphology, and bound and free roots provides some additional guidance.

Inflectional morphemes serve as grammatical markers that create different forms of the same word, such as plurals (*hat–hats, bus–buses*); tenses (*walk–walked–walking, spill–spilled–spilling, bite–biting–bitten*); possession (*Maria–Maria's*); or comparisons (*big–bigger–biggest*). These forms are acquired early in oral language and have been given less prominence in vocabulary research, probably because they seem to be readily learned without instruction. Research suggests that most primary-grade students whose first language is English can use inflected forms of root words effectively (Anglin et al., 1993) and that inflectional suffixes are generally mastered by age 9 or 10 (Berninger et al., 2010). While we concur with Scott et al. (2012) in recommending less instructional emphasis on them, it would be wise to assess knowledge of inflected forms, with an eye to instruction as needed, because they are encountered in a significant portion of written language, and irregular inflection forms (*break–broke; sing–sang–sung*) can cause problems, especially for English learners.

Derivational morphemes are prefixes or suffixes that are added to an existing word to create a new word while modifying the basic meaning (*happy–unhappy*) or the part of speech (*create–creation; clear–clearly*). *Bound roots* are morphemes that carry meaning similar to freestanding words, but they are not freestanding. These are most often Latin or Greek roots, for example *spect,* from Latin, meaning *to watch,* or *bio* from Greek, meaning *life.* Some bound roots have an additional designation as *combining forms.* Combining forms (e.g., *bio*) can join with other combining forms and with freestanding roots (words), and the new words that are formed can be further modified. Thus we can talk about *biology,* a combination of two combining forms *bio* and *logy,* and there is a word family that results from the combination: *biologic, biological,* and *biologically.* We can also talk about *biosphere, biography (biographer), biomass,* and others. In contrast, we cannot combine a prefix and a suffix without a root (e.g., we cannot have *misic* as *mis-* and *-ic* together). Combining forms are an important part of the vocabulary of science and technology (STEM) education.

Morphological Awareness

Given the above considerations and caveats, how do we best teach morphology? As should be clear from the approach to vocabulary that we have been developing, we would not recommend lessons that center on presenting a collection of prefixes and suffixes with their common meanings and words that contain them. Rather, a good starting point would be game-like activities that can heighten students' interest in morphology and support the acquisition of morphological awareness (Carlisle, 2000, 2010), specifically that words can be analyzed into parts, the same parts turn up in many words, and their effects on the root words is fairly predictable. These activities could start with common and relatively productive affixes (e.g., *-s, -ed, -ing, -er, -ness, de-, -ful, -ly,* and *un-*) that can be added to many words to help students begin to understand how the system works. An example is the Root Relay game described by Scott et al. (2012), in which teams of students complete a relay race to construct a word from a pile of roots, a pile of prefixes, and a pile of suffixes.

Other examples take common games like Jeopardy or Go Fish and transform them into games that focus on common roots (see Bear, Invernizzi, Templeton, & Johnston, 2016, for examples). These types of games help students put together meaningful words by paying attention to their component parts. Another game might move beyond real words by encouraging students to coin new words and definitions (e.g., *biofrostize* could be "to cause one's body to become frostbitten": *He was biofrostized after his 6-hour ordeal in the meat locker*). This is a powerful way to solidify the understanding of how morphological units are put together. This approach is captured well in the "verbum-struct-ion" game created by Moloney (2016).

Structured Word Inquiry

Morphology is one aspect of an innovative and systematic inquiry-based approach to English spelling that demonstrates connections to word structure and meaning. The approach, Structured Word Inquiry (SWI), developed by Bowers and Kirby (2010), prompts teachers and students to become "word scientists," investigating the interrelation of morphology, phonology, and etymology. SWI's key principles are that the *primary* function of English spelling is to represent meaning, and that the conventions by which English spelling represents meaning are so well ordered and reliable that spelling can be investigated and understood through scientific inquiry. Bowers's inquiry exploits the process of morphological problem solving using two linguistic tools: the morphological matrix and the word sum. These tools are meant to encourage and support teachers in designing their own ways to help students understand and appreciate how English morphology reveals meaningful connections between words.

The word sum uses standard linguistic notation to reveal the underlying morphological elements of a word. For example, *un + help + ful → unhelpful*. The second tool, the morphological matrix, represents members of a morphological family arranged into cells to show prefixes and suffixes that can combine with the base word.

un dis	**please**	ing	
		ure	*able*
		ant	*ly ness*

In an intervention study, Bowers and Kirby (2010) used the matrix and word sum extensively and found significantly better results in vocabulary learning for an experimental group when compared to a control group.

Bowers and Cooke (2012) suggest that teachers take on the role of word scientists, using word sums and matrices to investigate morphological structure. Their work shows how targeting the spelled base of a word can prompt discussion of changing pronunciations and can help students see consistent links between meaning and spelling. For example, conventional literacy instruction teaches the word *goes* as regular and *does* as irregular because of the pronunciation change of the vowel. However, if you attend to the underlying spelling rather than pronunciation, both are regular.

Figure 6.2, an excerpt from interactions with a kindergarten class around the word *healthy*, demonstrates the heart of the approach (Bowers, 2016, p. 3). What is so compelling about Bowers's approach is that rather than treating English spelling as a primarily flawed system filled with exceptions, it builds on the linguistic understanding of English spelling as a highly ordered and reliable system for meaning representation. It

A kindergarten class asked me to look at the word <healthy> from one of their units of study. I started by "writing-out-loud" the structure of the word like this:

"h – ea – l ----- th ----- y"

These students pay close attention to how I "write out loud" because they have learned that I plant meaning-structure cues that they want to find. Before I wrote this word out loud, most of the class assumed that the base of this word was <health>. But my spelling out suggested something different . . . .

They have learned that a long pause marks a boundary between morphemes and that announcing the <ea> together signals a digraph in a base. The first student hypothesis of a word sum read my spelling out perfectly.

heal + th + y → healthy

Seeing this concrete representation of the structure of <healthy> provoked a key question. They already knew the words <heal> and <health>, but a <-th> suffix would provide a concrete spelling–structure link between these words they had not seen before. This was a tempting hypothesis, but until I helped them see this word sum, the class had only thought of <th> as a digraph. Could it be a suffix too?

What impressed me most about these students was that they didn't just accept my word sum because I wrote it. They wanted to understand. The immediate response from the students when I completed the word sum was to ask for evidence of <-th> as a suffix in another word. What great scientists! When I gave them the words <grow> and <growth>, they were happy to add this new morpheme into their bank of understanding.

FIGURE 6.2. Example of structured word inquiry. From Bowers (2016). Used with permission from Peter Bowers.

also highlights how families of words are linked by meaning, structure, and history (Bowers, 2016).

Lexical Morphology (Latin Roots)

The examples just presented about morphology focus on derivational morphology—root or base words and the prefixes and suffixes that can be added to them. Bowers's inquiry approach also encompasses some exploration of bound morphemes as students try to figure out relationships among words. Bound morphemes such as *spec* in *speculate, specimen,* and *perspective* are most frequently the remnants of Latin in the English language.

Direct attention to teaching about Latin roots is another approach to morphology, which can be called *lexical morphology* (Crosson &

McKeown, 2016). Crosson and McKeown have worked with several formats of vocabulary instruction that included Latin roots. In each case, interactive instruction around academic words was the focus, and teaching about roots was one component of the instruction, which aligns with Bowers et al.'s (2010) findings about effective morphology instruction. The roots of targeted academic words were introduced, and other words that share the same roots were briefly presented. Students were asked to consider how the meaning of the root related to the word meanings. For example, here is how the roots *var* and *circum* were introduced (*variable* and *circumstances* were target words introduced in an earlier lesson):

> "*Var* is a Latin root that means change. How does the idea of change fit with the meaning of *variable*?" (Something *variable* can change often.)

> "*Circum* is a Latin root that means around. So the word *circumstances* means the conditions surrounding, or around, some event."

Activities that present root-related words asked students to engage in morphological problem solving to infer meanings of words containing taught roots. For example, in one activity, students are presented with sentences using root-related words and corresponding pictures. One sentence reads *The defunct truck was left to rust in the field*, accompanied by a picture of a broken-down truck. The teacher guides students to infer that something defunct is no longer working by asking:

> "Who sees a root hiding in *defunct*?"
> "What does *funct* mean?" (Work)
> "So if the truck is *defunct*, what does that mean?"

Another approach to developing conscious awareness of bound roots and morphological relationships to those roots is to develop a graphic way to demonstrate relationships in the form of a morphology tree. A morphology tree (see Figure 6.3) could be introduced by the teacher placing selected affixes and roots on the trees and by encouraging students to add related words as they encounter them in their reading or research materials. Posters outlining various deciduous trees have suffixes and roots (e.g., *-scribe, tele-, manu-,* and *-scope*) written on their trunks and, through group brainstorming and individual effort, words such as *telephone, telegraph, television, telescope, manuscript, transcribe, script, manual, manipulate, microscope, periscope, kaleidoscope,* and so on, are added to the branches as leaves.

FIGURE 6.3. Morphology tree.

Once there are enough leaves to see patterns emerging, the teacher guides students to uncover word meanings by asking:

> "How does knowing the meaning of *manu-* and *scribe* help you figure out the meaning of the word *manuscript*?"

> "How does knowing the meaning of *tele-* and *scope* help you figure out the meaning of *telescope*?"

Using words from their own reading materials adds interest and motivation to the task, and using known words to discover patterns helps students make the connection that morphological awareness is a useful strategy in their academic world.

Choosing words for instruction is particularly important, as teachers will want to focus on productive patterns while recognizing that seemingly transparent morphological relationships often have exceptions that deviate from an expected meaning. As Lederer (1989) points out: there is no *egg* in *eggplant*; *hammers* don't *ham*; and people drive on a *parkway* and *park* in the driveway. Patterns that are seen frequently seem to be likely candidates for instruction (Stahl & Nagy, 2006; White, Sowell, & Yanagihara, 1989), and it would be more productive to teach root words with larger morphological families than those with limited relatives. As Nagy and Hiebert (2010) point out, words like *impress* with variants such as *impressed, impresses, impressing, impression, impressive,* and *impressionable* afford a better learning opportunity than words like *throng,* which occurs just as frequently in English, but with the limited inflectional variants *thronged, throngs,* and *thronging.* Since Anglo-Saxon morphology tends to be used with more frequent words, it might make sense to teach these forms at earlier grades and concentrate on Latinate morphology, often found in relatively academic texts, in fourth grade and above.

Accounting for Grade-Level Differences

Another issue that teachers should be sensitive to is how the morphological demands of vocabulary learning shift across grade levels. Consider the following table, which lists some characteristic words according to grade level:

Grade level	Exemplars of morphological patterns
Grade 2	*cats, reading, puppies, took, mice*
Grade 4	*teacher, kindness, abbreviation, misread, unbelievable*
Grade 6	*photography, ignition, indirect, appropriation*
Grade 8	*biology, designation, legislation, hydrophobic, Herculean*
Grade 10	*bronchitis, hematoma, cytoplasm, leukocyte*

Note that these words are listed as exemplars of morphological phenomena tied to approximate grades and illustrate how vocabulary demands and instruction might change over time. Thus, in second grade, the teacher is most likely to be concerned that students can read and write using core vocabulary (root words) in different inflected forms, and will be concerned with such phenomena as adding vowel suffixes (-*ing*, -*es*, along with irregular past tenses and plurals).

The set of words for fourth grade is focused on the introduction of derivational morphology and to the differences between Germanic and Latinate affixes. The words *teacher* and *kindness* illustrate common Germanic suffixes that have a simple relationship to the root. *Unbelievable* and *misread* illustrate common prefixes that students need to learn early, while the word *abbreviation* provides a relatively easy example of the most common Latinate suffix *-ion*.

In the words for sixth grade, *photography* illustrates how stress can change for variant forms (compare *photograph, photographic,* and *photography*), resulting in different pronunciations of the vowels. The word *ignition* is provided to show how sound can shift when we convert words from one part of speech to another (*ignite/ignition, divide/division*). We chose *indirect* because the prefix *in-* is one of the most common a student is likely to acquire in subsequent grades. It also has two senses—negation (*inappropriate*) and inside (*inpatient*), showing the need for semantic flexibility. We chose *appropriation* because it illustrates the workings of multiple senses. Not only does *appropriate* have different meanings—*appropriate behavior, appropriated his ideas*—but the variant *appropriation* applies only to the second sense. In addition, this example shows interaction with phonology, where the final *-t* is pronounced differently when the suffix is applied.

The set of words for eighth grade contains two examples of combining forms (*biology* and *hydrophobic*). These words play an important role in high school courses and in STEM education. We used one word, *legislation*, that contains a bound root (*legalis*). Other words with the same root are *legislature, legal,* and *legitimate*. The word *designation* was chosen to show that it does not mean *de-sign-ation* but rather *designate-ion*. A similar example is *extradition*, which is a variant of *extradite* and not a variant of *tradition*. The word *Herculean* is chosen to show how a name can be incorporated into a word and how it carries a connotation associated with the individual. It also provides a basis for teaching a family of phrases, such as *Herculean effort/task/labor/ achievement*.

The set of words for 10th grade comes from Tier Three. The intent is to group these words according to some domain and show that specific affixes are associated with it. All of the ones in our grid are from the domain of *biomedicine*. The suffix *-itis* means *inflammation*, and other words with this ending include *tonsillitis, appendicitis, laryngitis, sinusitis, nephritis, hepatitis,* and *meningitis*. The words that are exemplified can be sorted according to expected grade level so that some of the words will be accessible, and some will be a stretch. The suffix *-oma* means *growth* and is intended to show that there are other Tier Three suffixes in this domain. The combining form *cyt-* means *cell*. The combining form *leuk-* means *white*. *Leukocyte* was chosen to show that *cyt-* can be both a final combining form and an initial form, as with *cytoplasm*.

As the vocabulary that students learn changes with grade level, the specific aspects of language that teachers need to make sure that students can handle also changes. It is important for teachers to familiarize themselves with the linguistic patterns that students are likely to find challenging at their grade level to ensure that they target these patterns in their lessons. More generally, morphological and other generative patterns provide powerful tools for helping students leverage what they know, so that they can benefit maximally from every opportunity they get to learn new words.

OTHER CONSIDERATIONS

Here we turn to two additional issues that may require attention and instructional adjustment as teachers find that their classrooms are increasingly culturally and linguistically diverse (Maxwell, 2014).

Register and Variant Forms of English

There is an increasing likelihood that teachers will not come from the same linguistic background as their students, which raises several issues. For instance, some variations of English use inflectional forms that are not part of standard academic English. A teacher who wishes to create a word-conscious classroom should be aware of the potential negative impact on students if they get the impression that their home language is incorrect or inappropriate, when in fact it is simply different and entirely normal within the student's native population group. The issue for such students is that they must be able to function comfortably within an academic context along with the use of more formal registers.

Everyone changes the language they use from one social situation to the next, adapting their vocabulary and even their grammar to fit the context. The technical linguistic term for this phenomenon is *code switching,* which applies to whenever people change the registers, dialects, or even languages they use, depending on their social situation (Wheeler, 2008). Teachers should encourage students to explore how people adjust their language—both the vocabulary they use and the grammatical patterns they prefer—from one context to the next. Making students aware of this flexibility and helping them learn how to code switch to use appropriate formal registers in an academic context can be accomplished without devaluing students' home languages.

Research indicates that when teachers approach language variation in this spirit, the results can be very positive, as they remove a potential barrier between teachers and students and give students a path toward engagement with academic English that does not require them to distance themselves from the communities in which they are raised. In particular, use of code-switching pedagogies has been successful in fostering the use of Standard English and boosting overall student writing performance among urban African American students at many different grade levels (Fogel & Ehri, 2000; Sweetland, 2006; Taylor, 1991).

Using traditional techniques as a teacher at an urban elementary school on the Virginia peninsula, Rachel Swords saw a 30-point gap in test scores between her African American and white third-grade students. In 2002, her first year of implementing code-switching strategies, she closed the achievement gap in her classroom—on standardized state assessments, her African American students did as well as her white students in English and history, and they outperformed her white students in math and science. These results have held constant in each subsequent year. In 2006, in a class that began below grade level, 100% of Sword's African American students passed Virginia's year-end state tests (Wheeler & Swords, 2006).

Code switching is central to the way people use language, and a word-conscious classroom will include code switching in its repertoire. This approach fosters metacognition by making students aware of how different contexts require different choices of words and grammatical structure. It teaches students to be sensitive to patterns and to form and test hypotheses, not just to learn what words mean, but also to learn when their use is appropriate.

Considerations for English Learners

We have thus far provided guidance about the general population of vocabulary learners, and much of the discussion applies equally well to all students. In this section we extend the discussion, specifically asking, "How might vocabulary acquisition differ for learners who have not yet mastered fluency in English?" People who speak English can be categorized in a number of ways. They can be a part of the mainstream population that speaks English or can be bilingual/multilingual, demonstrating equal proficiency across languages. They can also be users/learners of English as a lingua franca (ELF), where English may be the official language of communication, in a situation such as in a global company with offices in multiple countries where the national languages may not be the same. Here, the use of English is the common language that all employees around the world understand. While ELFs may need to learn English, their acquisition of vocabulary may be confined to workplace communication. Our focus is on yet another population, people who learn English in the classroom for academic or general purposes; henceforth we refer to them as "English learners" (ELs). This group includes those who learn English as a foreign language and those who learn English as a second language.

Unlike young children who learn English in an immersion setting where vocabulary is encountered during most of their waking hours, ELs are at a disadvantage in acquiring words, as their learning context often falls within the time limits available in the classroom. In relatively short periods of time, teachers are challenged with teaching vocabulary to all of their students as well as developing fluency in their ELs. Teachers may also encounter differences in literacy, in which students may be literate in languages that are character-based (such as Chinese) or languages that employ different alphabetic systems such as Korean or Cyrillic. A related and complicating issue is that a classroom may contain students who lack literacy skills both in English and in their native language.

A caveat faced with the instruction of ELs is that research on vocabulary instruction for this overall population often focuses on very specific age groups—either very young children or college-age students through adults. However, it appears that the results may be pedagogically generalizable across all age groups.

Vocabulary Learning through Context

Earlier in the chapter, we emphasized that interactions with books promote students' consciousness of words and word use. For ELs, Laufer (2003) challenges this "vocabulary through reading" hypothesis, because it assumes that ELs have enough word knowledge and reading fluency to comprehend context and make inferences correctly. According to Laufer, the claim that people acquire vocabulary through reading requires accepting the following assumptions: "the noticing assumption, the guessing ability assumption, the 'guessing-retention link' assumption, and the 'cumulative gain' assumption" (p. 568).

Learners need to first *notice* that a word in text is unknown (the noticing assumption). Learners who are not fluent in English may not recognize unfamiliar words as unfamiliar because their goal is to infer an overall message in a text rather than definitions of its individual words. Many of the words in texts may be encountered less frequently than words in a natural oral language or conversational learning context. Although many of those words may be familiar, they may not be well connected to other words and contexts in the learner's mental lexicon.

Laufer's guessing ability assumption refers to when the learner does make a conscious decision to infer a word's meaning from context, which calls on both linguistic and nonlinguistic clues. A limitation here is that sometimes clues are ignored because they do not fit into the EL's knowledge of the world. The clues that are needed to infer a word's meaning may be provided by other *unknown* words in the context, thus not serving ELs well because their own lexicon is not broad enough to allow a good guess.

The guessing-retention link assumes that learners can retain the meanings of words that they infer. Laufer indicates that, especially in the case of ELs, guessing does not promote comprehension, let alone retention. This is because the EL may deem an unknown word unimportant and thus ignore it; word meanings may be guessed incorrectly; and the EL may not want to interrupt his/her flow of reading to look up a word in a dictionary.

The cumulative gain assumption deals with the amount of exposure necessary for retaining the meaning of a word. Evidence suggests that as exposure increases, word knowledge deepens. Webb (2007) demonstrated that sizable gains were realized for receptive vocabulary with as few as one to three exposures to words and that gains on productive tasks were realized after seven exposures. Yet *after* 10 exposures to words, learners were still making sizable gains on word recall and retention of deeper meanings of words.

Work by Laufer (2003) and by Topkaraoğlu and Dilman (2014) provided an added dimension to considerations of amount of exposure necessary for word recall. Laufer (2003) examined learners' ability to recall the meaning of a word under three different conditions: after simply reading text, after reading text with dictionary look-ups, and reading text followed by participation in productive word-focused exercises (e.g., using the target words in an essay). The results showed that if a word was practiced in a productive word task, its meaning was more likely to be retained, even if it was noticed in the text and looked up in a dictionary. It is therefore important to use word-focused activities, which are more efficient and effective for ELs' vocabulary acquisition, as they force the learner to "notice" unknown words. Topkaraoğlu and Dilman demonstrated that word-focused activities such as word searches, crossword puzzles, fill-in-the-blanks, and unscrambling words are the kinds of activities that can boost ELs' productive vocabulary. The evidence about cumulative exposures to words for ELs seems to align with the key messages of this book: that multiple exposures are needed for vocabulary learning and that the productive, active use of words promotes more effective learning. Thus these ideas hold true for ELs as well as for native English-speaking students.

More about Dictionaries and Glosses

A common practice with ELs is using dictionaries and glosses. Glosses provide definitions of unknown words in reading, either in the margin of printed texts or as pop-up boxes in digital text (think portable glossary).

Glosses can be offered in English or translated into the EL's native language. Dictionaries and glosses help ELs with immediate comprehension of the text at hand, but they offer only minimal long-term retention of meanings compared to reading in context alone (Eckerth & Tavakoli, 2012; Laufer, 2011, 2014; Yoshii, 2014). As in other studies, these studies indicated that word-focused activities were still better for promoting retention and deeper understanding of vocabulary.

Morphological Awareness

Much like native speakers, ELs may begin to show difficulty in reading in fourth grade, when texts contain words that are longer and more complex and the vocabulary becomes more academic (Kieffer & Lesaux, 2007). Kieffer and Lesaux found that, for ELs, a change in pronunciation between a root and a word increased the difficulty of applying morphological knowledge, and concluded that an important aspect of instruction is pointing out this type of relationship, indicating that how a word sounds or how it is spelled may change when the root is isolated. Kieffer and Lesaux also suggest that it might be beneficial to ELs to teach some common Latin and Greek roots, as well as the relationships between cognates across languages.

Other researchers have also found that developing ELs' morphological awareness promotes vocabulary growth (Hayashi & Murphy, 2011). Effective instructional activities have included productive tasks, such as analyzing words into morphological units, identifying the root, and inferring the meaning of a word from its morphemes (Zhang & Koda, 2012).

Linguistic Distance

Linguistic distance, the extent of similarities between languages, can affect ELs' understanding of morphology. For example, English and Korean (both alphabetic languages) would have a shorter linguistic distance than English and Chinese, as English is an alphabetic language while Chinese is a character- (word-unity) based language. For languages that use other alphabetic systems (such as Korean or Persian), morphological awareness is a powerful contributor to reading comprehension for ELs, independent of phonological awareness (Ghafoori & Esfanjani, 2012; Jeon, 2011).

Many other linguistic features coincide with or are differentiated across languages; for example, compounding occurs in both English and Chinese, while derivation occurs primarily in English and at a minimal level in Chinese (Zhang, 2013). Another example is that some languages

may not contain the same kind of phonics as English, causing difficulty in both writing and pronunciation for some ELs (Akande, 2005;
Ellis, 2008). A review of cross-linguistic research concludes that role
of morphological awareness is likely to depend on how morphemes are
encoded in various languages (Kuo & Anderson, 2006). The general
point is that ELs with more linguistically distant native languages may
need additional support in learning morphology because they may not
have metalinguistic awareness mechanisms that can be transferred from
their native languages.

Polysemy

For ELs, it is particularly important to develop students' ability to distinguish multiple senses of the same word and to build their awareness of the
regular patterns. In doing so, explicit instruction about the relationships
among the different meanings of the polysemous words (without any
context) is more effective than simply having context from which one can
guess the different extended meanings (Rashidi, 2013). Teaching the core
sense of polysemous words, especially with techniques that ask students
to guess the figurative sense of a word based on its core sense, enables
ELs to make better connections between the core and figurative senses of
words and aids in the retention of multiple senses of words (Verspoor &
Lowie, 2003). Use of images, such as those found in *image-schema-based
vocabulary instruction* (ISBM) can help ELs better understand the additional meanings of words and integrate those meanings into their mental
lexicon (Makni, 2014). In ISBM, diagrams (i.e., image schemas) are used
to illustrate the core meaning of words. Other image schemas can be
used to demonstrate how the core meaning of a polysemous word can be
extended to other senses through metaphor. This research also indicates
that memorizing equivalents of meanings in students' native languages
was ineffective because it "ignor[es] the cross-linguistic semantic differences" (Makni, 2014, p. 15) between the languages. This is due to a lack
of parallelism between the core sense and figurative senses of different
languages (Karlsson, 2013). Karlsson recommends that after teaching
the core meaning of a word, teaching the most frequent senses of that
word first should be particularly effective with ELs.

Figurative Speech: Metonymy and Metaphor

Metonymy and metaphor fall along a continuum (Chen & Lai, 2012).
Metonymy refers to something through the use of a related entity, such
as "lend me your ears" meaning "listen to me"; metaphor is a mechanism
that crosses domains by referencing something that is experienced in one

domain and conceptually extends its use into another domain, such as saying someone has "a heart of gold." Chen and Lai demonstrated that ELs could distinguish between figurative expressions and literal meanings and that it was easier for them to understand metaphoric expressions than metonymic expressions.

Barcelona (2010) suggests that learning metonymy is particularly important for ELs because it varies significantly across languages. Metonymy may work differently conceptually and culturally in different languages, and the chains of inference may differ. ELs may better understand metonymies and metaphors if their origins are explained, so there is a point of reference to start with, for example, explaining that because gold is seen as valuable and good, someone with a "heart of gold" is a good person who is generous and kind. The more often ELs encounter metonymy and the more conventional the metonymy, the easier its acquisition.

It is important for instructors to contextualize metonymy so that ELs can understand it. This includes being explicit about culture-specific metonymies and teaching metonymic-guided reasoning across different domains so that ELs can understand how to generalize metonymy use effectively. Learning metonymy can assist ELs with better acquisition of metaphors by allowing them to understand levels of abstraction and decontextualization (Barcelona, 2010). Barcelona also suggests teaching polysemy at the same time can be useful because it can demonstrate the role that polysemy plays in the literal–metonymic–metaphoric continuum.

ALIGNING INSTRUCTION AND ASSESSMENT

While we have focused on instructional goals in this chapter, there is still a very strong link to assessment: instruction and assessment need to be aligned. This means that assessments should tap the vocabulary knowledge that is the focus of instruction—assess what you want to know about students' ability. Specifically, assessments should provide a good look at students' knowledge of word meanings, their facility with using words, and the abilities that underlie word learning such as their understanding of language patterns. In Chapter 5, we discussed the types of assessments that we think could address those goals. Here we turn our attention to assessments that teachers might create and employ in classrooms. Assessments that can be easily developed are important because a teacher's concern focuses on whether students have understood specific presented concepts or have learned words explicitly taught, and no off-the-shelf assessment is going to provide that for you.

A key point in thinking about classroom assessments is that many instructional activities can also serve as assessments. For example, the activities described for providing additional encounters, in which students are asked to explain implications of different uses of a word or how using different words changes the meaning of a specific context, make excellent assessment items. Asking students to write a sentence containing a taught word assesses their ability to apply the word. If students tend to write simple sentences of the *She was indirect* variety, the task can be modified, for example, by requiring the word *because* or *when* in each sentence. To assess whether students understand different senses of words, an assessment can be constructed of sentences that use polysemous words, and students can be asked either to explain the sentence or to write a paraphrase of it.

To assess the extent to which students are developing a sense of how authors use words, an assessment could present interesting language use from a text and ask students to discuss why they think the author chose specific words or what the author was trying to convey with a particular word choice. Examples from students' writing can also be used as items. Assessments that elicit students' responses to text could be framed around vocabulary.

For example, after reading *The Great Gatsby* (Fitzgerald, 1925), a teacher could ask students to respond to the following prompt: "Explain how these words apply to characters or situations in the novel: *delusion; fraud; naive; ostentatious.*"

Another approach to assessing vocabulary crosses the boundary between instruction and assessment, using items as embedded assessments. These are quick, specific activities presented amid instruction that can direct attention where it might be needed, but that also have intrinsic instructional value. One format is to have students indicate their responses with thumbs up/down to word meaning, word use, or to language patterns. For example:

"Is getting up at the same time each day an example of being *consistent?*"
"If something is *devalued,* is it worth more or less?"

FINAL THOUGHTS

In this chapter, we have exemplified creating a word-conscious classroom that includes focused vocabulary instruction and metalinguistic awareness of the generative language patterns, and suggested that this approach can facilitate the type of word learning that we have promoted throughout this book—indeed, promote a nation of word learners. From our perspective, effective vocabulary instruction invites students to develop a sensitivity to language, an enthusiasm for word learning, and an appreciation for how language is structured, as well as focusing on individual words. The approach might be likened to an apprenticeship model of learning that can be found among weavers, skateboarders, painters, carpenters, computer scientists, and musicians. For example, a musician learns to play music in part by listening to other musicians, by formal and informal conversations about techniques, by trial and error, and by picking up tips from others. In learning how to act, the apprentice also learns the language and the vocabulary associated with different activities (Lave & Wenger, 1991). In a word-conscious classroom, students become language apprentices as the teacher helps them understand how to focus their attention on patterns, scaffolds their use of new language in safe environments where they can learn from multiple contexts, develops a joyful attitude toward learning, and actively helps them use words well in speaking, writing, and other forms of representation. Within such environments, students come to appreciate language as a resource at their disposal rather than as a mysterious system with rules that they need to decipher and adhere to. In a word-conscious classroom, nearly every discussion is an opportunity to teach vocabulary, but it is also an opportunity to assess it by carefully observing how well students are able to handle new and unfamiliar words and word patterns. These opportunities also provide students with embedded activities that teach critical concepts while giving the teacher a clear indication of where students are in their understanding of words.

CHAPTER 7

The Role of Technology to Support Adaptive, Flexible, and Scalable Assessments

Throughout this book, we have expanded on ways to thoughtfully choose words for both vocabulary instruction and assessment. In this chapter, we explore some of the technological advances that can facilitate the use of principles presented thus far. In the early days of vocabulary assessment, developing the frequency ratings for words was done entirely by hand. Teams would read the Boy Scouts handbook, the Bible, Shakespeare, magazine articles, and other sources to manually count the frequencies of words (Thorndike, 1921). We now have computers that double in speed every 2 years and we can put thousands of books on a flash drive that costs less than $10. These advances have enabled significant progress in the kinds of software that can be developed to support vocabulary assessment and instruction. In particular, modern approaches to computational linguistics exploit statistical methods for analyzing massive collections of text (text corpora) and support a variety of methods for assessing vocabulary knowledge and supporting language learning that would have been impractical until recently.

In this chapter, we examine a number of these technological developments and highlight their potential to support more effective approaches to vocabulary assessment and instruction. We begin by introducing specific tutoring systems for reading and vocabulary and describing how they work. We then focus on some of the technologies that underlie the design of intelligent tutors, in particular, automated passage selection and automated item generation. Many of the innovations we discuss in this chapter have not yet found their way into commercial educational software but are likely to do so over the next several years. In particular, a number of researchers have been developing automated tutoring systems to support reading and vocabulary learning.

AUTOMATED READING AND VOCABULARY TUTORING SYSTEMS

The desire to provide mechanical assistance to support reading appeared surprisingly early. Antoniadis, Granger, Kraif, Ponton, and Zampa (2013) mention that a patent was awarded in 1809 for a machine to assist reading. Similarly, Bruillard (1997, pp. 33–34) noted that Edward Thorndike envisioned a mechanical book in 1913: "if, by some miracle of mechanical ingenuity, a book could be constructed in such a way that page 2 only became visible for those who have completed page 1 and so on, then much of that which currently requires personal instruction could be performed by the book." Experience has made clear, however, that the availability of an electronic book does not eliminate the need for instruction. Any attempt to automate learning requires a more complex form of software, which contains (at least implicitly) a model of what is to be taught and which implements methods for communicating that content.

Contemporary automated tutors fall under the label of intelligent tutoring systems, which are computer systems that use artificial intelligence techniques to help students learn a subject (Woolf, 2009). The aim is to provide customized feedback without intervention from a human teacher. They have been used, among other things, to teach arithmetic (Beal, Arroyo, Cohen, Woolf, & Beal, 2010; Canfield, 2001; VanLehn, 1988, 1990) and science (Graesser, Chipman, Haynes, & Olney, 2005; Van Lehn et al. 2005). An effective arithmetic tutoring system will generate arithmetic examples, give students an opportunity to solve them, and check whether student answers are correct. Artificial intelligence techniques come into play in order to recognize when a student's error reflects a common type of mistake, such as a failure to understand the concept of *carrying*. When a particular misconception is successfully identified, the computer can give students feedback about what they did wrong and generate examples to help them understand how to revise their practice. In practice, there are curricular tools that have many of the features of an intelligent tutoring system, but which function as supplementary tools or formative assessments under the control of a teacher.

Tutoring systems designed to teach students vocabulary knowledge fall into two major categories: word centered and reading centered. A word-centered system has targeted vocabulary instruction as its central goal and may include a variety of exercises and explicit assessments. A reading-centered system is designed to help students build their vocabularies as a byproduct of reading and has as its central goal the selection of reading materials that will be challenging enough to help students learn, but not so difficult that students become discouraged or lose interest.

The Role of Adaptive Assessment

Many intelligent tutoring systems take advantage of methods originally developed to support computerized adaptive testing, a type of test in which the questions are selected on the basis of a model of the student's ability level. This approach has a long history, going back to the early 20th century (Binet & Simon, 1904; Frandsen, McCullough, & Stone, 1950; Hutt, 1947). Computer adaptive testing emerged in the 1980s and has now become a standard assessment tool (Van der Linden & Glas, 2000; Wainer, Dorans, Flaugher, Green, & Mislevy, 2000; Wainer & Kiely, 1987; Weiss, 1982). The system starts by asking a student a set of questions that are known to be easy and progressively selects more difficult items (or, if the student does not perform well, goes back to easier questions). It obtains a more accurate estimate of a student's ability level by sampling preferentially from items at or near the student's probable level of attainment. Adaptive assessment is not necessarily diagnostic assessment (DiBello, Roussos, & Stout, 2006; Leighton & Gierl, 2007), which attempts to use results to make specific instructional decisions. While adaptive diagnostic systems have been designed and have important potential benefits by combining the efficiencies of adaptive testing with the focused feedback available from diagnostic assessments (Shute, Graf, & Hansen, 2006), these are relatively recent advancements that have not yet been reflected at the level of classroom practice, although there are working examples of the use of adaptive diagnostic feedback in intelligent tutoring systems (Nye, Graesser, & Hu, 2014). Thus, when assessments are carefully designed and calibrated to provide information about specific aspects of learning (Mislevy, Almond, & Lukas, 2003), assessment results can have the granularity and specificity needed to support automated decision making within an intelligent tutoring system (Shute & Zapata-Rivera, 2010). Up to this point, work on diagnostic vocabulary assessment appears to have been realized primarily in the form of placement tests designed to identify students in need of targeted intervention, often in a university context where the needs of English learners are an important consideration (Doe, 2014; Read, 2008; Read & Chapelle, 2001).

However, even the simplest forms of adaptive vocabulary testing provide efficient methods for estimating student levels of vocabulary attainment (Browne & Culligan, 2008; Gibson & Stewart, 2014; McBride & Weiss, 1974; Tseng, 2016), which can then be used to identify words a student is not likely to know. This kind of system can be turned into a learning tool by giving students multiple opportunities to answer questions about targeted words or by providing them with word lists or vocabulary exercises featuring those words. A number of systems have been developed along these lines, often involving the use of mobile phones or other personal digital devices (Browne & Culligan, 2008; Chen & Chung, 2008; Wauters, Desmet, & Van Den Noortgate, 2010). Various online services provide this kind of vocabulary testing and practice (see, e.g., such sites as *vocabulary.com*; cf. Abrams & Walsh, 2014).

The major limitation of adaptive vocabulary assessment is that it mainly uses simple multiple-choice items or relatively short cloze-type items that promote more of a drill-and-memorization tool than one that develops a rich knowledge of word use in context. Yet this kind of system offers significant advantages since it makes it possible to determine a student's vocabulary size efficiently, and quickly identify words that that student needs to learn. It is a first step toward providing automated support for personalized learning.

Word-Centered Tutoring Systems

Word-centered computer-assisted language learning (CALL) systems are common in second-language teaching. Many of these are not full-fledged intelligent tutoring systems and can more accurately be described as extended exercise and homework systems (Cooley, 2001; Goodfellow, 1995; Levy & Stockwell, 2013). For example, Stockwell (2007) describes a system designed for use on mobile devices for Japanese learners of English. It emphasizes a task-based paradigm in which students are asked to read lessons from a textbook and then complete tasks with targeted words drawn from each lesson. Item types include selecting the most appropriate word in a sentence context (a multiple-choice cloze item), matching words to definitions, translating Japanese words into English, filling in blanks with words that match English definitions, and writing an appropriate word into a blank in an English sentence (an open-response cloze item). Students then receive feedback regarding the accuracy of their performance and are allowed to attempt the tasks multiple times. Ma (2013) describes a similar system in which relatively simple lessons about target words are reinforced by a series of exercises.

Perhaps the most sophisticated word-centered system of which we are aware is DSCoVAR ("Discover")—a project focused on helping middle school students learn new word meanings (Frishkoff, Collins-Thompson, Nam, Hodges, & Crossley, 2017). Critically, the DSCoVAR system also includes a strategy-training module that focuses students on the kinds of context clues they can use to infer word meanings, as well as a contextual word-learning module in which students have the opportunity to learn words through repeated attempts to infer the meanings of words when they are presented in context. The acronym stands for Dynamic Support of Contextualized Vocabulary Acquisition for Reading, and as its name suggests, it is built around a discovery cycle meant to engage students in an inquiry process in which they are repeatedly exposed to different contexts that contain a targeted word and challenged to guess what it means in context. They receive feedback about how close they came, and are allowed to make additional attempts until they close in on a correct understanding of the word. DSCoVAR is built around the idea that word meaning is learned incrementally, as discussed in Chapter 4.

For DSCoVAR to work, a great deal of preparatory work is required—in particular, identifying large numbers of useful contexts for students to analyze for each target word. This problem is addressed by applying natural language processing (NLP) techniques to identify potentially useful contexts in a large text corpus. DSCoVAR also requires automated scoring and feedback. The typical learning cycle starts with the student reading an example sentence that contains the target word and guessing what it means. The student expresses that guess as a word or phrase. DSCoVAR then gives feedback about how well he or she did and the student moves on to a word-learning opportunity. In this way, DSCoVAR seeks to build the skills students need to learn to become effective word learners through repeated practice and feedback. For instance, a student may be presented with examples such as the following (Frishkoff et al., 2017): *Heather was ashamed of the dress because it was so garish.* The task instructions require the student to type in a word that has the same (or a similar) meaning as the underlined word. If a student types in a word that comes close to the intended meaning, such as *ugly,* he or she gets positive feedback; less accurate responses are identified as such, and students have the opportunity to revise their answers.

DSCoVAR has a variety of important features that distinguish it from typical practice-and-drill vocabulary modules. First is the quality of the instruction, which is based on contextual word learning rather than memorization or drill, and it provides for incremental word learning and immediate feedback to students. Second, the sequencing and spacing of instruction is maximized. Presentation of contexts is sequenced, with the easiest, most supportive contexts appearing during earlier stages of learning. This kind of sequencing has been shown to improve overall student performance (Frishkoff et al., 2016). Adaptive spacing of practice is also used, such that experiences with the same word are spaced out. Adaptive spacing has been shown to increase the probability students will remember what they have learned (cf. Pavlik & Anderson, 2005). Spacing between trials is adaptive as well, so that students are more frequently exposed to new contexts for words that they are having difficulty learning.

Reading-Centered Tutoring Systems

In a reading-centered system, the central feedback loop focuses on reading passages, not words. Students are first presented with a passage to read; answer vocabulary and reading questions based on the passage; and are assigned to an initial reading level. The system then gives them a second text to read, selected to fit within the range of reading abilities implied by their performance on the preceding passages. The goal of such systems is to build students' vocabulary knowledge by exposing them to a carefully graded series of texts, always just hard enough to hold their interest. Ultimately, such systems may be built into more general technology designed to make electronic books more effective as educational platforms (Huang, Liang, Su, & Chen, 2012; Korat, 2010; Korat & Shamir, 2008). There is some evidence that in the early grades, such technologically enabled e-books can be an effective resource to support vocabulary learning (Smeets & Bus, 2012).

Two long-standing research efforts to build reading-centered intelligent tutoring systems in which vocabulary plays a key role are: Project LISTEN and Project REAP. It is worth noting, however, that vocabulary plays a role in other reading-centered intelligent tutoring systems such as A2i (Ingebrand & Connor, 2017), which uses student scores on standardized assessments and its own internal assessments (including a simple vocabulary assessment game based on matching related words) to recommend relevant curricular materials to teachers.

Project LISTEN (Literacy Innovation that Speech Technology Enables) is a tutoring system that helps students by listening to them as they read selected passages aloud (Mostow, 2001; Mostow et al., 2003; Mostow, Hauptmann, Chase, & Roth, 1993; Mostow, Roth, Hauptmann, & Kane, 1994). It uses speech recognition to analyze what the student said and intervenes when the student makes a mistake. For example, the student might mispronounce the word *tear* and the computer can tell the student, "In this sentence, *tear* is pronounced as if it was spelled *tayr*. It means to rip something, especially clothing." The system also intervenes if the student gets stuck or asks for help. Speech recognition is a difficult problem in general, but it works much better if a limited vocabulary is used, as expected with children who are just learning how to read. Project LISTEN is focused on oral instead of silent reading and is optimized to provide specific feedback in response to student reading errors.

While vocabulary is not the main focus of Project LISTEN, it is an important subgoal, and as a result there has been significant work invested in developing supports for vocabulary assessment and instruction. In particular, there has been significant development of a tutorial intervention aimed at accelerating vocabulary learning. This has been accomplished by increasing the number of useful vocabulary words the student encounters and the number of encounters with these words, and by designing encounters to enrich the quality of the student's representation of word meaning, the ability to access it, and transfer that representation to related words (Heiner, Beck, & Mostow, 2006). The intervention is based on principles distilled from research on vocabulary instruction (Aist, 2002; Beck et al., 2013; Biemiller & Boote, 2006; Graves, 2000; Stahl & Nagy, 2006) that recommend providing both definitional and contextual information about individual words, eliciting active processing that ties target words to their contexts, and providing multiple exposures to meaningful information about words.

Project LISTEN begins with providing definitions for a set of words that the student encounters in a text while reading with the tutor. This is followed by a sequence of processing by asking the student to evaluate whether sentences containing a target word make sense, for example, *It takes courage to go to the dentist*; *It takes courage to make your bed.* Feedback is then provided, explaining "It DOES take courage to go to the dentist. Going to the dentist can be scary" and "It does NOT take courage to make your bed. There is nothing scary about making your bed." Another activity asks students to apply the word to other situations, for example, prompting the student to say the target word if it applies to that case and if not, to say "Nooo!" One example of a situation for the word *tradition* is *when a great-grandfather, grandfather, father, and son all have the SAME name.* Both examples, and non-examples (i.e., when a situation does not apply to the target word) are included in the activity.

In addition, the intervention presents the instruction orally (as well as showing the information on the screen), provides oral feedback, and asks students for oral input. This makes the intervention accessible to students for a wide range of reading levels and provides an interactive environment.

Project REAP keeps the core elements of a reading-based tutorial system but seeks to improve on that baseline along several dimensions

(Brown & Eskenazi, 2004; Collins-Thompson & Callan, 2004; Heilman, Collins-Thompson, Callan, & Eskenazi, 2006). The acronym REAP stands for REAder-specific Practice. In particular, the aims of Project REAP include developing a more sophisticated model of text readability, using a rich array of assessments to measure vocabulary knowledge, and maximizing student interest to increase the potential for effective word learning by fine-tuning its text selection process.

REAP searches the Web to identify potential reading materials that could be assigned to individual students. This approach supports the flexible retrieval of documents that meet very specific requirements. Documents can be selected to meet specific requirements such as reading level, topic, and genre. Since REAP is a true tutorial system that contains a student model that uses past activity to generate estimates of student interests and word knowledge, it is possible to personalize the texts retrieved to meet student needs and interests and ensure that the texts contain only a set percentage of words that student readers are unlikely to know or understand.

The innovations built into Project REAP are discussed separately at several points later in this chapter under several headings, so we will not discuss it in depth here. But it is worth noting that the range of innovations that have been undertaken as part of Project REAP include improvements in automated readability measurement (Callan & Eskenazi, 2007; Collins-Thompson, 2014; Heilman, Collins-Thompson, & Eskenazi, 2008; Heilman, Zhao, Pino, & Eskenazi, 2008). It also includes improvements in methods for matching students to texts on other dimensions, such as their personal interests, level of vocabulary attainment (Brown & Eskenazi, 2005; Heilman & Eskenazi, 2008; Heilman, Juffs, & Eskenazi, 2007; Rosa & Eskenazi, 2013), and in the automatic generation of vocabulary and reading comprehension items (Brown et al., 2005; Feeney & Heilman, 2008; Heilman & Eskenazi, 2006, 2007; Kulkarni, Heilman, Eskenazi, & Callan, 2008; Pino & Eskenazi, 2009).

THE TECHNOLOGIES
THAT SUPPORT TUTORING SYSTEMS

All of the systems described above critically depend on advances in computing technology, in particular NLP techniques, to automatically provide critical supports for the learning process. In this section, we discuss three key advances that have powered this progress. In particular, these systems depend on:

- *Digital and online language resources,* including large text corpora, online dictionaries, and thesauri.
- *Automated passage selection,* in which automated methods select passages matched to students for reading level, topical interest, and other variables.
- *Automated item generation,* in which vocabulary items are generated from templates or some more complex algorithm.
- *Nonintrusive vocabulary assessment,* in which information about student levels of knowledge is captured behind the scenes from performance on other educational activities.

Digital and Online Language Resources

There is now a wide variety of resources that can (and have) been used to create digital tools to support vocabulary instruction and assessment. These include a variety of reference word lists, word norm databases, text corpora, digital dictionaries, and other lexical resources.

Reference Word Lists

Various reference word lists have been compiled to help prioritize the words to be taught or assessed. All of these lists are focused on identifying critical words for vocabulary teaching. However, they have also been exploited as NLP features—a computer-calculated property of a word based on evidence about it, derived from a text corpus or linguistic database, to measure the difficulty and reading level of texts (Sheehan, Kostin, Futagi, & Flor, 2010).

The first efforts were made by Thorndike and Lorge (1944) and resulted in *The Teacher's Handbook of 30,000 Words.* The most frequent 2,000 words were used to create the *General Service List of English Words* (West, 1953)—roughly speaking, Tier One words that will generally be part of the oral vocabulary for native speakers and which will cover 70–90% of the words in written text (Gilner, 2011). It included not only words, but also a breakdown into senses and the relative distribution of the senses by percentages.

The *Academic Word List* was created to go to "the next level," and was focused on words that students would need to know to understand typical academic texts (Coxhead, 1998). It is based on a corpus of 3.5 million words and the words that occur at least 100 times in that corpus. The list contains 570 word families, where each word family includes inflectional and derivational variants of the roots; there are about 3,000 words altogether.

Revised versions have been proposed for both the *General Service List* and the *Academic Word List*. There are two lists named the "New General Service List." One was developed by Browne, Culligan, and Phillips (*newgeneralservicelist.org*; cf. Browne, 2013, 2014), and one was developed by Brezina and Gablasova (2013). These lists were created in order to find a different set of 2,000 words that would provide better coverage than the original *General Service List*. The original version has words such as *shilling*. The new lists are also based on much larger corpora—hundreds of millions to billions of words rather than millions. *The New Academic Word List* was also developed by Browne, Culligan, and Phillips (2013) and is based on the *Cambridge English Corpus*. Another successor to the *Academic Word List* was created from an academic subcorpus of the *Corpus of Contemporary American English,* called the *Academic Vocabulary List* (Gardner & Davies, 2014).

Word Norm Databases

A variety of databases have also been created by the psychology and linguistics communities to capture norms for various lexical properties of words.

- *The Living Word Vocabulary.* As discussed in Chapter 4, the *Living Word Vocabulary* (Dale & O'Rourke, 1976) is the only resource in which word senses are organized by grade level. It provides a sense-level breakdown for more than 29,000 words regarding the grades at which the sense is known and the percentage of students at that grade that know it. About 7,500 of the words have more than one sense, for a total of over 44,000 senses. The *Living Word Vocabulary* indicates the minimum grade level for which two-thirds or more of the students know the sense. The grades are broken down into 4th, 6th, 8th, 10th, 12th, 13th, and 16th. Although the original book is out of print, Biemiller (2009) created a revised and adapted version of the list that is accessible today.

- *Age-of-acquisition norms.* We mentioned this resource in Chapter 2. The dataset is a subjective assessment of the age when a word was learned for 30,000 English words, using crowdsourcing as a methodology (Kuperman et al., 2012).

- *Word-concreteness norms.* Concreteness refers to how easily a word can be perceived by the senses—things that can be touched, seen, heard, or tasted. It is the opposite of abstract words. We expect that words are easier to learn if they refer to something concrete. A set of ratings for 40,000 words is described in Brysbaert, Warriner, and Kuperman (2014).

- *Word-association norms and other attributes.* The MRC Psycho-linguistics Database (Coltheart, 1981) comprises information for more than 150,000 words and up to 26 linguistic and psychological attributes for each word. It includes the Edinburgh Associative Thesaurus, which contains elicited word associations for a set of 2,500 words. For example, for the stimulus *big,* the responses mentioned two or more times include *small, little, large, grand, huge, deal, girl, house.*

- *Word-frequency lists.* Various word-frequency lists have been developed to provide normed information about relative word frequencies. Among the best known and not already mentioned, such as the *General Service List* (which includes frequency information), are the Kučera-Francis word-frequency list (Kučera & Francis, 1967), the American Heritage word-frequency list (Carroll, Davies, & Richman, 1971), and the TASA word-frequency list (Zeno et al., 1995). Many other word-frequency resources can also now be obtained by analyzing word frequencies in a variety of readily available text corpora.

The availability of large, normed word databases like these provide important support for creating automated tools, as they allow targeted selection of vocabulary using criteria that have been shown to be important predictors of word difficulty in psycholinguistic studies (Brown & Watson, 1987; Coltheart, Laxon, & Keating, 1988; Monaghan & Ellis, 2010; Morrison et al., 1997).

Corpora of Written and Spoken English

The use of large corpora has revolutionized computational approaches to language. They allow us to address the difference between what is possible and what is likely. For example, consider the sentence *I see a bird.* It is a simple and straightforward sentence, but to a computer, it is not so simple. We understand the sentence to be a pronoun (*I*) followed by a verb (*see*) followed by a determiner (*a*) followed by a noun (*bird*). If we look up each word in a dictionary, there are other possibilities for the parts of speech. The word *I* could be a noun (a letter of the alphabet), and the same for *a.* *See* can also be a noun, a reference to the pope (*the Holy See*). It is thus logically possible (although extraordinarily unlikely) that the expression *I see a bird* is a sequence of nouns. Without knowing how often different uses of a word appear in context, but knowing only their possible part of speech, a computer will spend a lot of time sorting through all of the possibilities, many of which could have been discarded almost from the beginning. However, when a large text collection is available, it can be annotated (or in many cases, automatically analyzed) to extract various forms of information (such as part of speech or specific word senses). The resulting datasets can be used to support detailed analysis of what meanings (and parts of speech) words have, where those specific uses of the words appear, and how likely they are in context.

One of the first corpora to be widely used was the *Computational Analysis of Present-Day American English,* more commonly known as the Brown corpus (Kučera, & Francis, 1967). The Brown corpus was intended to sample equally from 15 different categories. Some of these categories focused on informational text (e.g., government documents, newspaper articles, editorials, reviews, scholarly articles, and popular nonfiction). Others focused on literary text (e.g., general fiction, mysteries, science fiction, Westerns, romance, and humor). In each of the 15 categories, 500 samples were selected, each about 2,000 words long. The samples were chosen carefully, and the overall corpus contains about 1 million words. The text was semiautomatically annotated with the part of speech for each word in context. The manual effort took years. The Brown corpus was followed up by the Lancaster-Oslo/Bergen Corpus (LOB; Johansson, Atwell, Garside, & Leech, 1986), which was organized the same way and taken from the same types of text, but assembled from British English rather than American. This allowed detailed comparisons to be made on how the two dialects differ not just qualitatively, but quantitatively. The Brown and LOB corpora were compiled in the 1960s. Updated versions of the Brown and LOB corpora were created 40 years later, allowing for a better understanding of the changes that occur over time (Mair, 1997).

For more information about corpus linguistics, see the proceedings of a Nobel Symposium on Corpus Linguistics (Svartvik, 1991) and Simpson and McCarthy (2005), which contains a set of seminal papers. Appendix 7.1 lists many of the major corpora. Many, but not all of these, are available from the Linguistic Data Consortium (*www.ldc.upenn.edu*), an organization that was created to facilitate the common use of corpora, whose website provides a good indication of the range of corpora now available. All of the corpora listed in the appendix are readily available, though usually after paying a fee to the sponsoring organization.

Lexical Resources

The availability of large corpora not only revolutionized computational linguistics, it also revolutionized the development of dictionaries. The Brown corpus was used as the basis for the *American Heritage Dictionary* (Morris, 1969), the first time a corpus was used for such a purpose. Dictionaries used to be created by manually scanning books and magazines and then putting contexts on 3″ × 5″ index cards. The cards were then sorted into piles by subjective assessment of their senses. Computerized corpora enabled automatic compilation of contexts. Computer tools were developed to assist lexicographers by providing a summary of how a word is used syntactically and some of its most common co-occurrences (Kilgarriff et al., 2014; Kilgarriff, Rychlý, Smrz, & Tugwell, 2004). The Collins COBUILD dictionary was also based on a corpus, but on a much larger scale than previous efforts (Sinclair, 1987). It not only used a large corpus, but it also introduced a new style of how a word is defined. As mentioned in Chapter 2, McKeown (1993) found that such changes in defining style supported a more effective learning of word meanings. The availability of computer tools and online presentation may yet lead to further improvements; thus far, most digital dictionaries are little more than paper dictionaries published online, with few changes in presentation or format.

A dictionary for learners of English has advantages over other dictionaries, even for native speakers, since learners' dictionaries are more likely to keep definitions simple and arrange word meanings from most to least common. The most important learner dictionaries are the *Collins COBUILD Advanced American English Dictionary, Second Edition* (2017), the *Oxford Advanced American Dictionary for Learners of English* (Folse, 2011), and the *Longman Dictionary of American English* (2014), which has the distinction of using a restricted set of words in the text of all of the definitions (based on the *General Service List of English Words*; West, 1953). The idea is that if a student knows these 2,000 words, he or she can understand the definitions of all the rest. Since modern dictionaries are digital and built on data from corpora, he or she often provide more useful resources to support the creation of language learning tools than older, traditional dictionaries. While some general-purpose dictionaries follow similar principles (such as the *American Heritage Dictionary of the English Language, Fifth Edition*, 2016), more traditional dictionaries (e.g., the *Merriam-Webster Collegiate Dictionary*, 2014, or the *Oxford English Dictionary, Third Edition*; Stevenson, 2010) organize word senses historically, with the oldest sense listed first.

In addition to general-purpose dictionaries, a variety of specialized resources have been developed to support NLP tools and applications. The teacher may have little direct contact with them, but under the hood, they are likely to play an ever-increasing role in developing advanced supports for instruction and assessment.

The lexical resource most commonly used to build automated tools is WordNet (Fellbaum, 1998), which we discussed in earlier chapters. It is a large, publicly available database based on lexical semantic relationships, capturing much of the information stored in both a dictionary and a thesaurus. In WordNet, word senses are organized into synsets (sets of word senses that are synonyms or near-synonyms). For example, the synset for *improve* is: *better, amend, ameliorate, meliorate*. Semantic relationships, such as part/whole, general/specific, or cause/effect, are indicated as relationships between synsets. The data files downloadable with WordNet include a semantic concordance, Semcor—a tool that allows users to find examples of specific sentences within a corpus of newspaper articles that have been marked up to indicate which word senses appear in which contexts (Landes, Leacock, & Tengi, 1998).

Other resources have been developed by computational linguists to understand more about language by bringing to light the patterns and associations that characterize language use. Levin (1993) compiled a rich collection for more than 3,000 verbs regarding how they differ in how the arguments (nouns) are expressed in connection with each verb. She clustered the verbs into different semantic sets, such as searching (*hunt, search, rummage, ferret*), grooming (*comb, braid, groom, floss, dress*), and communication (*tell, talk, say, complain, advise,* and many others). Levin's work focused on how such synonym sets tend to share similar usage patterns. For instance, verbs like *hunt, search, rummage,* or *ferret* all appear in contexts like "_____ around for" (someone *hunts/searches/rummages/ferrets* around for something he or she is looking for). Other words that might seem closely related in meaning do not share the same usage patterns, and those differences correspond to differences in meaning and in the parts of that meaning that are placed in focus. For instance, there is a class of words, *investigate* and *explore,* that might seem closely related in meaning to words like *hunt, search,* and *rummage,* but which require a direct object that names the object of the investigation. Yet there are subtle differences in what one can say using one or the other class of verb. We can *hunt, search, rummage,* or *ferret* around for a solution to a problem, but it means something very different to *hunt, search,* or *rummage* for a problem. By contrast, investigating or exploring a problem and investigating or exploring a solution to a problem are much more closely related in meaning. These kinds of subtleties in usage are a central problem in language learning.

In order to capture these and other subtleties about how words are used in context, a variety of other resources have been developed, including PropBank (Kingsbury & Palmer, 2002), VerbNet (Schuler, 2005), and Framenet (Baker et al., 1998). PropBank is a version of the Penn Treebank corpus (Marcus, Marcinkiewicz, & Santorini, 1993) in which the text has been annotated with semantic propositions (Palmer, Gildea, & Kingsbury, 2005). For example, the word *abdicate* involves a role of the *abdicator* and a role of what was *abdicated* (e.g., a throne, responsibility). PropBank focuses on verbs and provides a useful resource with which to study how the same verb meaning can be expressed in different syntactic patterns. VerbNet is a more specialized resource that maps the data in PropBank to the verb classes that were established in Levin's work. FrameNet is designed to provide a very broad resource in which verbs (and other words) are mapped to "semantic frames" that describe meaning and usage in great detail.

Teachers may never see these resources directly, but that does not detract from their importance. The richness and subtlety of word usage and its intrinsic link to meaning makes it nearly impossible to capture grammar and meaning using automated tools, without building up large databases that capture the facts of meaning and usage in very fine detail.

Automated Passage Selection

Providing passages at appropriate levels for individual readers is critical in education. Texts need to be available at various levels so that readers can access the content well enough to understand it, while assuring that the material still provides learning opportunities. Passages might be selected according to readability level, to match content to a desired topic or level of background knowledge, or based on a student's personal interests in order to motivate reading.

Readability

Finding ways to estimate the readability of texts has a long and checkered history. Early work (e.g., Dale & Chall, 1948; Dale & Tyler, 1934; Flesch, 1948; Gray & Leary, 1935; Lorge, 1939, 1948) identified a number of surface factors that accounted for much of the variability in text difficulty, including the difficulty of the vocabulary as measured rather crudely by word length or frequency and the complexity of phrasing as measured, for instance, by sentence length. These relatively simple formulas, in which two or three features are used to predict a criterion reading difficulty score, have the advantage of simplicity and ease of understanding. Variations on this traditional approach to readability have maintained currency up to the present day in the form of the revised Chall and Dale model (1995), the Lexile readability framework (Smith, Stenner, Horabin, & Smith, 1989; Stenner, Burdick, Sanford, & Burdick, 2007), and various other systems (Miltsakaki & Troutt, 2008; School Renaissance Institute, Inc., 2000).

One of the key issues with measuring text readability is providing an appropriate way to measure which texts are, in fact, easier for people to read. Performance on multiple-choice reading tests has been the most frequent measure, although other systems have used human estimates of the grade level of passages as the criterion variable (Spache, 1953).

Cloze items were originally developed as an empirical method to provide a direct measure of text readability (Bormuth, 1966): when blanks were introduced into a passage at regular intervals, readers on average had an easier time restoring the blanked-out words when the passages were easier to read and understand.

However, traditional readability measures suffer from well-known defects (Benjamin, 2012). They ignore the effects of text structure and text cohesion and the ways in which the readability of a text interacts with its specific content. The formulas also ignore the particular meaning sense of words in text, such that *left hand* and *left-wing politics* both add to the frequency count of *l-e-f-t*. Clearly, they are not equally comprehensible for young readers.

Many newer models attempt to exploit NLP techniques to capture a richer, more cognitively accurate model of text readability (Crossley, Greenfield, & McNamara, 2008; McNamara et al., 2002; Pitler & Nenkova, 2008; Todirascu et al., 2013). Traditional readability models ignore critical factors, including the role of background knowledge (Davison, 1985) and of genre, which can have a systematic impact on the language in a text (Biber, 1989; Biber & Conrad, 2009). However, Sheehan and colleagues (Deane, Sheehan, Sabatini, Futagi, & Kostin, 2006; Sheehan, Flor, & Napolitano, 2013; Sheehan, Kostin, & Futagi, 2007, 2008) show that it can be useful to build separate models to predict readability in different genres, yielding improvements in the prediction of readability.

The critical difference between the newer readability models and the older methods is that the newer methods tend to use a richer array of features (or employ factors derived from multiple features) and select features intended to capture specific aspects of the readability or text difficulty construct that go beyond the vocabulary and sentence complexity features built into traditional readability frameworks. They may include measures of topic cohesion (repetition of content words or clusters of related words), referential cohesion (pronouns and other devices for referring to the same entity at different points in the same text), text macrostructure (indicators of how a document is organized at the outline level), and genre (indicators that distinguish between different text types such as narrative and argument). Calculating such features requires relatively complex NLP techniques but makes a significant difference in text performance. Several research investigations have reached this conclusion. François and Miltsakaki (2012) and Feng, Jansche, Huenerfauth, and Elhadad (2010) both report that richer models that include NLP features classified documents more accurately by reading level than the traditional readability models.

Nelson, Perfetti, Liben, and Liben (2012) provide what is probably the best overall comparison between different methods for assessing text difficulty. They assessed six text difficulty models: REAP (REAder-specific Practice; Callan & Eskenazi, 2007), ATOS (Advantage, TASA Open Standard; cf. Milone, 2009), DRP (Degrees of Reading Power; Carver, 1985), Lexile (Stenner, 1996), Reading Maturity (Landauer & May, 2012), and SourceRater^SM (later renamed TextEvaluator™; Sheehan et al., 2010). Their results also confirm that models that incorporated a variety of NLP-based features, such as Reading Maturity and TextEvaluator, generally outperformed models that relied entirely on traditional readability features such as Lexile (Lennon & Burdick, 2004; Mesmer, 2008).

Content Matching

Research on matching texts to readers by content also indicates that NLP techniques can be effective. Wolfe et al. (1998) applied one NLP technique—latent semantic analysis, or LSA—to the problem of matching documents to readers, selecting texts whose content does not too greatly exceed the background knowledge that students already had. In this study, they chose texts intended to illustrate different levels of difficulty for the same subject, and had students write about the same topic both before and after they read one of the texts. LSA provided a method for judging whether the words in a student's essay were characteristic of the topic, essentially by indicating for any pair of words how likely that pair of words was to appear in the same contexts. Their results indicated that students improved most from pretest to posttest when they read texts whose content was not too far in advance of their pretest essay responses—that is, lower-knowledge students did better with more general, less technical texts, whereas higher-knowledge students learned more from more advanced texts.

LSA has also been used to match students to texts (and model answers) in the AutoTutor intelligent tutoring system architecture, which has been applied to developing tutoring systems for many different content domains (Graesser, Wiemer-Hastings, Wiemer-Hastings, Kreuz, & the Tutoring Research Group, 1999). These kinds of applications using LSA illustrate tasks that can be accomplished using a range of related NLP techniques. For instance, Miltsakaki (2009) demonstrated that techniques to classify texts into thematic categories could be used to customize searches for reading materials at appropriate levels.

Personalization

Personalization—matching texts to readers on a variety of dimensions—can increase motivation and engagement and make it more likely that students will get the full benefits of reading a text, including improvements in vocabulary (Heilman et al., 2010; Hsu, Hwang, & Chang, 2013). To aid vocabulary learning, texts need to offer words that are unfamiliar to the reader, but with a surrounding context that is accessible enough to provide meaningful information about the word.

The development of personalization in a reading and vocabulary intelligent tutoring system reflects a larger trend toward personalization of recommendations in modern information technology (Drachsler, Verbert, Santos, & Manouselis, 2015). The availability of large databases that capture user behavior, such as keyword searches, clicks on links, and reading time on a particular text, has made it much easier to train systems to match recommended content to user interest (Kelly & Belkin, 2001; Liu, Dolan, & Pedersen, 2010; Tan & Teo, 1998).

Automated Item Generation

Automatically generating assessment items is a goal that, when feasible and well controlled, offers obvious potential advantages: inexpensive item development, an explicit item design, and, in the best-case scenarios, control of item properties using a model of the processes readers use to respond to specific types of items. Automatic item generation would also allow assessments to be tailored to assess selected words or address specific texts or curricula.

Initial interest in automated item generation emerged in the field of educational measurement. Methods for item generation initially were conceptualized as standardized procedures for item writers developing criterion-referenced tests, where the goal was to determine whether individuals could perform a specified task, rather than compare their performance to a population norm (Anderson, 1972; Bormuth, 1970; Hiveley, 1974; Millman, 1974; Roid & Haladyna, 1978). Interest in computerized automated item generation followed naturally, with significant interest emerging in the 1980s, as expressed in the research program outlined in Millman and Westman (1989). This line of endeavor identified several criteria that need to be satisfied by an automated item generation system. First, of course, there needs to be an algorithm that generates test questions automatically. For the items produced by an algorithm to be valid, there must be a cognitive theory underlying the design of the items, linking the design template to the construct to be tested. In addition, for the output of an automated item generation system to be immediately useful, without an intervening stage of human evaluation and pilot testing of the resulting items, there must be a predictive statistical model that links the properties of the items—that is, their difficulty and discrimination—to features of the design template.

Automated item generation has been successful primarily in non-language domains where the relevant design features are easily identified and controlled for difficulty and discrimination. For example, Bejar and Yocom (1991) examine ways to generate items based on transformations of figures that test student understanding of mental rotations, and Singley and Bennett (2002) and Bejar et al. (2002) examined the use of automated item generation to create mathematical test questions. Gorin (2005) and Gorin and Embretson (2006) tried to apply the same methodology to reading comprehension questions with less success, where the critical issue was whether the difficulty of generated test questions could be adequately controlled. Gorin showed that significant aspects of reading comprehension item difficulty can be predicted (typically, those associated with literal understanding), but other aspects were less easy to model (typically, those more strongly associated with inference). Certain features, such as the presence of negation, strongly affected difficulty. Others, such as the order in which ideas were presented, affected reaction times, but not the actual difficulty of the items.

In general, the greater the complexity of the cognitive processes involved, the more difficult it is to reduce the generation process to an effective algorithm or to model the properties of automatically generated items. In particular, automated item generation of vocabulary items appeared to be feasible, but with some problems in controlling the difficulty of the items generated. For instance, Janssen and De Boeck (1997) were able to generate multiple-choice synonym items effectively, but reported problems in predicting difficulty, although some of these issues have to do with the mathematical properties of the statistical model used, rather than with the item generation system, although this is also a significant consideration. Gierl and Lai (2012) discuss some of the issues involved in creating strong item models. The quality of automatically generated items can be significantly improved if a strong cognitive theory underlies the item model, allowing the selection of elements to correspond to elements likely to drive discrimination and difficulty.

Generating Open-Response Definitional Items

Let us begin with the simplest kind of test question: providing students with a target word and asking them to define it—as used, for instance, in the DSCoVAR vocabulary tutor discussed earlier in this chapter. Such items are by definition easy to generate—one needs only to generate a list of target words and choose which words to present—but less easy to score. However, there is an implicit function that distinguishes between good answers and bad answers. It is obvious, for instance, that *struggle* or *attack* are reasonable one-word attempts to define a word like *fight*; that *hurt* is related to *fight*, but more weakly; whereas words like *jump* or *fish* are essentially unrelated. Humans can be trained to score such questions. If a statistical model can be trained to predict human scores on such questions, the result will be a completely automated way to score vocabulary knowledge. Collins-Thompson and Callan (2007) and Collins-Thompson, Frishkoff, and Crossley (2012) built such a system, drawing upon both human-compiled vocabulary databases, such as WordNet and corpus-based methods for estimating whether words are similar in meaning, such as LSA (Landauer, Foltz, & Laham, 1998). They developed an algorithm that combined these resources to estimate the similarity of the meanings of words and phrases and then evaluated how well their system agreed with human ratings. They found that their method correlated moderately with human ratings (Collins-Thompson & Callan, 2007). While agreement between humans was much higher, the performance of the automated system was good enough to track student learning when they were given multiple opportunities to learn targeted words (Frishkoff, Collins-Thompson, Perfetti, & Callan, 2008).

Generating Multiple-Choice Synonym Items

Traditional, discrete synonym items (i.e., items that have only one correct answer) are one step more complicated. Instead of asking students to produce a synonym or a definition and scoring their answers on a scale that ranges from good definitions to nondefinitions, a multiple-choice synonym question provides respondents with a list of possible synonyms or definitions and asks them to choose the best one.

Implicitly, such questions ask examinees to distinguish between likely synonyms and likely nonsynonyms—a distinction that corresponds rather closely to the kinds of semantic similarity functions we discussed as being needed to generate open-response definitional items. The correct answers—the key—should be highly valued by whatever function we are using to measure semantic similarity, whereas incorrect answers—distractors—should not be highly valued by such a function. Ideally, we would also be able to establish functions that would identify attractive distractors, such as strong word associations (such as between *horse* and *stable*) or similarities in spelling or pronunciation. NLP methods can be used to approximate such functions mathematically, for instance, by using LSA to judge the quality of keys, as in Landauer and Dumais (1997), who used LSA to judge which of a set of options was most similar to the key in a set of TOEFL vocabulary items.

Generating Word Association Items

Another kind of discrete item—word association items—ask the student to select among a set of words to identify those that have an association with a key word's meaning. In this method, a corpus is analyzed to identify associations among words. If we pick the words most strongly associated with a target word in the corpus, we can generate a list of associates. If we pick words that are not associated with the target word, and generate lists of associated words for them, we can create a list of option choices, one of which is related to the target (the key) and the rest of which are not (distractors). This is the method employed by Heilman and Eskenazi (2007), who demonstrated that the method could be used to generate usable items.

Taking Advantage of Polysemy When Generating Multiple-Choice Definition Items

There is an obvious problem with any test item that asks a respondent to define a word without providing any kind of sentence or passage context: it does not take polysemy into account. When people read a word in context, they have to disambiguate it; and if they are sufficiently sophisticated to be able to apply dictionary definitions, they should be able to select the dictionary definition that best matches the meaning of a polysemous word. This defines a relatively simple type of vocabulary item that is easy to generate automatically—simply choose a word that has multiple definitions in the dictionary and generate an item where the examinee must select the right definition for that word in the context in which it is used. However, this item type presents one significant challenge: the problem of defining the key. That is, given a passage containing a targeted word and a list of definitions, how can we automatically decide which is the correct definition of the targeted word in the passage?

This is the NLP problem of word-sense disambiguation (Agirre & Edmonds, 2006; Mihalcea, 2011; Stevenson & Wilks, 2003). Word-sense disambiguation software has not yet reached a sufficient standard of accuracy that we can rely on to identify keys without human quality assurance. However, even though word-sense disambiguation algorithms do not always correctly identify which definition is intended in a specific sentence context, Kulkarni et al. (2008) and Dela Rosa and Eskenazi (2011) used NLP methods for word-sense disambiguation to generate items of this type and found that a vocabulary tutoring system that was sensitive to word senses in this way had a positive impact on student learning.

Generating Synonym-in-Context Items

Another way to take advantage of polysemy in automated item generation is to use synonyms or antonyms of a contextually inappropriate sense as distractors. For instance, *easy* can mean either *comfortable* (someone can have an *easy* manner), or *simple* (someone can undertake an *easy* job). This method is applied by Lin, Sung, and Chen (2007, p. 2), whose system generates items like the following:

> In this sentence *Learning English is not an easy job*, the meaning of the adjective *easy* is similar to:
>
>   (a) *available*
>   (b) *comfortable*
>   (c) *light*
>   (d) *simple*

Similar methods are applied by Susanti, Iida, and Tokunaga (2015), but with selections of target sentences from larger passages. For instance, one of the passages their system uses contains the following partial sentence: *She was a bright young PhD graduate from Yale University, and her research on thermal dynamics* . . . (p. 78). Use of word-sense disambiguation techniques allows Susanti et al.'s system to identify the intended sense of *bright* (synonymous with *smart*, which becomes the key). The system generated the following distractors, each related to an irrelevant sense: *cheerful, lively, dazzling,* and *valuable.*

Generating Cloze Items

Thus far, we have considered variations on synonym and definition items. Considerable work has also focused on automatically generating various kinds of cloze items, where a word or phrase in a source text is replaced with a blank. The properties of a cloze item are heavily contingent on how strongly the blanked-out word is related to the rest of the sentence. Some sentence blanks can be filled by practically any word drawn from the correct part of speech. For instance, the sentence *Let's have a talk about* _____ can be filled by practically any noun. On the other end of the spectrum, a sentence like the following is highly constraining: *The painting was obscured by several layers of* _____ *that had been added over the years by overzealous restorers.* Very few words can reasonably be used to fill in the blank, and *varnish* is one of those few.

In the simplest form of a cloze item, an open-response cloze item, respondents are expected to produce a word that fills the blank, and what we learn from the question depends entirely on the relationship between the sentence and the blank. Automatic generation of open-response cloze items to test vocabulary knowledge can thus be reduced to the task of identifying highly constraining contexts and of building automated models that identify sentences containing such contexts.

Automatically identifying appropriate sentences for cloze items is a problem that has received a great deal of attention in the literature. At the very least, any word that correctly fills the blank in a cloze item must fit appropriately into the syntactic structure of the target sentence. Collocations matter, too. For instance, the collocational pattern *layers of* _____ requires not only that the word filling the blank be a noun, but also that it should be a noun describing some kind of physical substance. The larger context matters too; for instance, in the highly constraining sentence just mentioned, the use of words like *painting* and *restorers* strongly suggests physical materials used in *painting,* such as oils, paint, or varnish. Ultimately, background knowledge and verbal inference play a role. A *restorer* might apply a layer of varnish to a *painting,* but it seems unreasonable to infer that even an overzealous *restorer* would cover a masterpiece with a new layer of paint. Much of the relevant information, such as grammaticality, sentence complexity, the presence of collocations, and the presence of important related words in the surrounding context can be modeled with reasonable accuracy using NLP techniques (Becker, Basu, & Vanderwende, 2012; Correia, Baptista, Eskenazi, & Mamede, 2012; Pino, Heilman, & Eskenazi, 2008; Skory & Eskenazi, 2010).

The problem of identifying the constraints that must be imposed on cloze sentence contexts is closely connected to the larger problem of identifying useful example sentences for vocabulary learners. The methods described above, which typically involve ranking sentences drawn from a corpus by how well they are likely to function as the stem for a cloze item, are very close relatives to methods for ranking sentences by their likelihood of working well as dictionary examples (Kilgarriff, Husák, McAdam, Rundell, & Rychlý, 2008) or for generating such example sentences from corpus data (Liu, Mostow & Aist, 2013). In nearly all of these lines of research, higher-ranked sentences tend to be more readable (as measured by the frequency of the words and the complexity of the sentence structures they contain), while also exemplifying typical patterns of usage (as measured by the frequency with which a target word appears in those contexts or the strength of word–context associations). For example, Liu et al.'s system generated sentences like the following for the word *declare*: *Members are asked to declare that you are 18*; *He was forced to declare a state of emergency*; *It is time to declare victory and go home.*

Open-response cloze items can be further constrained by providing a hint—one or more initial letters for the targeted word (Pino & Eskenazi, 2009). For example, an item like the following is likely to be significantly easier than the original open-response cloze item without the hint: *The painting was obscured by several layers of va*_____ *that had been added over the years by overzealous restorers.*

The most common type of automatically generated cloze item, at least in the context of vocabulary assessment, is the multiple-choice cloze item where the respondent must decide which of a set of options best fits into the blank rather than produce a response. Various principles have been proposed to govern the creation of distractors for multiple-choice cloze items. The simplest, baseline method is to choose words that are of the same part of speech and of comparable frequency to the key (Coniam, 1997, 1998), though some approaches include a grammatically inappropriate distractor, especially if the items are designed for a second-language population (Lee & Seneff, 2007; Mostow & Jang, 2012). More difficult distractors can be generated by selecting words that are syntactically plausible but never appear in the same exact phrasal patterns (collocations) as the key (Lee & Seneff, 2007; Liu, Wang, Gao, & Huang, 2005), or by selecting words that appear in the same collocations but do not make sense in the larger sentence or paragraph context (Hill & Simha, 2016).

The type of vocabulary knowledge tested by automatically generated multiple-choice cloze items will vary depending on the word type being tested, the grammatical context in which that word is placed, and the principle used for selecting the distractors. For instance, in the following example from Lee and Seneff (2007, p. 2176), the item primarily tests knowledge of the specific grammatical requirements of the verb *drive*, as reflected in the choice of prepositions:

It's really different driving _____ the right side of the street.

    (a) on [key]
    (b) [leave blank]
    (c) with
    (d) to

On the other hand, an example like the following from Liu et al. (2005, p. 3) only requires the respondent to recognize whether the key can be used grammatically in context:

Huang increasingly _____ that his fans have high expectations of him, although the upside is that their support helps provide the momentum that keeps him going.

    (a) prevents
    (b) controls
    (c) finds [key]
    (d) aims

Items can also be automatically generated using distractors in which any choice would be grammatically acceptable, so that the correct choice is governed by the logical connection between the key word and the context, such as between *hurricane* and *safe* in this example (Hill & Simha, 2016):

Follow these tips to stay _____ during a hurricane.

    (a) open
    (b) safe
    (c) quiet
    (d) active

Generating Multiple Types of Tasks from the Same Passage

Most of the systems we have reviewed focus on creating individual items. When an assessment is passage based, the focus has typically been on finding the best passages to illustrate particular vocabulary items. A different approach starts from the idea that teachers have a large supply of passages they want students to read anyway—and a shortage of appropriate tasks to help students practice their vocabulary (and other language skills). Burstein and Sabatini (2016), and Madnani, Burstein, Sabatini, Biggers, and Andreyev (2016) take this tack and present a system, Language Muse®, The Language Muse™ Activity Palette (the "Palette"), designed to generate large sets of classroom activities based on a single text. This allows a teacher to assign activities to students based on their specific needs, without having to adapt or personalize the texts they assign.

In the Language Muse Activity Palette system, automated item generation is applied to create several vocabulary-related tasks, including selecting correct homonyms, selecting correct inflectional forms, selecting correct synonyms, selecting the correct preposition to complete phrasal verbs, and selecting the correct option(s) to answer a set of multiple-choice cloze items.

The system also includes a range of other item types, such as summary tasks to support reading comprehension. Within the Language Muse Activity Palette system, teachers can input new texts, create new tasks based on those texts, assign those tasks to students, and view automatically scored student responses to better understand content comprehension and language skills development, especially for English learners. Capabilities like these—which automatically create and score student activities from teacher-selected texts—greatly expand the potential for the use of item generation in classroom teaching.

General Considerations about Item Generation

The examples we have presented illustrate that most of the types of vocabulary items that can be created and scored automatically are relatively simple in structure. When context plays a role in these items, it functions primarily to indicate which sense of the target word is intended. The most challenging kinds of vocabulary questions, such as the GRE sentence completion items discussed in an earlier chapter, require verbal inferences that are relatively difficult to model using current NLP techniques, although some features of these items can be predicted using NLP features (Bejar, Deane, Flor, & Chen, 2016). However, in the current state of the art, a very broad range of vocabulary items can be generated and scored automatically, sufficient to support the deployment of automated vocabulary items in software designed to support language learning and to develop reading comprehension. Nonetheless, evaluations of automated item generation systems in the NLP literature focus most often on the usability of the items created, with state-of-the-art systems producing between 60% and as much as 96% usable items, possibly depending on the specific grammatical pattern being tested and the rules for creating distractors (Lee & Seneff, 2007; Lin et al., 2007; Liu et al., 2005). There is currently relatively little research on predicting the difficulty and discrimination of automatically generated vocabulary items, but when this gap is filled, the automatic generation of vocabulary items is likely to become a staple element in reading- and vocabulary-focused intelligent tutoring systems.

Nonintrusive Vocabulary Assessment

A major new direction in assessment research focuses on the idea that we do not always need to test students' knowledge directly, using specially designed items. Instead, we can collect information about student behavior while the students are interacting with a digital environment and use features of that behavior to support inferences about what students know and can do. This approach, sometimes termed "stealth assessment" (Shute, 2011; Shute & Kim, 2014) or "nonintrusive assessment," can make it much easier to collect assessment information without disrupting ongoing teaching and learning. It can also make it easier for teachers to get assessment information quickly when they need it to help narrow the gap between higher- and lower-performing students.

The key idea is that students are producing evidence of their skills and abilities all the time. For example, as students read and write they may look up words they do not know or hesitate when typing a word of whose spelling they are uncertain. While students communicate with other students and with the teacher, the words they use and the way they combine them with other words reflects the vocabulary they have mastered. Outside of a digital environment, most of that information is lost very quickly or never collected in the first place, but in a digital environment it is possible to keep detailed records of student behavior and to analyze the logs of students' keystrokes for features that help to predict what students know and can do (Shute, Ventura, Bauer, & Zapata-Rivera, 2009).

Allen and McNamara (2015) report on using a writing tutorial system, The Writing Pal (W-Pal), as a nonintrusive assessment of student vocabulary knowledge. This tool allows students to write essays in a digital environment in which various tutorial supports are provided. Allen and McNamara's study focused on determining whether features of students' writing performance could be used to predict their performance on a standard assessment of vocabulary knowledge, the Gates–MacGinitie (MacGinitie et al., 2000). The researchers extracted a variety of features from student essays, including the mean age of acquisition, concreteness, frequency, and academic status of the words produced by each student, and built a regression model that predicted student performance on the Gates–MacGinitie vocabulary test from these features. Their model predicted vocabulary test performance relatively strongly between the predicted and actual scores. These results were obtained for a single student essay for each student, containing an average of 410 words. In a literacy classroom that required students to write regularly (and possibly also to communicate with one another digitally as part of their classroom work), much larger numbers of student essays could be created. These results suggest that we could obtain accurate estimates of student vocabulary size from students' ongoing classroom work without ever administering an explicit vocabulary assessment. This methodology may have the potential to provide richer measurement of students' depth of vocabulary knowledge in a nonintrusive way, although to date no studies have done so.

Various other behaviors have been shown to have significant relations with reading level. For instance, in a modern digital environment, students frequently engage in online searches, where they create queries to find material they need to address personal or educational needs. Liu, Croft, Oh, and Hart (2004) show that the vocabulary used in a student's search queries can be used to predict overall vocabulary level. There is also an established relationship between how well a reader can predict what is coming up in a text, including which words will appear in a text, and reading time (Smith & Levy, 2013). Readers speed up when parts of a text are predictable and slow down when they are less so, which also leads to the observation that more readable texts are also read more quickly (Nishikawa, Makino, & Matsuo, 2013). Thus it is quite probable that an intelligent tutoring system that tracked the relationship between reading time and the readability and predictability of a text could be used to generate additional evidence about students' reading and vocabulary levels. In addition, as technology becomes available to track eye movements during reading, the pattern of fixations—for instance, the amount of time spent fixating on unknown versus familiar words—may also provide indirect evidence that could be used to provide nonintrusive evidence of reading comprehension and vocabulary knowledge (Rayner, 1998; Williams & Morris, 2004).

At this point, the use of nonintrusive evidence to assess vocabulary knowledge is very much in its infancy. However, there are significant benefits to be gained from nonintrusive assessment—most notably, the ability to track how students are doing from their performance on regular classwork, reducing the total time spent on formal assessment tasks.

FINAL THOUGHTS

Teaching vocabulary is hard work. It can be very difficult for a teacher to keep track of students' progress in their vocabulary learning and to intervene—either directly, by teaching targeted words, or indirectly, by guiding students to engage in reading at their level and help them develop effective word-learning strategies. The developments in the technology we review in this chapter promise to make that job easier by providing automated supports for teachers and students. However, it is important to note that this kind of technology is an enabler, not a substitute for effective teaching. In the classroom of the future, teachers may have access to much richer information about how their students are doing and they may have a much richer palette of activities they can build into their instruction to support student learning. Nevertheless, the usefulness of the tools and their effectiveness will depend on the extent to which they support and encourage learning and are wedded to effective classroom practice. Teachers need to be informed consumers of these kinds of products. Ultimately, technology is a tool, and its effectiveness depends on the use we make of it.

APPENDIX 7.1. SOME IMPORTANT CORPORA

Written, Edited Text

Many different corpora are available containing digital versions of edited, written documents. These include the following.

- The *British National Corpus* (BNC), specifically for British English (Leech, 1992), was created to yield more reliable statistics than the Brown or LOB corpora. It contains almost 100 million words, primarily written text, but also a smaller sample of transcribed speech.
- The *Touchstone Applied Science Associates* (TASA) *corpus,* a collection designed to match the kinds of texts students would be exposed to in school, contains samples from 37,520 texts totaling 10,828,757 words. The texts are drawn from nine genres, including language arts, science, and social studies/history.
- The *Corpus of Contemporary American English* (COCA) database contains more than 400 million words (Davies, 2010). Like the BNC and TASA, it is designed to provide a balance between different types of text, including spoken language, fiction, popular magazines, newspapers, and academic journals.
- The *English Gigaword Corpus (5th Edition),* a comprehensive archive of newswire text maintained by the Linguistic Data Consortium at the University of Pennsylvania (Graff & Cieri, 2003; Parker, Graff, Kong, Chen, & Maeda, 2011), contains about 4 billion words of running text.
- *Abstracts from Medline (www.nlm.nih.gov/pubs/factsheets/medline. html)* is a citation database for several thousand medical journals and totals about 2 billion word tokens.
- The *Juris corpus* is a public-domain corpus maintained by the Linguistic Data Consortium at the University of Pennsylvania, containing 694,000 U.S. legal documents and totaling 99 million words (Canavan & Morgovsky, 1998).
- The *International Corpus of Learner English* (ICLE; Granger, 2003; Granger, Dagneaux, Meunier, & Paquot, 2002) contains 2.5 million words of text from 3,640 college essays written by L1 speakers of Czech, Dutch, Finnish, French, German, Japanese, Polish, Russian, Spanish, and Swedish.

Spoken English

A variety of corpora have been collected to document spoken English in various situations, such as academic speech and telephone conversation for both first- and second-language learners. Many of these corpora were originally collected in order to support the development of speech recognition software such as currently found in cellphone digital assistant software, such as Siri and Cortana (Godfrey & Holliman, 1993; Lemon, 2012). These include:

- The *Switchboard Telephone Speech Corpus* (Godfrey & Holliman, 1993) contains 2,400 conversations among 543 speakers from all parts of the United States, totaling about 3 million words.
- The *Fisher English Training Corpus* (Cieri, Miller, & Walker, 2004) contains 16,454 telephone calls totaling 17 million word tokens. The collection is drawn from a representative U.S. population sample, associated with a rich array of demographic variables including age, gender, and American dialect region.

Other speech corpora were specifically collected to support the development of resources for second-language learners of English (Cieri et al., 2004; Simpson, 2002; Thompson & Nesi, 2001). These include:

- The *Michigan Corpus of Academic Spoken English* (MICASE) comprises 1.8 million word tokens and 200 hours of academic speech (lectures, seminars, office hours, etc.) recorded at the University of Michigan. The collection is associated with variables for academic position/role, native speaker status, first language, speech event type, academic division/discipline, and degree of interactivity (Simpson, 2002).
- The *Corpus of British Academic Spoken English* (BASE) contains 160 lectures and 39 seminars from two U.K. universities, totaling about 1.6 million word tokens (Thompson & Nesi, 2001).

CHAPTER 8

Resources for Developing
a Nation of Word Learners

This chapter provides annotated lists of resources that might be useful for teachers, researchers, and publishers in implementing the ideas presented in this book. These resources include online tools and published books that are particularly valuable and readily available. In the lists, we present both educational resources for teachers with lesson plans and ideas for instructional practice, as well as easily accessible resources for those who wish to dive more deeply into particular topics. There is a huge variety of potential resources online. Google searches of terms like "vocabulary resources" yield thousands of hits! The problem with many of those sources is that they are descriptions of programs for sale, sites with very little content and an abundance of ads, or sites that are mostly lists of links to other sites—many of which lead nowhere or to places where, let's say, you really don't want to go. There are also many gems out there, but given the noise-to-signal ratio, we are certain that this is far from a comprehensive account of what is useful. However, we think the following curated lists of some resources and tools will be very useful, informative, and fun.

ONLINE RESOURCES FOR IMPLEMENTING EFFECTIVE VOCABULARY INSTRUCTION

Ready-to-Use Lesson Plans

The VINE (Vocabulary Innovations in Education) Consortium
http://vineconsortium.org/vase/lessons

This site has lesson plans for word-conscious activities, including collecting words, word sorts, word predictions, vocabulary walks, and morphology based on words found in fourth- and fifth-grade science, math, social studies, and English materials. Topics include physical, life and earth sciences, geometry, algebra, measurement, English language development, history, careers, compound words, and morphology.

Exceptional Expressions for Everyday Events (E4)
and Super Synonym Sets for Stories (S4)
http://textproject.org/classroom-materials/vocabulary
E4 is a set of 32 lessons to support students' curiosity and awareness of the richness of language. The heart of each lesson is a word web with multiple meanings for each word, words with similar meanings, idioms, common phrases, and English–Spanish cognates related to each word. S4 is an extension of E4 with 20 additional narrative concepts.

Word Generation
www.wordgen.serpmedia.org
This site provides set of four programs for grades 4–5 and 6–8 (science, social studies, English language arts, and math) that provide semantically rich contexts for learning a predetermined set of words. Classroom activities also support word-learning strategies, word awareness, and multiple exposures to words.

Reading Educator: Vocabulary Strategies
www.readingeducator.com/strategies/vocabulary.htm
This site contains 14 activities and lesson plans for encouraging active word exploration.

Western Washington University Linguistics in Education
https://teachling.wwu.edu
This site provides lesson plans for teaching linguistics as a part of K–12 education. It also provides some useful links, including links to Greek and Latinate word roots for middle school, associated lesson plans, and language-related blogs.

General Resources for Instruction

Vocabulary.com
www.vocabulary.com/about
This multipurpose site can be used as a learning tool for students, but it also has abundant teacher resources. This consists of lists of words from literature, speeches, current events, and words that characterize many standardized tests including the SAT, GRE, PARCC, Smarter Balanced, and so

on. Part of the site is a subscription service that teachers can use to create and track learning programs for their students. The site has its roots in the *Visual Thesaurus,* an interactive thesaurus and dictionary developed by *Thinkmap,* a software company that uses visualization to facilitate communication, learning, and discovery. Vocabulary.com was created to "empower learners to unpack the complexity and nuances of the English language in a way that was systematic, engaging, and adaptive."

Learn That Word
www.learnthat.org

This site was created by the LearnThat Foundation, an organization of parents, educators, and English learners who were looking for an effective solution for vocabulary learning. The site provides free online individualized tutoring and images, audio, and video resources to help children learn vocabulary words. The tutor also provides customized quizzes and spaced review. Teachers can create personal accounts for individual students. Both free and premium options are available.

TextProject
http://textproject.org

This nonprofit site offers a plethora of resources, including free downloadable books with multiple exposures to conceptually rich words, word pictures, lists of Spanish–English cognates, research reports, teacher development modules, and much more.

Vocabulary Spelling City
www.spellingcity.com

Originally launched as SpellingCity in 2008, in 2011 it became VocabularySpellingCity to reflect the addition of significant vocabulary capabilities. Their mission is "efficient game-based study of literacy skills using any word list." Word lists include those from published reading programs that can be paired with interactive learning games and free printable worksheets. In addition to word lists, the Teaching Resources pages provide free lesson plan ideas and supplemental materials for teachers in all subject areas and grade levels. These resources include background information on grade-level topics to assist in creating lesson plans focusing on areas such as grammar or figurative language. A premium option is also available.

WordWorks
www.wordworkskingston.com

This site offers an abundance of resources for Structured Word Inquiry (SWI), the approach that teaches about word structure and meaning through spelling (Bowers & Kirby, 2010). Users can also access the teacher resource book *Teaching How the Written Word Works* (Bowers, 2009), which includes a series of structured word inquiry lessons that provide instruction about the interrelation of morphological word families with the matrix and word sums. This book helps teachers make sense of how the English spelling system works while teaching their students. The WordWorks website has countless free resources and illustrations of scientific inquiry of the written word from preschool to high school. Some practical links from WordWorks include:

- **WordWorks YouTube page:** Videos of SWI in action.
- **Beyond the Word:** Lyn Anderson's blog, with a particular focus on SWI for the early years.
- **Real Spellers:** Teacher discussions and SWI resources, including archives of WordWorks newsletters and more.

Word Games and Puzzles

Frame Games
www.terrystickels.com/frame-games

This site offers a set of visual images that create common words or phrases (e.g., LUN CH = lunch break; LANGU4AGES = foreign languages). Students enjoy guessing both the words and word phrases, as well as using them as models to create their own.

Literal Pictures of Idioms
www.boredpanda.com/funny-idioms-proverbs-illustrations-keren-rosen
www.henry4school.fr/Language/pdf/Illustrated%20Idioms2.pdf
http://idiomsbykids.com/index.php

These sites provide literal pictures of idioms (e.g., cats and dogs raining down from the sky), which can be used to draw attention to how idioms do not represent actual meanings of words, through guessing games and as examples of ways that students could also illustrate idioms and multiword phrases literally.

Hinky Pinkies
www.readwritethink.org/resources/resource-print.html?id=30651
www.thinkablepuzzles.com/hinkpinks

These sites provide word puzzles based on rhyming words (e.g., obese feline = fat cat).

Word Tagul Clouds
https://tagul.com

This site provides a tool for creating word clouds from text you input, similar to Wordles (*www.wordles.com*) but with a series of predefined word cloud shapes. Word clouds are great way to help students become aware of words they overuse in their writing, because the words they use multiple times increase in size. The activities on the site are fun for playing with words to create particular images or impressions. Users can customize shapes, fonts, layouts, colors, and animation. This resource is free for personal or noncommercial use.

Word Sift
https://wordsift.org

This is another site where users can input text to create word clouds. Bonus features include different styles of clouds and identification of words in the text on the Academic and General Service word lists and by frequency. The site also includes example sentences, a visual thesaurus, and pictures for the most frequent words used in the text.

Vocabulary.co.il
www.vocabulary.co.il

This site provides an extensive selection of free games that are already populated with words, including activities to create compound words, identify the meanings of idioms, match words for oxymorons, find the meaning of roots, select appropriate parts of speech, reveal antonyms and synonyms, and engage in wordplay. The activities are offered at different grade levels, with instructional videos for some of the concepts (e.g., how to divide words into syllables).

Language Blogs

Lingholic
www.lingholic.com

This blog was founded in 2012 to provide information, experiences, and opinions on language learning from a wide range of perspectives. Although most information is directed toward acquiring a new language, there are also posts on general topics such as:

- How many words do I need to know? The 95/5 rule in language learning.
- "It's Raining Husbands" and other idioms translated into different languages.
- Language learning, scaffolding, and the zone of proximal development.

Linguist-Educator Exchange (LEX)
https://linguisteducatorexchange.com

Linguist Gina Cooke created this blog to provide linguistically accurate resources for teachers and online courses. It offers linguistic information and reliable, logical strategies for teachers and English learners who want to know more about English and its instruction. Blog posts, archived since 2010, address a variety of topics, including etymology, morphology, history of reading instruction, and language education.

The English Blog
www.englishblog.com/vocabulary/#.V63Ib1f92JU

Jeffrey Hill, a teacher of English at the EM Normandie Business School in Le Havre, France, developed this blog for English learners, but most of the language is very advanced. A key feature is crossword puzzles on current topical themes like Brexit, Tour de France, and soccer, as well as more general themes.

About Education
www.about.com/education

This site makes users wade through an enormous number of ads, but contains two pieces of highly useful content. One is a usage glossary of 600 commonly confused words, including usage explanation and quizzes. The other, on the site's ESL link (*http://esl.about.com*) provides sets of text passages for learning idioms and expressions in context.

Reference Resources

There are plenty of conventional dictionaries available online, which we will not detail here. Rather, we limit the recommendations we include to some specialized word resources.

Reverso Dictionary
http://dictionary.reverso.net/english-cobuild

Reverso offers a free English dictionary that explains the use of words and phrases in natural, informal language and provides real-life examples. It is based on the Collins *COBUILD English Dictionary for Advanced Learners, Fourth Edition* (Collins, 2003), a dictionary expressly for English learners, but its explanatory style of defining words is helpful for native English speakers as well.

The Online Etymology Dictionary
www.etymonline.com

This site provides descriptions of the origins of English words. As described on the front page of the website, "This is a map of the wheel-ruts of modern English. Etymologies are not definitions; they're explanations of what our words meant and how they sounded 600 or 2,000 years ago." The page also offers a link to a full set of resources that were used to create the site (*www.etymonline.com/sources.php*), including books on a range of topics, such as slang, names of Hollywood stars, and place names.

OneLook Dictionary Search
www.onelook.com

This site provides links to word definitions in up to 129 different dictionaries. There is also a reverse option (*www.onelook.com/reverse-dictionary.shtml*) where users can enter a definition to search for a word. This link also searches for related words.

The General Service List
http://jbauman.com/aboutgsl.html

Adapted from West's (1953) list, this is a list of approximately 2,000 words selected to be of greatest "general service" to English learners.

The Academic Word List
www.victoria.ac.nz/lals/resources/academicwordlist

This site provides a list of 570 word families that occur frequently across disciplines in college and university settings.

Word Families
www.LexicalResearch.com

The word families on this site are separated into inflectional variants and derivational variants, created using the open-source program KSTEM (Krovetz 1993). The coverage of roots and variants is larger than the Academic Word List, and these datasets are freely available under the Creative Commons license.

Lexipedia
www.lexipedia.com

This site is a type of visual thesaurus that gives definitions for various parts of speech. When a user enters a word, the site identifies morphologically related words, synonyms, antonyms, and "fuzzynyms" (strongly related words that are not synonyms). A nice feature is the ease of use and the ability to obtain the information for all parts of speech separately.

Wordnik
www.wordnik.com

This site provides extensive definitions to a much larger set of words than in typical dictionaries. It also provides a wide range of other information about words, such as use in context, pictures, synonyms, antonyms, hypernyms, words found in similar contexts, rhyming words, and a reverse dictionary of words that contain the target word in their definition. Wordnik's material is sourced from the Internet by automatic programs.

A Word a Day (AWAD) Sites
www.merriam-webster.com/word-of-the-day
www.dictionary.com/wordoftheday
http://wordsmith.org/words/today.html

These sites provide daily vocabulary words. Wordsmith, for instance, presents five thematically related words each week with pronunciation, etymology, and a sample context.

AudioEnglish
www.audioenglish.org

This site was created for adult English learners and has a searchable dictionary that provides various senses of words and how they are classified, as well as hypernyms, hyponyms, synonyms, context examples, and pronunciation. In addition, it shows the use of the words in phrases for various contexts, such as travel, talking on a telephone, and practical everyday phrases.

My Vocabulary Size
http://my.vocabularysize.com

This site provides a free service that was created by students from Victoria University of Wellington in New Zealand as a tribute to the research of Paul Nation, who created the Vocabulary Size Test (VST). Teachers can use the available tests (multiple choice) to measure students' vocabulary range and size. Teachers can also create customized tests.

SELECTED BOOKS FOR DEVELOPING WORD AWARENESS

For Use in Any Classroom

Aliki. (1998). *Marianthe's story: painted words, spoken memories.* New York: Greenwillow Books.

Marianthe's journey to a new life and a new language in the United States is told through her paintings and her storytelling in a classroom with a remarkably sensitive teacher. The lyrical language of this book is a wonderful way to introduce personal narratives.

Banks, K., & Kulikov, B. (2006). *Max's words.* New York: Farrar, Straus & Giroux.

This picture book is great for introducing the concept of collecting words.

Base, G. (1986). *Animalia.* New South Wales: Harcourt Brace Jovanovich.

This book's delightful illustrations depict numerous words for each letter of the alphabet. It makes great use of alliteration for the captions (e.g., *lazy lions lounging in the local library*).

van Allsburg, C. (1987). *The Z was zapped: A play in 26 acts.* New York: Houghton Mifflin.

This "guess the picture" book uses alliteration to introduce each letter of the alphabet.

Yolen, J. (1987). *Owl moon.* New York: Philomel Books

This book tells the story of a father and child who go owling one winter's night. The poetic language creates a sense of magic and mystery.

Particularly Useful in K–3 Classrooms

Brown, R. (1996). *The tale of the monstrous toad.* London: Andersen Press.

The clever use of adjectives and strong verbs in this book describes a monstrous toad that is too poisonous to be eaten by a monster.

Browne, A. (2001). *My dad.* New York: Doubleday

Similes and idioms in this story describe how a child feels about his dad.

Cameron, A. (1988). *The most beautiful place in the world.* New York: Random House Children's Books.

Juan, the little boy in the story, lives with his grandmother because his mother cannot care for him. This story of courage and resilience in Guatemala is an unforgettable introduction to the realities of life for children in developing countries.

Curtis, J. L., & Cornell, L. (2008). *Big words for little people.* New York: Joanna Cotler Books.

This book presents expressive vocabulary words (e.g., *superb, stupendous*) through clever rhymes.

Edwards, P. D., & Cole, H. (1996). *Some smug slug.* New York: HarperCollins.

The authors introduce sophisticated vocabulary using alliteration with "s" words (e.g., *Slowly the slug started up the steep surface, stringing behind it scribble sparkling like silk*).

Fleming, D. (1995). *In the tall tall grass.* New York: Scholastic.

The book uses rhyme to introduce expressive vocabulary words (e.g., *crunch, munch, caterpillars lunch*).

Lawson, J. (1992). *A morning to polish and keep*. Markham, ON: Red Deer Press.

A family goes fishing in the early morning. The title is indicative of the lovely, lyrical nature of the language in this story.

London, J. (1995). *Like butter on pancakes*. London: Viking Kestrel Picture Books.

Metaphor and simile abound in this delightful account of a boy's day on a farm. Jonathan London also wrote *The Condor's Egg*.

O'Connor, J., & Preiss-Glasser, R. (2006). *Fancy Nancy series*. New York: HarperCollins.

This is an "I Can Read" series in which Nancy uses "fancy" words for descriptions.

Parish, P. (1963). *Amelia Bedelia series*. New York: Harper & Row.

These humorous beginning chapter books feature Amelia Bedelia, a housekeeper who misunderstands just about everything.

Particularly Useful in Fourth- to Eighth-Grade Classrooms

Picture Books

Frasier, D. (2000). *Miss Alaineus: A vocabulary disaster*. New York: Harcourt Children's Books.

This humorous picture book highlights the misunderstandings of the meanings of words.

Gwynne, F. (1970). *The king who rained*. New York: Windmill Books/ Simon & Schuster.

Literal pictures accompany humorous homonyms and homophones.

Gwynne, F. (1976). *A chocolate moose for dinner*. New York: Simon & Schuster.

Gwynne continues the theme with more literal pictures of humorous homonyms and homophones.

Heller, R. (1988). *Kites sail high: A book about verbs*. New York: Grosset & Dunlap.

Heller, R. (1989). *Many luscious lollipops: A book about adjectives*. New York: Grosset & Dunlap.

Heller, R. (1990). *Merry-go-round: A book about nouns*. New York: Grosset & Dunlap.

Heller, R. (1991). *Up, up, and away: A book about adverbs*. New York: Grosset & Dunlap.

Heller, R. (1997). *Mine, all mine: A book about pronouns*. New York: Grosset & Dunlap.

In this series of books, Heller uses rhyme and colorful illustrations to introduce different parts of speech.

McGugan, J. (1994). *Josepha: A prairie boy's story*. Markham, ON: Red Deer Press.

In 1900, an immigrant boy unable to speak English sits in the classroom with the younger children—"a blushing bull in primary row." The book employs metaphor and simile as well as strong verbs and nouns.

Schotter, R., & Potter, G. (2006). *The boy who loved words*. New York: Schwartz & Wade.

This is a great picture book for developing the concept of collecting interesting words.

Scieszka, J., & Smith, L. (2001). *Baloney (Henry P.)*. New York: Viking.

This is an entertaining tall tale by a boy from outer space who uses weird words.

*Poetry**

Alarcon, F. (1997). *Laughing tomatoes and other spring poems*. San Francisco: Children's Book Press.

This book contains a collection of bilingual Spanish/English poems. Also see: *Iguanas in the Snow and Other Winter Poems; Angels Ride Bikes and Other Fall Poems; From the Bellybutton of the Moon and Other Summer Poems*.

Creech, S. (2001). *Love that dog*. New York: HarperCollins.

Creech presents a series of free-verse diary entries to a teacher from a boy who does not write poems.

Janeczko, P. (2009). *A kick in the head: An everyday guide to poetic forms*. Somerville, MA: Candlewick Press.

These 29 poems are great for teaching about different poetic forms.

---

*These can be used in any grade level.

O'Neill, M. (1961). *Hailstones and halibut bones: Adventures in color.* New York: Doubleday.

These poems about colors illustrate semantic patterns of polysemy.

Ruurs, M. (2001). *The power of poems: Teaching the joy of writing poetry.* Chicago: Maupin House.

This short book is packed with teaching ideas for choosing just the right word for poems.

Short Novels about Words

Clements, A. (1998). *Frindle.* New York: Aladdin Paperbacks.

Clements spins an entertaining story about a fifth grader who coins a new word.

DeGross, M., & Hanna, C. (1998). *Donavan's word jar.* New York: Harper Trophy.

This is an easy-to-read chapter book about collecting words.

RECOMMENDED NOVELS
WITH SUPERB GIFTS OF WORDS

Agosín, M. (2015). *I lived on Butterfly Hill.* New York: Atheneum Books for Young Readers.

This moving story, loosely based on a true story, captures the life of an 11-year-old refugee when Chile is overrun by a dictator.

Avi. (2002). *Crispin: The cross of lead.* New York: Hyperion Books for Children.

Avi is a prolific and powerful writer. Set in 14th-century England, this tale is full of intrigue and adventure. Also see the sequels: *At the Edge of the World; The End of Time;* and his other award-winning books: *Poppy;* and *The True Confessions of Charlotte Doyle.*

Babbitt, N. (1975). *Tuck everlasting.* New York: Farrar, Strauss & Giroux.

When Winnie meets Tuck she is confronted by an extraordinary decision.

Burnford, S. (1960). *The incredible journey.* Toronto: Elan Press.

This classic story follows three house pets trying to find their way home across the wilderness.

Dahl, R. (1961). *James and the giant peach.* New York: Knopf.

In this daring and hilarious fantasy, Dahl uses language in scrumptious and unusual ways. See also *Danny, The Champion of the World* and *Charlie and the Chocolate Factory.*

Ellis, D. (2000). *The breadwinner.* Toronto: Groundwood Books.

Eleven-year-old Parvana lives in Kabul during Taliban rule. When her father is imprisoned, she disguises herself as a boy in order to work in the market-place. Also see *Parvana's Journey.*

Fleischman, P. (1980). *The half-a-moon inn.* New York: HarperCollins.

Fleischman's powerful language tells a fantastical tale of wicked highway-men, evil innkeepers, and a brave boy.

Garfield, L. (1967). *Smith.* New York: Viking Penguin/Puffin Books.

Smith is a lively, complicated mystery whose main character is a 12-year-old pickpocket.

Hiaasen, C. (2002). *Hoot.* New York: Knopf.

Hiassen's offbeat and hilarious tale uses language to great effect to describe characters.

Holm, A. (1965). *I am David.* London: Methuen & Company.

Having escaped from concentration camp, David travels across Europe, silently and watchfully, avoiding involvement with anyone who shows inter-est in him. He gradually begins to gain hope and lose mistrust, regaining his own identity in the process.

Juster, N. (1971). *The phantom tollbooth.* New York: Scholastic.

This classic wears well and is full of puns and plays on words.

Lowry, L. (1990). *Number the stars.* New York: Bantam Doubleday Dell.

During World War II, a 10-year-old Danish girl learns bravery as she hides a friend from the Nazis.

MacLachlan, P. (1985). *Sarah, plain and tall.* New York: Harper & Row.

Now a classic, the language of this book reflects the tenderness and poi-gnancy of the story. Sarah comes to look after Caleb and Anna, and the family relationship gradually becomes permanent.

Magorian, M. (1981). *Goodnight Mr. Tom*. New York: Harper & Row.

In this heartwarming story about a boy evacuated to the countryside in World War II, Willie Beech begins to blossom as he builds a friendship with Tom Oakley, but his healing cannot begin until the dark secret of his abuse at the hands of his mother is revealed.

Naidoo, B. (1986). *Journey to Jo'Burg: A South African story*. New York: Harper.

Mma lives and works in Johannesburg, far away from her children. When the baby becomes sick, Naledi and Tiro set off on a journey to the city to find Mma and bring her back.

Park, L. (2001). *A single shard*. New York: Clarion Books.

Tree-ear, an impoverished orphan in 12th-century Korea, dreams of becoming a potter.

Paterson, K. (1977). *Bridge to Terabithia*. New York: Harper & Row.

Katherine Patterson, one of the greatest writers for children, writes in rich and melodious language. See also *The Great Gilly Hopkins; Lyddie; The Master Puppeteer*.

Paulsen, G. (1988). *Hatchett*. New York: Penguin Random House.

A story of a boy's survival and courage.

Reynolds Gardiner, J. (1983). *Stone fox*. New York: Harper & Row.

In the story of Little Willie and the sled dog race, Searchlight proves to be a dog in a million and Stone Fox, another sledder, makes a generous gesture.

Rowling, J. K. (1998). *Harry Potter* series. New York: Scholastic.

Rowling makes eloquent use of language and puns in this fantasy series.

Ryan, P. M. (2000). *Esperanza rising*. New York: Scholastic.

In the 1930s, Esperanza's wealthy family experiences tragedy in Mexico and immigrates to California to become migrant farmworkers. Ryan is a skillful author who also wrote *Becoming Naomi León* and *The Dreamer*.

Spinelli, J. (1990). *Maniac Magee*. New York: HarperCollins

This action-packed novel explores themes of racism and homelessness with rich, descriptive language. See also: *Stargirl*.

Staples, S. (1989). *Shabanu, daughter of the wind.* New York: Random House.

Eleven-year-old Shabanu is facing an arranged marriage, but her parents fear she is too strong-willed to make a good wife. The sequel is *Haveli.*

Taylor, M. (1976). *Roll of thunder, hear my cry.* New York: Puffin.

This Newbery Award–winning book is a deep and powerful portrayal of racism in the 1930s. Other books about the same family include *Let the Circle Be Unbroken; The Road to Memphis;* and *The Land.*

White, E. B. (1952). *Charlotte's web.* New York: Harper Collins.

An old-fashioned story of life, death, and friendship expressed in lyrical language.

Woodson, J. (2014). *Brown girl dreaming.* New York: Puffin Books.

A memoir in verse about a girl's first attempts at becoming a writer.

RESOURCES AUTHORED BY OUR CONFERENCE PARTICIPANTS

We thought it fitting to include this final set of resource suggestions because, after all, our participants' contributions are what initiated this book. So we polled our participants and asked them to suggest which of their works could serve as resource tools for teachers and researchers. Our participants responded with the following resources.

Camille Blachowicz

Blachowicz, C. L. Z., Baumann, J. F., Manyak, P., & Graves, M. (2013). *Flood, fast, focus: Integrating vocabulary in the classroom. IRA e-essentials-reading, what's new?* Newark, DE: International Reading Association.

Blachowicz, C., & Fisher, P. (2014). *Teaching vocabulary in all classrooms* (5th ed.). Boston: Pearson.

Blachowicz, C., Fisher, P., Ogle, D., & Watts-Taffe, S. (2013). *Teaching academic vocabulary K–8: Effective practices across the curriculum.* New York: Guilford Press.

Cobb, C., & Blachowicz, C. (2014). *No more "look up the list" vocabulary instruction.* Portsmouth, NH: Heinemann.

Ogle, D., Blachowicz, C., Fisher, P., & Lang, L. (2016). *Academic vocabulary in middle and high school: Effective practices across the disciplines.* New York: Guilford Press.

Michael D. Coyne

Coyne, M. D., Capozzoli, A., Ware, S., & Loftus, S. (2010). Beyond RTI for decoding: Supporting early vocabulary development within a multitier approach to instruction and intervention. *Perspectives on Language and Literacy, 36*(2), 18.

Coyne, M. D., Capozzoli-Oldham, A., Cuticelli, M., & Ware, S. M. (2015). Using assessment data to make a difference in vocabulary outcomes. *Perspectives on Language and Literacy, 41*(3), 52.

Amy C. Crosson

Crosson, A. C. (2016). Supporting linguistically diverse students to develop deep, flexible knowledge of academic words. In C. P. Proctor, A. Boardman, & E. Hiebert (Eds.), *English learners and emergent bilingualism in the Common Core era* (pp. 62–98). New York: Guilford Press.

Bonnie J. Dorr

Dorr, B. J. (1997). Large-scale dictionary construction for foreign language tutoring and interlingual machine translation. *Machine Translation, 12*(4), 271–322.

Habash, N., & Dorr, B. J. (2003). A categorical variation database for English. *Proceedings of North American Association for Computational Linguistics* (pp. 96–102). Stroudsburg, PA: Association for Computational Linguistics. Available at *https://clipdemos.umiacs.umd.edu/catvar.*

A Categorial-Variation Database (or Catvar) is a database of clusters of uninflected words (lexemes) and their categorial (i.e. part-of-speech) variants. For example, the words *hunger* (verb), *hunger* (noun), *hungry* (adjective), and *hungriness* (noun) are different English variants of some underlying concept describing the state of being hungry.

Madnani, N., & Dorr, B. J. (2013). Generating targeted paraphrases for improved translation. *ACM Transactions on Intelligent Systems and Technology, 4*(3). Available at *http://dl.acm.org/citation.cfm?doid=2483669.2483673.*

Gwen Frishkoff and Kevyn Collins-Thompson

Frishkoff, G., Collins-Thompson, K., Nam, S. J., Hodges, L., & Crossley, S. (2017). Dynamic Support of Contextual Vocabulary Acquisition for Reading (DSCoVAR): An intelligent tutor for contextual word learning. In S. A. Crossley & D. S. McNamara (Eds.), *Adaptive educational technologies for literacy instruction* (pp. 69–81). New York: Routledge.

Michael J. Kieffer

Kelley, J. G., Lesaux, N. K., Kieffer, M. J., & Faller, S. E. (2010). Effective academic vocabulary instruction in the urban middle school. *The Reading Teacher, 64*(1), 5–14.

Kieffer, M. J., & Lesaux, N. K. (2010). Morphing into adolescents: Active word learning for English language learners and their classmates in middle school. *Journal of Adolescent and Adult Literacy, 54,* 47–56.

Joshua F. Lawrence

The most current site with all versions of Word Generation curricula is *www.wordgen.serpmedia.org.*

The Word Generation assessments and many other vocabulary assessments can be found at *www.iris-database.org.*

The direct link to the Word Generation assessments is *www.iris-database.org/iris/app/home/detail?id=york:807715.*

Lawrence, J. F., Maher, B., & Snow, C. E. (2013). Research in vocabulary: Word power for content-area learning. In J. Ippolito, J. F. Lawrence, & C. Zaller (Eds.), *Adolescent literacy in the era of the Common Core: From research into practice* (pp. 61–72). Cambridge, MA: Harvard Education Press.

Lawrence, J. F., White, C., & Snow, C. E. (2010). The words students need. *Educational Leadership, 68*(2), 23–26.

William Nagy

Nagy, W. (2009). Understanding words and word learning: Putting research on vocabulary into classroom practice. In S. Rosenfield & V. Berninger (Eds.), *Implementing evidence-based academic interventions in school settings* (pp. 479–500). New York: Oxford University Press.

Nagy, W., & Hiebert, E. (2011). Toward a theory of word selection. In M. L. Kamil, P. D. Pearson, E. B. Moje, & P. P. Afflerbach (Eds.), *Handbook of reading research: Volume IV* (pp. 388–404). New York: Routledge.

Nagy, W., & Scott, J. (2000). Vocabulary processes. In M. Kamil, P. Mosenthal, P. D. Pearson, & R. Barr (Eds.), *Handbook of reading research: Volume III* (pp. 269–284). Mahwah, NJ: Erlbaum.

Nagy, W., & Townsend, D. (2012). Words as tools: Learning academic vocabulary as language acquisition. *Reading Research Quarterly, 47*(1), 91–108.

Stahl, S. A., & Nagy, W. (2006). *Teaching word meanings.* Mahwah, NJ: Erlbaum.

P. David Pearson and Elfrieda H. Hiebert

Cervetti, G. N., Hiebert, E. H., Pearson, P. D., & McClung, N. (2015). Factors that influence the difficulty of science words. *Journal of Literacy Research, 47*(2), 153–185.

Pearson, P. D., Hiebert, E. H., & Kamil, M. L. (2007). Vocabulary assessment: What we know and what we need to learn. *Reading Research Quarterly, 42*(2), 282–296.

Pearson, P. D., Hiebert, E. H., & Kamil, M. L. (2012). Vocabulary assessment: Making do with what we have while we create the tools we need. In E. J. Kame'enui & J. F. Baumann (Eds.), *Vocabulary instruction: Research to practice* (2nd ed., pp. 231–255). New York: Guilford Press.

Glossary

accessible words—higher-frequency words that may not be known by students who have limited vocabulary knowledge, but are important for comprehension (Graves et al., 2014).

accountability—when standardized high-stakes assessments are used politically to report how well students are performing against their peers in a particular grade and content area.

acronym—a word that is created from the first letter of each word in a series of words.

adaptive spacing—controlling the sequencing of words and the spacing of instruction in a tutoring system to provide the easiest, most supportive contexts during earlier stages of learning.

affixes—prefixes or suffixes that are added to the beginning or end of a bound root or an existing word to form a new word.

age of acquisition—the estimated age when a learner acquires specific words.

algorithm—step-by-step computer commands that are used to make calculations or perform a set of tasks.

annotation—a set of standardized notes or comments that are added to existing text to document specific linguistic features of that text.

antonyms—words that mean the opposite of each other.

artificial intelligence—the development of computer systems that are able to perform tasks normally carried out by humans.

assessment—a test to determine proficiency in a given task.

association (associates)—a type of relationship between words that are similar in theme, context, or topic.

automated readability index—a computer-calculated statistic that indicates the grade level at which a student is supposed to be able to understand a particular text.

bound morphemes—morphemes that cannot appear as independent words but must be part of a larger word, which contains affixes and bound roots.

bound roots—parts of words that have meanings similar to the meanings of nouns, verbs, adjectives, or adverbs, but which cannot stand alone as a word. Bound roots can be combined with prefixes and suffixes to create a derived word whose meaning is related to that of the bound root (e.g., *ept* as in inept or adept, *ject* as in project or subject, *chron* as in chronic or synchronize).

breadth—the overall size of one's vocabulary; the number of words that a learner knows something about.

capacity theory—the proposal that a lack of linguistic fluency is a critical bottleneck in the development of writing expertise.

cloze item—a fill-in-the-blank test question in which words are blanked out from a larger passage, and the reader must use the surrounding context to infer what word should appear in the blank.

code switching—the ability to switch from one language or register to another depending on the social situation or context.

collocation—a sequence of words that characteristically appear together, reflecting normal usage.

combining forms—root words that are combined with other root words or with freestanding roots (i.e., complete words) to form new words that can be further modified through the use of affixes.

compound nouns—a word that is made up of two or more nouns and carries its own definition.

compound words—words that are formed by combining two or more root words.

computational linguistics (natural language processing)—the branch of linguistics that uses computer science techniques to analyze text and speech.

computer adaptive testing—an approach to testing in which the test questions are administered to students based on their demonstrated ability level on previously administered test questions.

concreteness—a measure of how easily the referent of a word is perceived by the senses. Concrete words denote things that can be touched, seen, heard, or tasted.

congruent word meaning—closely related definitions of a word.

connotation—shades of meaning and implications carried by a word that cannot be captured in a simple definition.

construct—See *vocabulary construct.*

context—where a word appears. We differentiate between two kinds of context: the social context in which a word is used (who is using the word, to whom, in what kinds of social situations), and the passage context (where the word appears in relation to other words).

co-occurrences of words—a measurement of how often words appear together in a corpus.

corpus (corpora)—a large computerized collection of "real-life" texts upon which linguistic analyses can be conducted to identify different types of patterns associated with words or grammatical features in a language.

crowdsourcing—a means of collecting large amounts of data through the Internet.

decoding—the ability to convert printed letters that comprise a word into the correct pronunciation of the word.

depth—simultaneous knowledge of many different aspects of word meaning and usage, including knowledge of multiple meanings for the same word.

derivational morphemes—prefixes or suffixes that are added to an existing word to create a new word while modifying the original word's basic meaning or part of speech.

derived forms—words that have been formed by adding prefixes or suffixes.

determiner—a class of words used to introduce noun phrases. Determiners comprise several traditional parts of speech, including articles (*the, a, any, all, what*), possessive adjectives (*his, her, your, my*), demonstrative adjectives (*this, that, these*), and interrogative adjectives (*which*).

discrete item—in assessment, a test question that that has a short, specific answer that can be scored as right or wrong, often in the form of multiple-choice or cloze questions.

discriminate—in the context of test questions, the ability to differentiate between the correct answer and the alternatives that are provided.

dispersion—the extent to which words appear in a variety of contexts, across a wide range of subject matter.

distractor (option choice)—in a multiple-choice item, an option choice would be one of the possible answers to the question. A distractor is an incorrect option, in contrast to the correct option, or key.

domain—content or subject area.

dynamic assessment—a highly interactive procedure in which an examiner takes a student through stages of a learning process in order to identify the skills that an individual student possesses as well as his or her learning potential.

essential words—words that are crucial for comprehending a specific text that students are reading.

etymologies of words—word origins.

foil words—words that are provided in an assessment as possibly associated with a given word, but are, in fact, unrelated. See also *distractor.*

functional relations—the way that words work together to create meaning.

generative patterns (generative mechanisms)—morphological, syntactic, and semantic patterns, often implicitly recognized, that facilitate the comprehension of words.

genre—a classification of the different types of written or spoken text. Some of the most important genre distinctions include informational text, narratives, and argument.

glos—short, simple definitions of unknown words in context. A gloss may be provided either in the margin for texts that appear in hardcopy or as pop-up boxes when text is delivered by computer.

grammatical constructions—See *syntactic patterns.*

graphic organizer—a visual representation of information that is used as an aid to organize one's thoughts. Graphic organizers are often used to organize material collected from one or more reading passages or to plan the content and organization of an extended piece of writing.

high-stakes tests—any kind of test that is used by some authority, such as a state, to make important educational decisions about students, teachers, schools, or districts. See also *accountability.*

homonyms (homonymous)—two distinct words with unrelated meanings that happen to have the same spelling and pronunciation.

homophones—distinct words that sound the same but are spelled differently and have different meanings (e.g., *read/reed* or *two/too/to*).

hypernyms—words that describe a broader concept or category that includes the meaning of a more specific word (e.g., an *eagle* is a kind of *bird,* where *bird* is the hypernym of *eagle*).

hyponyms—words that fall under the broader category named by some other word (e.g., a *throne* is a kind of *chair,* where *throne* is the hyponym of *chair*).

idiom or idiomatic expression—a sequence of words that conveys a different meaning than one would expect from the meaning of its component words.

imported words—words that may not appear in a text, but are related to the text, and which might help students understand and extend what they are learning (Graves et al., 2014).

incidental word learning—learning words that one has not been explicitly taught.

incremental word learning—word learning that happens gradually, as the learner's depth of knowledge about individual words increases.

inflectional morphemes (inflectional variants)—morphemes that serve as grammatical markers. Inflectional morphemes create different forms of the same word, such as plurals, tenses, possession, or comparisons. Inflectional variants are different forms of the same word that differ only by the presence or absence of specific inflectional morphemes.

intelligent tutoring systems—computer systems that use artificial intelligence techniques to help students learn a particular subject.

intransitive verbs—verbs that do not have a direct object.

item—test question.

key—the correct answer in a discrete item.

L1—native speaker of English.

L2—second-language learner (i.e., English is not the student's native language; it may be his or her second language).

latent semantic analysis (LSA)—a technique based on the linguist J. R. Firth's idea that "you shall know a word by the company it keeps." It creates a mathematical model that measures how often two words that show up in the same places and treats them as more similar in meaning the more often they appear in the same company.

lexical access—the process of retrieving word knowledge from memory.

lexical inferencing—the process of inferring what a word means, using all available clues, including morphological form, passage context, and social context.

lexical knowledge—knowledge of words.

lexical morphology—the ways in which words are built up from component parts (roots, prefixes, and suffixes), especially relationships among words based on their Latin roots.

lexical quality—the extent to which reader's knowledge of a word represents the word's form and meaning, including knowledge of word use and the ability to retrieve aspects of a word's meaning that are relevant to a given context.

lexicographer—someone who compiles dictionaries.

lexicon—the vocabulary of a person or language.

linguistic distance—the extent to which languages are similar based on each language's grammar, phonics, and orthography (i.e., whether the languages are both alphabetic or character based and whether they exhibit similar morphological and syntactic patterns).

Matthew effect—the learning phenomenon whereby the "rich get richer and the poor get poorer," such that those with an initial advantage in skill are likely to increase their advantage over less-advantaged peers.

meta-analysis—a statistical procedure for combining data from multiple studies.

metacognitive skills/knowledge/awareness—the self-awareness in which a person is aware of his or her own thought processes and uses this knowledge to choose more effective strategies or procedures.

metalinguistic skills/knowledge/awareness—explicit knowledge about language (as opposed to the implicit ability to use a language), such as the awareness of how words work in English and the ability to reflect on and manipulate that awareness.

metaphor—taking concepts from one domain and applying them by analogy to a second domain (e.g., using words for fighting to describe arguments).

metonymy—using the name of an object or concept to refer to a related object or concept (e.g., the use of *turquoise* as a color and as a stone).

morpheme—the smallest meaningful part of a word.

morphological awareness—recognition of how morphemes are used to change or create different meanings.

morphological inference—the process of using morphological knowledge to guess what a word means.

morphological patterns—parallels between words that are formed using the same roots, prefixes, and suffixes. See also *word families*.

morphological relatedness—when two words belong to the same word family or exemplify the same or similar morphological patterns (e.g., *magnet, magnets, magnetic, magnetize*).

morphology—the study of how word forms are built up from smaller component parts (morphemes).

multiword expression—a sequence of words that has an independent meaning from its component words. Types of multiword expressions include collocations, idioms, phrasal verbs, and multiword named entities.

named entity—proper nouns that are composed of a sequence of multiple words (e.g., *Bank of England* or *White House*).

natural language processing (NLP)—See *computational linguistics*.

norm—the average level of performance of a group of people, such as grade level.

open-response item—a kind of test question that requires students to answer in their own words, typically in the form of an essay.

option choice—See *distractor*.

orthography (orthographic representation of a word)—the study of how words are expressed in written form, as distinct from their pronunciation, or phonology. The orthographic representation of a word is how it is spelled.

passage—reading passage.

personalization—adapting instruction to the specific needs of individual learners.

phonology—the study of how words sound.

phrasal verbs—a multiword expression formed by combining a verb with a particle (e.g., *up, down, in, out, away, across, at, into, on*).

polysemy (polysemous)—multiple but related meanings for the same word. The different meanings of a polysemous word are called its *senses*.

prefix—a letter or group of letters that are added to the beginning of a root word to make a new grammatically complete word or to change the meaning of an existing word.

productive vocabulary—words (from memory or from one's active vocabulary) that a person can use appropriately in context.

prototypical attributes—features of word meaning that apply to typical examples but do not necessarily apply to every example (e.g., mammals have hair, but there are hairless mammals).

pseudoword—a nonword that resembles a real word in terms of pronunciation and morphological structure.

psycholinguistics—the study of the psychological processes behind language acquisition and use.

readability—how easy or difficult a text is to read, usually based on an algorithm that considers factors such as sentence length and number of syllables in words.

receptive vocabulary—words that a person may understand but may not be able to produce orally (or in writing).

referential cohesion—the use of pronouns and other devices in a language that are used for referring to the same entity at different points in the same text.

referential understanding—understanding what words in a passage refer to in terms of references to the subject and objects in and across the sentences.

register—a language variant, characterized primarily by differences in word choice and details of pronunciation, appropriate to a specific situation. People use different registers in oral versus written contexts, in formal versus informal situations, and in academic versus nonacademic contexts, among others.

root words—words that consist of a single morpheme.

rote information—information that is learned mechanically or superficially through repetition.

scale—a mechanism for interpreting differences in test scores to describe how much two individuals' abilities differ on the construct measured by the test.

semantic category—a classification based on word meanings. Words that belong to the same semantic category are similar in overall meaning and describe things that fall into the same general class.

semantic drift—a situation in which words gradually change meaning, coming to be applied more narrowly or more broadly over time.

semantic frames—a theoretical concept that links the grammatical patterns in which a word is used to the way its meaning combines with other words in the sentence.

semantic pattern—patterns of word meanings that are commonly extended to describe additional situations and concepts (i.e., polysemy).

semantic propositions—a meaning that can be true or false. A sentence may express several propositions (e.g., a sentence like *The clever fox barked loudly* expresses three propositions: the fox barked, the fox was clever, and the barking was loud).

semantic relationship—relationships among words with similar or associated meanings. See *synonyms, antonyms, hypernyms, hyponyms, metonymy.*

semantics—the study of meaning.

SES—socioeconomic status.

simile—an expression that compares one thing to another.

specialization (or generalization)—the use of a word to describe something more narrowly or more loosely, giving it a different, more specialized (or more general) meaning.

standardized test scores—used with standardized tests (often used in high-stakes situations) in which student performances can be compared to each other because the meaning of the score points and ranges have a consistent interpretation. See also *scale.*

stealth (nonintrusive) assessment—a method of assessing students' knowledge by collecting information about their behavior from how they interact with a digital environment. Features of the displayed behaviors are used to support inferences about what students know and can do.

suffix—a letter or group of letters that are added to the end of a root word to make a new grammatically complete word or to change the meaning of an existing word.

surface factors—easily measurable features of words and expressions.

synonym—words that mean roughly the same thing.

synsets—sets of word senses that are synonyms or near synonyms.

syntactic knowledge—the ability to apply grammatical patterns or to identify instances of a grammatical concept.

syntactic patterns—common patterns regarding how words are regularly arranged to form sentences.

syntax—how words are arranged into sentences, based on the rules of grammar.

tacit knowledge—knowledge of words, phrases, or generative patterns that is implicit and indirectly learned through personal experience, not explicitly acquired from a book or lesson.

taxonomic knowledge—how a person organizes information into a hierarchy of semantic categories. Taxonomic knowledge facilitates the storage and recall of information from memory.

test reliability—how consistently a test measures a construct across time and people.

test validity—the accuracy of how well a test measures a construct.

text macrostructure—how a document is organized. Text macrostructure is signaled by a variety of clues, including paragraph boundaries, transitional words, coherence between related words, and other linguistic cues.

Tier One vocabulary—high-frequency, conversational vocabulary.

Tier Two vocabulary—academic vocabulary.

Tier Three vocabulary—domain-specific vocabulary.

topic cohesion—a measure of the extent to which the words in a passage are related to the same ideas, as measured by repetition of content words or clusters of related words in a text.

topical association—the associations between words that are associated or are used in connection with roughly the same ideas or topics.

transitive verbs—verbs that have a direct object.

valuable words—words that may be challenging for most students and important for reading a variety of texts in the future (Graves et al., 2014).

vocabulary acquisition—word learning.

vocabulary construct—those aspects of word knowledge that one is interested in assessing.

word bank—a collection of words compiled by a classroom from materials students have encountered during their studies, containing words and phrases that may be useful to them when they write about the subject they are studying.

word-conscious classroom—a class in which learning about words is infused in classroom activities and integrated with the curriculum, and where students are encouraged to engage actively in developing their own vocabularies.

word consciousness—an alertness to language use and word encounters; developing metacognitive and metalinguistic understanding of vocabulary.

word families—groups of words that share a common root. See also *morphological patterns*.

word frequency—an estimate of how common a word is in the language, as measured by how often it appears in some large corpus of text.

word norm databases—information about the approximate time in a person's life when he or she might learn and retain a word; measures about word difficulty or concreteness; measures of associations between words; or the frequency of a word.

wordplay—activities in which a teacher draws students' attention to multiple senses of words through the use of jokes and puns to create metalinguistic awareness.

word sense—a particular definition of a word.

zeugma—a situation in which a single word is used in two different parts of a sentence but carries a different meaning in each part.

References

Abbott, R., & Berninger, V. (1993). Structural equation modeling of relationships among developmental skills and writing skills in primary and intermediate grade writers. *Journal of Educational Psychology, 85*(3), 478–508.

Abrams, S. S., & Walsh, S. (2014). Gamified vocabulary. *Journal of Adolescent and Adult Literacy, 58*(1), 49–58.

Adams, M. J. (1990). *Beginning to read: Thinking and learning about print.* Boston: MIT Press.

Adolphs, S., & Schmitt, N. (2003). Lexical coverage of spoken discourse. *Applied Linguistics, 24*(4), 425–438.

Afflerbach, P. (2005). National reading conference policy brief: High-stakes testing and reading assessment. *Journal of Literacy Research, 37*(2), 151–162.

Agirre, E., & Edmonds, P. (2006). *Word sense disambiguation: Algorithms and applications.* New York: Springer.

Aist, G. S. (2002). Helping children learn vocabulary during computer-assisted oral reading. *Journal of Educational Technology and Society, 5*(2), 147–163.

Aitchison, J. (2012). *Words in the mind: An introduction to the mental lexicon.* Hoboken, NJ: Wiley.

Akande, A. T. (2005). Morphological errors in the English usage of some Nigerian learners: Causes and remedies. Retrieved from *www.academia. edu/1804961/Morphological_errors_in_the_English_usage_of_some_ Nigerian_learners_causes_and_remedies.*

Alderson, J. C., & Kremmel, B. (2013). Re-examining the content validation of a grammar test: The (im)possibility of distinguishing vocabulary and structural knowledge. *Language Testing, 30*(4), 535–556.

Alexander, P. A. (2003). The development of expertise: The journey from acclimation to proficiency. *Educational Researcher, 32*(8), 10–14.

Allan, K. (2007). The pragmatics of connotation. *Journal of Pragmatics, 39*(6), 1047–1057.

Allen, L. K., & McNamara, D. S. (2015). You are your words: Modeling students' vocabulary knowledge with natural language processing tools. In *Proceedings of the 8th international conference on Educational Data Mining* (pp. 258–265). Retrieved from *http://educationaldatamining.org/EDM2015/index.php?page=proceedings*.

American Educational Research Association, American Psychological Association, & National Council on Measurement in Education. (2014). *Standards for educational and psychological testing*. Washington, DC: Author.

The American Heritage Dictionary (5th ed.). (2016). Boston: Houghton Mifflin.

Anderson, R. C. (1972). How to construct achievement tests to assess comprehension. *Review of Educational Research, 42*(2), 145–170.

Anderson, R. C., & Nagy, W. E. (1991). Word meanings. In R. Barr, M. L. Kamil, P. Mosenthal, & P. D. Pearson (Eds.), *Handbook of reading research* (Vol. 2, pp. 690–724). White Plains, NY: Longman.

Anglin, J. M. (1970). *The growth of word meaning*. Cambridge, MA: MIT Press.

Anglin, J. M., Miller, G. A., & Wakefield, P. C. (1993). Vocabulary development: A morphological analysis. *Monographs of the Society for Research in Child Development, 58*(10), i–186.

Antoniadis, G., Granger, S., Kraif, O., Ponton, C., & Zampa, V. (2013). NLP and CALL: Integration is working. *arXiv:1302.4814v1* [cs.CL].

Apthorp, H. S., Randel, B., Cherasaro, T., Clark, T., McKeown, M. G., & Beck, I. L. (2012). Effects of a supplemental vocabulary program on word knowledge and passage comprehension. *Journal of Research on Educational Effectiveness, 5*(2), 160–188.

Attali, Y., & Burstein, J. (2005, November). Automated essay scoring with e-Rater® v.2.0. *ETS Research Report* (RR-04-45), i–21.

Attali, Y., & Powers, D. (2008, April). A developmental writing scale. *ETS Research Report* (RR-08-19), pp. i–59.

Baayen, R. H., Piepenbrock, R., & van Rijn, H. (1993). *The CELEX lexical database* [CD-ROM]. Philadelphia: Linguistic Data Consortium.

Babbitt, N. (1975). *Tuck everlasting*. New York: Farrar, Straus & Giroux.

Bachman, L. F. (1982). The trait structure of cloze test scores. *TESOL Quarterly, 16*(1), 61–70.

Baker, C. F., Fillmore, C. J., & Lowe, J. B. (1998). The Berkeley Framenet project. In *Proceedings of the 17th international conference on computational linguistics* (Vol. 1, pp. 86–90). Stroudsburg, PA: Association for Computational Linguistics.

Banas, J. A., Dunbar, N., Rodriguez, D., & Liu, S. (2011). A review of humor in educational settings: Four decades of research. *Communication Education, 60*(1), 115–144.

Banks, K., & Kulikov, S. (2006). *Max's words*. New York: Farrar, Straus & Giroux.

Barcelona, A. (2010). Metonymic inferencing and second language acquisition. *AILA Review, 23*(1), 134–154.

Barfield, A. (2003). *Collocation recognition and production: Research insights.* Tokyo: Chuo University.

Bauer, L., & Nation, P. (1993). Word families. *International Journal of Lexicography, 6*(4), 253–279.

Beal, C. R., Arroyo, I., Cohen, P. R., Woolf, B. P., & Beal, C. R. (2010). Evaluation of AnimalWatch: An intelligent tutoring system for arithmetic and fractions. *Journal of Interactive Online Learning, 9*(1), 64–77.

Bear, D. R., Invernizzi, M., Templeton, S., & Johnston, F. (2016). *Words their way* (6th ed). Upper Saddle River, NJ: Pearson.

Beck, I. L., McKeown, M. G., & Kucan, L. (2002). *Bringing words to life: Robust vocabulary instruction.* New York: Guilford Press.

Beck, I. L., McKeown, M. G., & Kucan, L. (2013). *Bringing words to life: Robust vocabulary instruction* (2nd ed.). New York: Guilford Press.

Beck, I. L., Perfetti, C. A., & McKeown, M. G. (1982). Effects of long-term vocabulary instruction on lexical access and reading comprehension. *Journal of Educational Psychology, 74*(4), 506.

Becker, L., Basu, S., & Vanderwende, L. (2012). Mind the gap: Learning to choose gaps for question generation. In *Proceedings of the 2012 conference of the North American chapter of the Association for Computational Linguistics: Human Language Technologies* (pp. 742–751). Stroudsburg, PA: Association for Computational Linguistics.

Bejar, I. I., Chaffin, R., & Embretson, S. (1991). *Cognitive and psychometric analysis of analogical problem solving.* New York: Springer Verlag.

Bejar, I. I., Deane, P. D., Flor, M., & Chen, J. (2016). *Evidence of the generalization and construct representation inferences for the GRE sentence equivalence item type* (GRE Board Report No. RR-17-02). Princeton, NJ: Educational Testing Service.

Bejar, I. I., Lawless, R. R., Morley, M. E., Wagner, M. E., Bennett, R. E., & Revuelta, J. (2002). A feasibility study of on-the-fly item generation in adaptive testing. *ETS Research Report* (RR-02-23), pp. i–44.

Bejar, I. I., & Yocom, P. (1991). A generative approach to the modeling of isomorphic hidden-figure items. *Applied Psychological Measurement, 15*(2), 129–137.

Benjamin, R. G. (2012). Reconstructing readability: Recent developments and recommendations in the analysis of text difficulty. *Educational Psychology Review, 24*(1), 63–88.

Berninger, V. W., Abbott, R. D., Nagy, W., & Carlisle, J. (2010). Growth in phonological, orthographic, and morphological awareness in grades 1 to 6. *Journal of Psycholinguistic Research, 39*(2), 141–163.

Biber, D. (1989). A typology of English texts. *Linguistics, 27*(1), 3–44.

Biber, D. (1995). *Dimensions of register variation: A cross-linguistic comparison.* Cambridge, UK: Cambridge University Press.

Biber, D., & Conrad, S. (2009). *Register, genre, and style.* New York: Cambridge University Press.

Biber, D., & Finegan, E. (1989). Styles of stance in English: Lexical and grammatical marking of evidentiality and affect. *Text: An Interdisciplinary Journal for the Study of Discourse, 9*(1), 93–124.

Biemiller, A. (2001). Teaching vocabulary: Early, direct, and sequential. *American Educator, 25*(1), 24–28.

Biemiller, A. (2005). Size and sequence in vocabulary development: Implications for choosing words for primary grade vocabulary instruction. In A. Hiebert & M. Kamil (Eds.), *Teaching and learning vocabulary: Bringing research to practice* (pp. 223–242). Mahwah, NJ: Erlbaum.

Biemiller, A. (2006). Vocabulary development and instruction: A prerequisite for school learning. In D. K. Dickinson & S. B. Neumann (Eds.), *Handbook of early literacy research* (Vol. 2, pp. 41–51). New York: Guilford Press.

Biemiller, A. (2009). *Words worth teaching: Closing the vocabulary gap.* Columbus, OH: McGraw-Hill SRA.

Biemiller, A. (2015). Which words are worth teaching? *Perspectives on Language and Literacy, 41*(3), 9–13.

Biemiller, A., & Boote, C. (2005). *Selecting useful word meaning for instruction in the primary grades.* Paper presented at the annual meeting of the American Educational Research Association, Montreal.

Biemiller, A., & Boote, C. (2006). An effective method for building meaning vocabulary in primary grades. *Journal of Educational Psychology, 98*(1), 44–62.

Biemiller, A., & Slonim, N. (2001). Estimating root word vocabulary growth in normative and advantaged populations: Evidence for a common sequence of vocabulary acquisition. *Journal of Educational Psychology, 93*(3), 498–520.

Binet, A., & Simon, T. A. (1904). Méthode nouvelle pour le diagnostic du niveau intellectuel des anormaux. *L'Année Psychologique, 11*, 191–244.

Blachowicz, C. L. Z. (1987). Vocabulary instruction: What goes on in the classroom? *The Reading Teacher, 41*(2), 132–137.

Blachowicz, C. L. Z., Fisher, P. J. L., Ogle, D., & Watts-Taffe, S. (2006). Vocabulary: Questions from the classroom. *Reading Research Quarterly, 41*(4), 524–539.

Blanton, W., & Moorman, G. (1990). The presentation of reading lessons. *Reading Research and Instruction, 29*(3), 35–55.

Bolger, D. J., Balass, M., Landen, E. & Perfetti, C.A. (2008). Contextual variation and definitions in learning the meaning of words. *Discourse Processes, 45*(2), 122–159.

Bonk, W. J. (2003). *A psycholinguistic investigation of collocation.* Master's thesis, University of Colorado, Boulder, CO.

Booher-Jennings, J. (2006). Rationing education in an era of accountability. *Phi Delta Kappan, 87*(10), 756–761.

Bormuth, J. R. (1966). Readability: A new approach. *Reading Research Quarterly, 1*(3), 79–132.

Bormuth, J. R. (1967). Comparable cloze and multiple-choice comprehension test scores. *Journal of Reading, 10*(5), 291–299.

Bormuth, J. R. (1968). Cloze test readability: Criterion reference scores. *Journal of Educational Measurement, 5*(3), 189–196.

Bormuth, J. R. (1969). *Development of readability analysis* (United States Office of Education, Project No. 7-0052). Chicago: University of Chicago.

Bormuth, J. R. (1970). *On the theory of achievement test items*. Chicago: University of Chicago Press.

Borovsky, A., Elman, J. L., & Kutas, M. (2012). Once is enough: N400 indexes semantic integration of novel word meanings from a single exposure in context. *Language Learning and Development, 8*(3), 278–302.

Boshuizen, H. P., & Van de Wiel, M. W. (2014). Expertise development through schooling and work. In A. Littlejohn & A. Margaryan (Eds.), *Technology enhanced professional learning: Processes, practices, and tools* (pp. 71–84). New York: Routledge.

Bowers, P. (2009). Teaching how the written word works. Available at *www.wordworkskingston.com*.

Bowers, P. N. (2016). The evolution of a community of learners: SWI at Nueva and beyond (Word Works Newsletter #81). Retrieved August 1, 2016, from *http://files.realspellers.org/PetesFolder/Newsletters/WW_Newsletter_81_Nueva.pdf*.

Bowers, P. N., & Cooke, G. (2012). Morphology and the Common Core building students' understanding of the written word. *Perspectives on Language and Literacy, 38*(4), 31.

Bowers, P. N., & Kirby, J. R. (2010). Effects of morphological instruction on vocabulary acquisition. *Reading and Writing, 23*(5), 515–537.

Bowers, P. N., Kirby, J. R., & Deacon, S. H. (2010). The effects of morphological instruction on literacy skills: A systematic review of the literature. *Review of Educational Research, 80*(2), 144–179.

Brezina, V., & Gablasova, D. (2013). Is there a core general vocabulary?: Introducing the New General Service List. *Applied Linguistics, 36*(1), 1–22.

Brillhart, J. (2002). *Molly rides the school bus*. Park Ridge, IL: Albert Whitman.

Brown, G. D., & Watson, F. L. (1987). First in, first out: Word learning age and spoken word frequency as predictors of word familiarity and word naming latency. *Memory and Cognition, 15*(3), 208–216.

Brown, J., & Eskenazi, M. (2004). *Retrieval of authentic documents for reader-specific lexical practice*. Paper presented at the 2004 InSTIL/ICALL symposium, Venice, Italy.

Brown, J., & Eskenazi, M. (2005). *Student, text and curriculum modeling for reader-specific document retrieval*. Paper presented at the IASTED International Conference on Human-Computer Interaction, Phoenix, AZ.

Brown, J. C., Frishkoff, G. A., & Eskenazi, M. (2005). Automatic question generation for vocabulary assessment. In *Proceedings of the conference on Human Language Technology and Empirical Methods in Natural Language Processing* (pp. 819–826). Stroudsburg, PA: Association for Computational Linguistics.

Brown, J. S., Collins, A., & Duguid, P. (1989). Situated cognition and the culture of learning. *Educational Researcher, 18*(1), 32–41.

Browne, C. (2013). The new General Service List: Celebrating 60 years of vocabulary learning. *The Language Teacher, 37*(4), 13–16.

Browne, C. (2014). A new General Service List: The better mousetrap we've been looking for. *Vocabulary Learning and Instruction, 3*(1), 1–10.

Browne, C., & Culligan, B. (2008). Combining technology and IRT testing to build student knowledge of high-frequency vocabulary. *JALT CALL Journal, 4*(2), 3–16.

Browne, C., Culligan, B., & Phillips, J. (2013). The New Academic Word List, version 1.0. Retrieved August 2, 2016, from *www.newacademicwordlist. org.*

Bruillard E. (1997). *Les machines à enseigner.* Paris: Hermès.

Brysbaert M., Warriner B. A., & Kuperman V. (2014). Concreteness ratings for 40 thousand generally known English word lemmas. *Behavior Research Methods, 26*(3), 904–911.

Burgess, C. (1998). From simple associations to the building blocks of language: Modeling meaning in memory with the HAL model. *Behavior Research Methods, Instruments, and Computers, 30*(2), 188–198.

Burgess, C., & Livesay, K. (1998). The effect of corpus size in predicting reaction time in a basic word recognition task: Moving on from Kučera and Francis. *Behavior Research Methods, Instruments, and Computers, 30*(2), 272–277.

Burstein, J., & Sabatini, J. (2016). The Language Muse Activity Palette. In S. A. Crossley & D. S. McNamara (Eds.), *Adaptive educational technologies for literacy instruction* (pp. 275–280). New York: Routledge.

Bybee, J. (2006). From usage to grammar: The mind's response to repetition. *Language, 82*(4), 711–733.

Cain, K., & Oakhill, J. (2011). Matthew effects in young readers' reading comprehension and reading experience aid vocabulary development. *Journal of Learning Disabilities, 44*(5), 431–443.

California Department of Education. (2005). California English language development test regulations. Retrieved from *www.cde.ca.gov/ta/tg/el.*

Callan, J., & Eskenazi, M. (2007). Combining lexical and grammatical features to improve readability measures for first and second language texts. In *Proceedings of the Human Language Technology Conference* (pp. 460–467). Stroudsburg, PA: Association for Computational Linguistics.

Canavan, A., & Morgovsky, P. (1998). JURIS LDC98T32. Philadelphia: Linguistic Data Consortium.

Canfield, W. (2001). ALEKS: A Web-based intelligent tutoring system. *Mathematics and Computer Education, 35*(2), 152–158.

Carlisle, J. F. (2000). Awareness of the structure and meaning of morphologically complex words: Impact on reading. *Reading and Writing, 12*(3), 169–190.

Carlisle, J. F. (2010). Effects of instruction in morphological awareness on literacy achievement: An integrative review. *Reading Research Quarterly, 45*(4), 464–487.

Carlisle, J. F., & Feldman, L. B. (1995). Morphological awareness and early reading achievement. In L. B. Feldman (Ed.), *Morphological aspects of language processing* (pp. 189–209). New York: Erlbaum.

Carlisle, J. F., & Katz, L. A. (2006). Effects of word and morpheme familiarity on reading of derived words. *Reading and Writing, 19*(7), 669–693.

Carroll, J. B. (1962). Factors in verbal achievement. In P. L. Dressel (Ed.),

Proceedings of the 1961 Invitational Conference on Testing Problems (pp. 11–18). Princeton, NJ: Educational Testing Service.

Carroll, J. B. (1970). An alternative to Juilland's usage coefficient for lexical frequencies. *ETS Research Bulletin* (RB—10-48), i–15.

Carroll, J. B. (1972). A new word frequency book. *Elementary English, 49*(7), 1070–1074.

Carroll, J. B. (1979). Measurement of abilities constructs. In A. P. Maslow & R. H. McKillip (Eds.), *Construct validity in psychological measurement* In *Proceedings of colloquium on theory and application in education and employment* (pp. 23–41). Princeton, NJ: Educational Testing Service.

Carroll, J. B., Davies, P., & Richman, B. (1971). *The American Heritage word frequency book*. Boston: Houghton Mifflin.

Carroll, J. B., & White, M. N. (1973). Age-of-acquisition norms for 220 picturable nouns. *Journal of Verbal Learning and Verbal Behavior, 12*(5), 563–576.

Carroll, L., & Tenniel, J. (1872). *Through the looking glass: And what Alice found there*. Boston: Lee and Shepard.

Carver, R. P. (1985). Measuring readability using DRP units. *Journal of Literacy Research, 17*(4), 303–316.

Chaffin, R. (1997). Associations to unfamiliar words: Learning the meanings of new words. *Memory and Cognition, 25*(2), 203–226.

Chall, J. S., & Dale, E. (1995). *Readability revisited: The new Dale–Chall readability formula*. Cambridge, MA: Brookline Books.

Chen, C. M., & Chung, C. J. (2008). Personalized mobile English vocabulary learning system based on item response theory and learning memory cycle. *Computers and Education, 51*(2), 624–645.

Chen, Y.-C, & Lai, H.-I. (2012). EFL learners' awareness of metonymy–metaphor continuum in figurative expressions. *Language Awareness, 21*(3), 235–248.

Christ, T. (2011). Moving past "right" or "wrong": Toward a continuum of young children's semantic knowledge. *Journal of Literacy Research, 43*(2), 130–158.

Cieri, C., Miller, D., & Walker, K. (2004). The Fisher corpus: A resource for the next generations of speech-to-text. In *Proceedings of the Fourth International Conference on Language Resources and Evaluation* (pp. 69–71). Paris: European Language Resources Association.

Collins COBUILD advanced American English dictionary (2nd ed.). (2017). London: HarperCollins UK.

Collins COBUILD English dictionary for advanced learners (4th ed.). (2003). London: HarperCollins UK.

Collins-Thompson, K. (2014). Computational assessment of text readability: A survey of current and future research. *International Journal of Applied Linguistics, 165*(2), 97–135.

Collins-Thompson, K., & Callan, J. (2004). Information retrieval for language tutoring: An overview of the REAP project. In *Proceedings of the 27th annual international ACM SIGIR conference on research and development in information retrieval* (pp. 544–545). New York: Association for Computing Machinery.

Collins-Thompson, K., & Callan, J. (2007). Automatic and human scoring of word definition responses. In *Proceedings of the North American Association for Computational Linguistics: Human Language Technology* (pp. 476–483). Stroudsburg, PA: Association for Computational Linguistics.

Collins-Thompson, K., Frishkoff, G., & Crossley, S. A. (2012). Definition response scoring with probabilistic ordinal regression. In *Proceedings of the International Conference on Computers in Education* (Vol. 6, pp. 101–105). Singapore: National Institute of Education, Nanyang Technological University.

Coltheart, M. (1981). The MRC psycholinguistic database. *Journal of Experimental Psychology, 33*(4), 497–505.

Coltheart, V., Laxon, V. J., & Keating, C. (1988). Effects of word imageability and age of acquisition on children's reading. *British Journal of Psychology, 79*(1), 1–12.

Common Core State Standards Initiative. (2010). Common Core State Standards for English language arts and literacy in history/social studies, science, and technical subjects. Available at *www.corestandards.org/wp-content/uploads/ELA_Standards1.pdf*.

Coniam, D. (1997). Preliminary inquiry into using corpus word frequency data in the automatic generation of English language cloze tests. *CALICO Journal, 16*(2–4), 15–33.

Coniam, D. (1998). From text to test, automatically: An evaluation of a computer cloze-test generator. *Hong Kong Journal of Applied Linguistics, 3*(1), 41–60.

Connor, C. M., Spencer, M., Day, S. L., Giuliani, S., Ingebrand, S. W., McLean, L., et al. (2014). Capturing the complexity: Content, type, and amount of instruction and quality of the classroom learning environment synergistically predict third graders' vocabulary and reading comprehension outcomes. *Journal of Educational Psychology, 106*(3), 762–778.

Conrad, S., & Biber, D. (2004). The frequency and use of lexical bundles in conversation and academic prose. *Lexicographica: International Annual for Lexicography 20*, 56–71.

Cooley, R. E. (2001). Vocabulary acquisition software: User preferences and tutorial guidance. In *AIED 2001 Workshop Papers—Computer Assisted Language Learning* (pp. 17–23).

Correia, R., Baptista, J., Eskenazi, M., & Mamede, N. (2012). Automatic generation of cloze question stems. In *Proceedings of the International Conference on Computational Processing of the Portuguese Language* (pp. 168–178). Berlin: Springer Verlag.

Corrigan, R. (2007). An experimental analysis of the affective dimensions of deep vocabulary knowledge used in inferring the meaning of words in context. *Applied Linguistics, 28*(2), 211–240.

Corson, D. J. (1985). *The lexical bar.* Oxford, UK: Pergamon Press.

Coxhead, A. (1998). An academic word list (ELI Occasional Publications #18, School of Linguistics and Applied Language Studies). Wellington, New Zealand: Victoria University of Wellington.

Coxhead, A. (2000). A new academic word list. *TESOL Quarterly, 34*(2), 213–238.

Coxhead, A., & Byrd, P. (2007). Preparing writing teachers to teach the vocabulary and grammar of academic prose. *Journal of Second Language Writing, 16*(3), 129–147.

Coyne, M. D., McCoach, D. B., Loftus, S., Zipoli, R., Ruby, M., Crevecoeur, Y., et al. (2010). Direct and extended vocabulary instruction in kindergarten: Investigating transfer effects. *Journal of Research on Educational Effectiveness, 3*(2), 93–120.

Cromley, J. G., & Azevedo, R. (2007). Testing and refining the direct and inferential mediation model of reading comprehension. *Journal of Educational Psychology, 99*(2), 311–325.

Crossley, S. A., Greenfield, J., & McNamara, D. S. (2008). Assessing text readability using cognitively based indices. *TESOL Quarterly, 42*(3), 475–493.

Crossley, S. A., Salsbury, T., & McNamara, D. S. (2015). Assessing lexical proficiency using analytic ratings: A case for collocation accuracy. *Applied Linguistics, 36*(5), 570–590.

Crosson, A. C., & McKeown, M. G. (2016). Middle school learners' use of Latin roots to infer the meaning of unfamiliar words. *Cognition and Instruction, 34*(2), 1–24.

Crosson, A. C., & McKeown, M. G. (2017). *An innovative approach to assessing depth of knowledge of academic words.* Manuscript under review.

Crovitz, D., & Miller, J. A. (2008). Register and charge: Using synonym maps to explore connotation. *English Journal, 97*(4), 49–55.

Dahl, R. (1982). *The BFG.* New York: Farrar, Straus & Giroux.

Dale, E., & Chall, J. S. (1948). A formula for predicting readability. *Educational Research Bulletin, 27*, 11–20.

Dale, E., & O'Rourke, J. (1976). *The living word vocabulary.* Boston: Houghton Mifflin.

Dale, E., & Tyler, R. (1934). A study of factors influencing the difficulty of reading materials for adults of limited reading ability. *Library Quarterly, 4*(3), 384–412.

Dale, P. S., & Fenson, L. (1996). Lexical development norms for young children. *Behavior Research Methods, Instruments and Computers, 28*(1), 125–27.

Davies, M. (2009). The 385+ million word Corpus of Contemporary American English (1990–2008+): Design, architecture, and linguistic insights. *International Journal of Corpus Linguistics, 14*(2), 159–190.

Davies, M. (2010). The Corpus of Contemporary American English as the first reliable monitor corpus of English. *Literary and Linguistic Computing, 25*(4), 447–464.

Davis, F. B. (1944). Fundamental factors of comprehension in reading. *Psychometrika, 9*(3), 185–197.

Davison, A. (1985). *Readability: The situation today* (Center for the Study of Reading Technical Report No. 359). Urbana–Champaign: University of Illinois Center for the Study of Reading.

Deane, P., Lawless, R., Li, C., Sabatini, J. S., Bejar, I. I., & O'Reilly, T. (2014).

Creating vocabulary item types that measure students' depth of semantic knowledge. *ETS Research Report* (RR-14–02). Available at *http://dx.doi.org/10.1002/ets2.12001.*

Deane, P., Lawless, R. R., Sabatini, J., & Li, C. (2015). *Measuring students' depth of knowledge in domain-specific vocabulary.* Unpublished manuscript. Princeton, NJ: Educational Testing Service.

Deane, P., Sheehan, K. M., Sabatini, J., Futagi, Y., & Kostin, I. (2006). Differences in text structure and its implications for assessment of struggling readers. *Scientific Studies of Reading, 10*(3), 257–275.

DeGross, M., & Hanna, C. (1998). *Donovan's word jar.* New York: Harper-Collins.

Dela Rosa, K., & Eskenazi, M. (2011). *Effect of word complexity on L2 vocabulary learning.* Paper presented at the sixth annual Workshop on Innovative Use of NLP for Building Educational Applications, Portland, OR.

Deno, S. L., Marston, D., & Mirkin, P. (1982). Valid measurement procedures for continuous evaluation of written expression. *Exceptional Children, 48,* 368–371.

DiBello, L. V., Roussos, L. A., & Stout, W. (2006). 31A review of cognitively diagnostic assessment and a summary of psychometric models. *Handbook of Statistics, 26,* 979–1030.

Doe, C. (2014). Diagnostic English Language Needs Assessment (DELNA). *Language Testing, 3*(4), 537–543.

Dowty, D. (1991). Thematic proto-roles and argument selection. *Language, 6*(3), 547–619.

Drachsler, H., Verbert, K., Santos, O. C., & Manouselis, N. (2015). Panorama of recommender systems to support learning. In F. Ricci, L. Rokach, & B. Shapira (Eds.), *Recommender systems handbook* (2nd ed., pp. 421–451). New York: Springer.

Duff, D., Tomblin, J. B., & Catts, H. (2015). The influence of reading on vocabulary growth: A case for a Matthew effect. *Journal of Speech, Language, and Hearing Research, 58*(3), 853–864.

Dunn, L. M., & Dunn, D. M. (2007). *Peabody Picture Vocabulary Test— Fourth edition.* Minneapolis, MN: Pearson.

Dunsmuir, S., & Blatchford, P. (2004). Predictors of writing competence in 4- to 7-year-old children. *British Journal of Educational Psychology, 74*(3), 461–483.

Durso, F. T., & Shore, W. J. (1991). Partial knowledge of word meanings. *Journal of Experimental Psychology, 120*(2), 190–202.

Eckerth, J., & Tavakoli, P. (2012). The effects of word exposure frequency and elaboration of word processing on incidental L2 vocabulary acquisition through reading. *Language Teaching Research, 16*(2), 227–252.

Educational Developmental Laboratories. (1989). *EDL core vocabularies in reading, mathematics, science, and social studies.* Austin, TX: Steck-Vaughn.

Educational Testing Service. (2016a). TOEFL IBT test questions. Retrieved July 7, 2016, from *www.ets.org/Media/Tests/TOEFL/pdf/SampleQuestions_largeprint.doc.*

Educational Testing Service. (2016b). GRE Revised General Test: Text completion. Retrieved July 7, 2016, from *www.ets.org/gre/revised_general/prepare/verbal_reasoning/text_completion/sample_questions*.

Educational Testing Service. (2016c). GRE Revised General Test: Sentence equivalence. Retrieved July 7, 2016, from *https://www.ets.org/gre/revised_general/prepare/verbal_reasoning/sentence_equivalence/sample_questions*.

Ellis, N. C. (2003). Constructions, chunking, and connectionism: The emergence of second language structure. In C. Doughty & M. H. Long (Eds.), *Handbook of second language acquisition* (pp. 33–68). Oxford, UK: Blackwell.

Ellis, N. C. (2008). The dynamics of second language emergence: Cycles of language use, language change, and language acquisition. *Modern Language Journal, 92*(2), 232–249.

Enright, M. K., & Bejar, I. I. (1989). An analysis of test writers' expertise: Modeling analogy item difficulty. *ETS Research Report*(2), i–26.

Ericsson, K. A., & Charness, N. (1994). Expert performance: Its structure and acquisition. *American Psychologist, 49*(8), 725–747.

Eskildsen, S. W. (2008). *Constructing a second language inventory: The accumulation of linguistic resources in L2 English*. Doctoral dissertation, University of Southern Denmark, Odense, Denmark.

Feeney, C. M., & Heilman, M. (2008). Automatically generating and validating reading-check questions. In *Proceedings of the International Conference on Intelligent Tutoring Systems* (pp. 659–661). Berlin: Springer Verlag.

Fellbaum, C. (Ed). (1998). *WordNet: An electronic lexical database*. Cambridge, MA: MIT Press.

Feng, G., Deane, P., Lawless, R. R., Sabatini, J. P., Halderman, L., O'Reilly, T., et al. (2013). *Mapping the development of domain-specific vocabulary* [Unpublished manuscript]. Princeton, NJ: Educational Testing Service.

Feng, L., Jansche, M., Huenerfauth, M., & Elhadad, N. (2010). A comparison of features for automatic readability assessment. In *Proceedings of the 23rd International Conference on Computational Linguistics: Posters* (pp. 276–284). Stroudsburg, PA: Association for Computational Linguistics.

Fillmore, C. (1966). *Toward a modern theory of case* (Project on Linguistic Analysis report). Columbus: Ohio State University.

Firth, J. (1957). A synopsis of linguistic theory, 1930–1955. In *Studies in linguistic analysis* (pp. 1–32). Oxford, UK: Blackwell.

Fisher, D., & Frey, N. (2014). Content area vocabulary learning. *The Reading Teacher, 67*(8), 594–599.

Fitzgerald, F. S. (1925). *The great Gatsby*. New York: Charles Scribner's Sons.

Fleishman, P. (1980). *The half-a-moon-inn*. New York: HarperCollins.

Flesch, R. (1948). A new readability yardstick. *Journal of Applied Psychology, 32*(3), 221–233.

Flinspach, S. L., Castaneda, R., Vevea, J., & Scott, J. A. (2014). *Exploring bilingual students' performance overall and on cognate words in a large-scale multidimensional vocabulary test*. Paper presented at the annual meeting of the American Educational Research Association, Philadelphia, PA.

Flinspach, S. L., Scott, J. A., & Vevea, J. (2012). *Assessing breadth of academic vocabulary: Testing "new" words from across the fourth-grade and fifth-grade curriculum.* Paper presented at the annual meeting of the American Educational Research Association, Vancouver, BC, Canada.

Fogel, H., & Ehri, L. (2000). Teaching elementary students who speak Black English vernacular to write in Standard English: Effects of dialect transformation practice. *Contemporary Educational Psychology, 25*(2), 212–235.

Folse, K. (2011). *Oxford advanced American dictionary for learners of English.* Oxford, UK: Oxford University Press.

Foltz, P. W. (2007). Discourse coherence and LSA. In T. K. Landauer, D. S. McNamara, S. Dennis, & W. Kintsch (Eds.), *Handbook of latent semantic analysis* (pp. 167–184). New York: Routledge.

Foltz, P. W., Kintsch, W., & Landauer, T. K. (1998). The measurement of textual coherence with latent semantic analysis. *Discourse Processes, 25*(2–3), 285–307.

Foraker, S., & Murphy, G. L. (2012). Polysemy in sentence comprehension: Effects of meaning dominance. *Journal of Memory and Language, 67*(4), 407–425.

Francis, D., Rivera, M., Lesaux N., Kieffer, M., & Rivera, H. (2006). *Practical guidelines for the education of English language learners: Research-based recommendations for instruction and academic interventions.* Portmouth, NH: RMC Research Corportion, Center on Instruction.

François, T., & Miltsakaki, E. (2012). Do NLP and machine learning improve traditional readability formulas? In *Proceedings of the First Workshop on Predicting and Improving Text Readability for Target Reader Populations* (pp. 49–57). Stroudsburg, PA: Association for Computational Linguistics.

Frandsen, A. N., McCullough, B. R., & Stone, D. R. (1950). Serial versus consecutive order administration of the Stanford-Binet Intelligence Scales. *Journal of Consulting Psychology, 14*(4), 316–320.

Frankenberg-Garcia, A. (2012). Learners' use of corpus examples. *International Journal of Lexicography, 25*(3), 273–296.

Frishkoff, G. A., Collins-Thompson, K., Hodges, L. E., & Crossley, S. (2016). Accuracy feedback improves word learning from context: Evidence from a meaning-generation task. *Reading and Writing, 29*(4), 609–632.

Frishkoff, G. A., Collins-Thompson, K., Nam, S., Hodges, L., & Crossley, S. A. (2017). Dynamic support of contextual vocabulary acquisition for reading (DSCoVAR). In S. A. Crossley & D. S. McNamara (Eds.), *Educational technologies and literacy development: Adaptive educational technologies for literacy instruction* (pp. 69–81). New York: Routledge.

Frishkoff, G. A., Collins-Thompson, K., Perfetti, C., & Callan, J. (2008). Measuring incremental changes in word knowledge: Experimental validation and implications for learning and assessment. *Behavioral Research Methods, 40*(4), 907–925.

Frishkoff, G. A., Perfetti, C. A., & Collins-Thompson, K. (2011). Predicting robust vocabulary growth from measures of incremental learning. *Scientific Studies of Reading, 15*(1), 71–91.

Fry, E. B., Kress, J. E., & Fountoukidis, D. L. (2004). *The reading teacher's book of lists.* Upper Saddle River, NJ: Prentice Hall.

Gardner, D. (2004). Vocabulary input through extensive reading: A comparison of words found in children's narrative and expository reading materials. *Applied Linguistics, 25*(1), 1–37.

Gardner, D., & Davies, M. (2014). A new academic vocabulary list. *Applied Linguistics, 35*(3), 305–327.

Ghafoori, N., & Esfanjani, F. J. (2012). The effect of morphological awareness on vocabulary knowledge of Iranian high school students. *Iranian EFL Journal, 8*(3), 174.

Gibbs, R. W. (2006). Metaphor interpretation as embodied simulation. *Mind and Language, 21*(3), 434–458.

Gibson, A., & Stewart, J. (2014). Estimating learners' vocabulary size under item response theory. *Vocabulary Learning and Instruction, 3*(2), 78–84.

Gierl, M. J., & Lai, H. (2012). The role of item models in automatic item generation. *International Journal of Testing, 12*(3), 273–298.

Gilhooly, K. J., & Gilhooly, M. L. M. (1979). Age-of-acquisition effects in lexical and episodic memory tasks. *Memory and Cognition, 7*(3), 214–223.

Gilhooly, K. J., & Gilhooly, M. L. M. (1980). The validity of age of acquisition ratings. *British Journal of Psychology, 71*(1), 105–110.

Gilhooly, K. J., & Logie, R. H. (1980). Age-of-acquisition, imagery, concreteness, familiarity, and ambiguity measures for 1,944 words. *Behavior Research Methods and Instrumentation, 12*(4), 395–427.

Gilner, L. (2011). A primer on the General Service List. *Readings in a Foreign Language, 23*(1), 65–83.

Giora, R. (2012). Happy new war: The role of salient meanings and salience-based interpretations in processing utterances. In H.-J. Schmid (Ed.), *Cognitive pragmatics* (pp. 233–260). Berlin: De Gruyter Mouton.

Godfrey, J., & Holliman, E. (1993). *Switchboard-1 release 2 LDC97S62* [DVD]. Philadelphia: Linguistic Data Consortium.

Goldberg, A. E. (1995a). *Construction grammar.* Hoboken, NJ: Wiley.

Goldberg, A. E. (1995b). *Constructions: A construction grammar approach to argument structure.* Chicago: University of Chicago Press.

Goldberg, A. E. (2006). *Constructions at work: The nature of generalization in language.* Oxford, UK: Oxford University Press.

Goldberg, A. E. (2016). Partial productivity of linguistic constructions: Dynamic categorization and statistical preemption. *Language and Cognition, 8*(3), 369–390.

Goodfellow, R. (1995). A review of the types of CALL programs for vocabulary instruction. *Computer Assisted Language Learning, 8*, 205–226.

Goodman, J. C., Dale, P. S., & Li, P. (2008). Does frequency count?: Parental input and the acquisition of vocabulary. *Journal of Child Language, 35*(3), 515–531.

Gorin, J. S. (2005). Manipulating processing difficulty of reading comprehension questions: The feasibility of verbal item generation. *Journal of Educational Measurement, 42*(4), 351–373.

Gorin, J. S., & Embretson, S. E. (2006). Item difficulty modeling of paragraph comprehension items. *Applied Psychological Measurement, 30*(5), 394–411.

Graesser, A. C., Chipman, P., Haynes, B. C., & Olney, A. (2005). AutoTutor: An intelligent tutoring system with mixed-initiative dialogue. *IEEE Transactions on Education, 48*(4), 612–618.

Graesser, A. C., Wiemer-Hastings, K., Wiemer-Hastings, P., Kreuz, R., & the Tutoring Research Group. (1999). AutoTutor: A simulation of a human tutor. *Cognitive Systems Research, 1*(1), 35–51.

Graff, D., & Cieri, C. (2003). English gigaword corpus. *Linguistic Data Consortium.* Retrieved from *http://catalog.ldc.upenn.edu/ldc2003t05.*

Granger, S. (2003). The international corpus of learner English: A new resource for foreign language learning and teaching and second language acquisition research. *TESOL Quarterly, 37*(3), 538–546.

Granger, S., Dagneaux, E., Meunier, F., & Paquot, M. (Eds.). (2002). *International corpus of learner English.* Louvain-la-Neuve, Belgium: Presses Universitaires de Louvain.

Graves, M. F. (1980, December). *Skill with polysemous words: A measurement of the depth of children's word knowledge.* Paper presented at the annual meeting of the National Reading Conference, San Diego, CA.

Graves, M. F. (2000). A vocabulary program to complement and bolster a middle-grade comprehension program. In B. M. Taylor, M. F. Graves, & P. van den Broek (Eds.), *Reading for meaning: Fostering comprehension in the middle grades* (pp. 116–135). New York: Teachers College Press.

Graves, M. F. (2004). Teaching prefixes: As good as it gets? In J. F. Baumann & E. J. Kame'enui (Eds.), *Vocabulary instruction: Research to practice* (pp. 81–99). New York: Guilford Press.

Graves, M. F., Baumann, J. F., Blachowicz, C. L., Manyak, P., Bates, A., Cieply, C., et al. (2014). Words, words everywhere, but which ones do we teach? *The Reading Teacher, 67*(5), 333–346.

Graves, M. F., & Prenn, M. C. (1986). Costs and benefits of various methods of teaching vocabulary. *Journal of Reading, 29*(7), 596–602.

Gray, W. S., & Leary, B. A. (1935). *What makes a book readable.* Chicago: University of Chicago Press.

Greene, B. (2001). Testing reading comprehension of theoretical discourse with cloze. *Journal of Research in Reading, 24*(1), 82–98.

Grobe, C. (1981). Syntactic maturity, mechanics, and vocabulary as predictors of quality ratings. *Research in the Teaching of English, 15*(1), 75–85.

Gruber, J. S. (1965). *Studies in lexical relations.* Bloomington: Indiana University Linguistics Club.

Gyllstad, H. (2007). *Testing English collocations: Developing receptive tests for use with advanced Swedish learners.* Lund, Sweden: Lund University.

Habash, N., & Dorr, B. (2003). A categorical variation database for English. In *Proceedings of the 2003 Human Language Technology Conference and the North American Chapter of the Association for Computational Linguistics (HLT-NAACL)* (pp. 96–102). Stroudsburg, PA: Association for Computational Linguistics.

Halderman, L. K., Sabatini, J. S., Deane, P., Lawless, R., Feng, G., & Bejar, I. (2013). *Breadth of vocabulary knowledge: Mapping domain-specific vocabulary and validating with expert and student judgments* [Unpublished manuscript]. Princeton, NJ: Educational Testing Service.

Hart, B., & Risley, T. R. (1995). *Meaningful differences in the everyday experience of young American children.* Baltimore: Brookes.

Hayashi, Y., & Murphy, V. (2011). An investigation of morphological awareness in Japanese learners of English. *Language Learning Journal, 39*(1), 105–120.

Heilman, M., Collins-Thompson, K., Callan, J., & Eskenazi, M. (2006). Classroom success of an intelligent tutoring system for lexical practice and reading comprehension. Retrieved from *http://citeseerx.ist.psu.edu/viewdoc/download?doi=10.1.1.70.5828&rep=rep1&type=pdf.*

Heilman, M., Collins-Thompson, K., Callan, J., Eskenazi, M., Juffs, A., & Wilson, L. (2010). Personalization of reading passages improves vocabulary acquisition. *International Journal of Artificial Intelligence in Education, 20*(1), 73–98.

Heilman, M., Collins-Thompson, K., & Eskenazi, M. (2008). An analysis of statistical models and features for reading difficulty prediction. In *Proceedings of the Third Workshop on Innovative Use of NLP for Building Educational Applications* (pp. 71–79). Stroudsburg, PA: Association for Computational Linguistics.

Heilman, M., & Eskenazi, M. (2006). Authentic, individualized practice for English as a second language vocabulary. *Interfaces of Intelligent Computer-Assisted Language Learning Workshop at the Ohio State University, Columbus, 12*(6).

Heilman, M., & Eskenazi, M. (2007). Application of automatic thesaurus extraction for computer generation of vocabulary questions. In *Proceedings of the SLaTE workshop on Speech and Language Technology in Education* (pp. 65–68). Retrieved from *http://www.isca-speech.org/archive/slate_2007.*

Heilman, M., & Eskenazi, M. (2008). Self-assessment in vocabulary tutoring. In *Intelligent Tutoring Systems* (pp. 656–658). Berlin: Springer Verlag.

Heilman, M., Juffs, A., & Eskenazi, M. (2007). Choosing reading passages for vocabulary learning by topic to increase intrinsic motivation. *Frontiers in Artificial Intelligence and Applications, 158,* 566.

Heilman, M., Zhao, L., Pino, J., & Eskenazi, M. (2008). Retrieval of reading materials for vocabulary and reading practice. In *Proceedings of the Third Workshop on Innovative Use of NLP for Building Educational Applications* (pp. 80–88). Stroudsburg, PA: Association for Computational Linguistics.

Heiner, C., Beck, J., & Mostow, J. (2006, June). Automated vocabulary instruction in a reading tutor. In *International Conference on Intelligent Tutoring Systems* (pp. 741–743). Berlin: Springer Verlag.

Henriksen, B. (1999). Three dimensions of vocabulary development. *Studies in Second Language Acquisition, 31,* 303–317.

Hiebert, E. H. (2005). In pursuit of an effective, efficient vocabulary curriculum for elementary students. In E. H. Hiebert & M. L. Kamil (Eds.), *Teaching and learning vocabulary* (pp. 243–263). Mahwah, NJ: Erlbaum.

Hiebert, E. H. (2011). *WordZones profiler.* Santa Cruz, CA: TextProject.

Hiebert, E. H., & Cervetti, G. N. (2011). *What differences in narrative and informational texts mean for the learning and instruction of vocabulary* (Reading Research Report 11.01). Santa Cruz, CA: TextProject.

Hill, J., & Simha, R. (2016, June). *Automatic generation of context-based fill-in-the-blank exercises using co-occurrence likelihoods and Google n-grams.* Paper presented at the 11th Workshop on Innovative Use of NLP for Building Educational Applications, San Diego, CA.

Hively, W. (1974). Introduction to domain-referenced testing. *Educational Technology, 14,* 5–10.

Hoff, E. (2003). The specificity of environmental influence: Socioeconomic status affects early vocabulary development via maternal speech. *Child Development, 74*(5), 1368–1378.

Hoffmann, T., & Trousdale, G. (Eds.). (2013). *The Oxford handbook of construction grammar.* Oxford, UK: Oxford University Press.

Hsu, C. K., Hwang, G. J., & Chang, C. K. (2013). A personalized recommendation-based mobile learning approach to improving the reading performance of EFL students. *Computers and Education, 63,* 327–336.

Huang, Y. M., Liang, T. H., Su, Y. N., & Chen, N. S. (2012). Empowering personalized learning with an interactive e-book learning system for elementary school students. *Educational Technology Research and Development, 60*(4), 703–722.

Hunt, L. C. (1957). Can we measure specific factors associated with reading comprehension? *Journal of Educational Research, 51*(3), 161–172.

Hutt, M. L. (1947). A clinical study of "consecutive" and "adaptive" testing with the revised Stanford-Binet. *Journal of Consulting Psychology, 11*(2), 93–103.

Ingebrand, S. W., & Connor, C. M. (2017). Assessment-to-instruction (A2i): An online platform for supporting individualized early literacy instruction. In S. A. Crossley & D. S. McNamara (Eds.), *Adaptive educational technologies for literacy instruction* (pp. 33–48). New York: Routledge.

International Reading Association. (1999). *High-stakes assessments in reading: A position statement of the International Reading Association.* Newark, DE: Author.

Jackendoff, R. S. (1972). *Semantic interpretation in generative grammar.* Cambridge, MA: MIT Press.

Janssen, R., & De Boeck, P. (1997). Psychometric modeling of componentially designed synonym tasks. *Applied Psychological Measurement, 21*(1), 37–50.

Jeon, E. H. (2011). Contribution of morphological awareness to second-language reading comprehension. *Modern Language Journal, 95*(2), 217–235.

Johansson, S. E., Atwell, R., Garside G., & Leech, G. (1986). *The Tagged LOB Corpus: User's manual.* Bergen, Norway: Norwegian Computing Centre for the Humanities.

Joseph, H. S., Wonnacott, E., Forbes, P., & Nation, K. (2014). Becoming a written word: Eye movements reveal order of acquisition effects following incidental exposure to new words during silent reading. *Cognition, 133*(1), 238–248.

Juhasz, B. J., & Rayner, K. (2006). The role of age of acquisition and word frequency in reading: Evidence from eye fixation durations. *Visual Cognition, 13*(7–8), 846–863.

Kapantzoglou, M., Restrepo, M. A., & Thompson, M. S. (2012). Dynamic assessment of word learning skills: Identifying language impairment in bilingual children. *Language, Speech, and Hearing Services in Schools, 43*(1), 81–96.

Karlsson, M. (2013). Quantitative and qualitative aspects of advanced learners' L1 and L2 mastery of polysemous words. *Hermes: Journal of Language and Communication Studies, 51*, 79–112.

Kelly, D., & Belkin, N. J. (2001). Reading time, scrolling and interaction: Exploring implicit sources of user preferences for relevance feedback. In *Proceedings of the 24th annual international ACM SIGIR conference on research and development in information retrieval* (pp. 408–409). New York: Association for Computing Machinery.

Keuleers, E., Lacey, P., Rastle, K., & Brysbaert, M. (2012). The British Lexicon Project: Lexical decision data for 28,730 monosyllabic and disyllabic English words. *Behavior Research Methods, 44*(1), 287–304.

Kieffer, M. J., & Lesaux, N. K. (2007). Breaking down words to build meaning: Morphology, vocabulary, and reading comprehension in the urban classroom. *The Reading Teacher, 61*(2), 134–144.

Kieffer, M. J., & Lesaux, N. K. (2012). Direct and indirect roles of morphological awareness in the English reading comprehension of native English, Spanish, Filipino, and Vietnamese speakers. *Language Learning, 62*(4), 1170–1204.

Kilgarriff, A., Baisa, V., Bušta, J., Jakubíček, M., Kovář, V., Michelfeit, J., et al. (2014). The Sketch Engine: Ten years on. *Lexicography, 1*(1), 7–36.

Kilgarriff, A., Husák, M., McAdam, K., Rundell, M., & Rychlý, P. (2008). GDEX: Automatically finding good dictionary examples in a corpus. In *Proceedings of the XIII EURALEX International Congress* (pp. 425–432). Barcelona: Institut Universitari de Linguistica Aplicada.

Kilgarriff, A., Rychlý, P., Smrz, P., & Tugwell, D. (2004). Itri-04–08 the Sketch Engine. *Information Technology, 105*, 116.

Kim, Y., Otaiba, S. A., Puranik, C., Folsom, J. S., Greulich, L., & Wagner, R. K. (2011). Componential skills of beginning writing: An exploratory study. *Learning and Individual Differences, 21*(5), 517–525.

Kingsbury, P., & Palmer, M. (2002). From TreeBank to PropBank. In *Proceedings of the International Conference on Language Resources and Evaluation (LREC)*. Retrieved from *http://lrec.elra.info/proceedings/lrec2002/pdf/283.pdf.*

Kirby, J. R., Deacon, S. H., Bowers, P. N., Izenberg, L., Wade-Woolley, L., & Parrila, R. (2012). Children's morphological awareness and reading ability. *Reading and Writing, 25*(2), 389–410.

Klages, E. (2006). *The green glass sea.* New York: Viking Books for Young Readers.

Korat, O. (2010). Reading electronic books as a support for vocabulary, story comprehension and word reading in kindergarten and first grade. *Computers and Education, 55*(1), 24–31.

Korat, O., & Shamir, A. (2008). The educational electronic book as a tool for supporting children's emergent literacy in low versus middle SES groups. *Computers and Education, 50*(1), 110–124.

Krovetz, R. (1993). Viewing morphology as an inference process. In R. Korfhage, E. Rasmussen, & P. Willet (Eds.), *Proceedings of the 16th Annual International ACM-SIGIR Conference on Research and Development in Information Retrieval* (pp. 191–202). New York: Association for Computing Machinery.

Kučera, H., & Francis, W. (1967). *Computational analysis of present-day American English.* Providence, RI: Brown University Press.

Kulkarni, A., Heilman, M., Eskenazi, M., & Callan, J. (2008). Word sense disambiguation for vocabulary learning. In *Proceedings of the International Conference on Intelligent Tutoring Systems* (pp. 500–509). Berlin: Springer Verlag.

Kuo, L. J., & Anderson, R. C. (2006). Morphological awareness and learning to read: A cross-language perspective. *Educational Psychologist, 41*(3), 161–180.

Kuperman, V., Stadthagen-Gonzalez H., & Brysbaert, M. (2012). Age-of-acquisition ratings for 30,000 English words. *Behavior Research Methods, 44*(4), 978–990.

Lakoff, G., & Johnson, M. (1980). *Metaphors we live by.* Chicago: University of Chicago Press.

Landau, S. I. (1984). *Dictionaries: The art and craft of lexicography.* New York: Scribner.

Landauer, T. K., & Dumais, S. T. (1997). A solution to Plato's problem: The latent semantic analysis theory of acquisition, induction, and representation of knowledge. *Psychological Review, 104*(2), 211.

Landauer, T. K., Foltz, P. W., & Laham, D. (1998). An introduction to latent semantic analysis. *Discourse Processes, 25*(2–3), 259–284.

Landauer, T. K., Kireyev, K., & Panaccione, C. (2011). Word maturity: A new metric for word knowledge. *Scientific Studies of Reading, 15*(1), 92–108.

Landauer, T. K., & May, D. (2012, April). *Improving text complexity measurement through the reading maturity metric.* Paper presented at the annual meeting of the National Council on Measurement in Education Vancouver, BC, Canada.

Landes, S., Leacock, C., & Tengi, R. (1998). Building semantic concordances. In C. Fellbaum (Ed.), *WordNet: An electronic lexical database* (pp. 199–217). Cambridge, MA: MIT Press.

Larsen, J. A., & Nippold, M. A. (2007). Morphological analysis in school-age children: Dynamic assessment of a word learning strategy. *Language, Speech and Hearing Services in Schools, 38*(3), 201–212.

Laufer, B. (2003). Vocabulary acquisition in a second language: Do learners really acquire most vocabulary by reading?: Some empirical evidence. *Canadian Modern Language Review/La Revue Canadienne des Langues Vivantes, 59*(4), 567–587.

Laufer, B. (2011). The contribution of dictionary use to the production and retention of collocations in a second language. *International Journal of Lexicography, 24*(1), 29–49.

Laufer, B. (2014). Vocabulary in a second language: Selection, acquisition, and testing: A commentary on four studies for JALT vocabulary SIG. *Vocabulary Learning and Instruction, 3*(2), 38–46.

Laufer, B., & Nation, P. (1999). A vocabulary-size test of controlled productive ability. *Language Testing, 16*(1), 33–51.

Lave, J., & Wenger, E. (1991). *Situated learning: Legitimate peripheral participation.* Cambridge, UK: Cambridge University Press.

Lawrence, J. F., Hwang, J. K., Deane, P., & Lawless, R. (2015, December). *Exploring the interface of language development and semantic knowledge with depth measures of academic vocabulary.* Paper presented at the 65th annual Conference of the Literacy Research Association, Carlsbad, CA.

Lederer, R. (1989). *Crazy English: The ultimate joy ride through our language.* New York: Pocket Books.

Lee, J., & Seneff, S. (2007). *Automatic generation of cloze items for prepositions. Proceedings of the 2007 INTERSPEECH conference* (pp. 2173–2176). Red Hook, NY: Curran Associates, Inc.

Leech, G. (1992). 100 million words of English: The British National Corpus (BNC). *Language Research, 28*(1), 1–13.

Leech, G., & Rayson, P. (2014). *Word frequencies in written and spoken English: Based on the British National Corpus.* New York: Routledge.

Leighton, J., & Gierl, M. (Eds.). (2007). *Cognitive diagnostic assessment for education: Theory and applications.* Cambridge, UK: Cambridge University Press.

Lemon, O. (2012). Conversational interfaces. In O. Pietquin & O. Lemon (Eds.), *Data-driven methods for adaptive spoken dialogue systems* (pp. 1–4). New York: Springer.

Lennon, C., & Burdick, H. (2004). The Lexile framework as an approach for reading measurement and success. Available at *www.lexile.com.*

Lesaux, N. K., Kieffer, M. J., Faller, E., & Kelley, J. (2010). The effectiveness and ease of implementation of an academic vocabulary intervention for linguistically diverse students in urban middle schools. *Reading Research Quarterly, 45*(2), 198–230.

Levenston, E. A., Nir, N., & Blum-Kulka, S. (1984). Discourse analysis and the testing of reading comprehension by cloze techniques. In A. K. Pugh & J. M. Ulijn (Eds.), *Reading for professional purposes: Studies and practices in native and foreign languages* (pp. 202–212). London: Heinemann Educational.

Levin, B. (1993). *English verb classes and alternations: A preliminary investigation.* Chicago: University of Chicago Press.

Levy, M., & Stockwell, G. (2013). *CALL dimensions: Options and issues in computer-assisted language learning.* New York: Routledge.

Lewis, C. S. (1955). *The magician's nephew* (*The Chronicles of Narnia*, Book 6). New York: Collier Books.

Lidz, C. S. E. (1987). *Dynamic assessment: An interactional approach to evaluating learning potential.* New York: Guilford Press.

Lin, Y. C., Sung, L. C., & Chen, M. C. (2007, November). *An automatic multiple-choice question generation scheme for English adjective understanding.* Paper presented at the Workshop on Modeling, Management and Generation of Problems/Questions in eLearning, the 15th International Conference on Computers in Education.

Liu, C.-L., Wang, C.-H., Gao, Z.-M., & Huang, S.-M. (2005). *Applications of lexical information for algorithmically composing multiple-choice cloze items.* Paper presented at the second annual Workshop on Building Educational Applications Using NLP, Ann Arbor, MI.

Liu, J., Dolan, P., & Pedersen, E. R. (2010, February). *Personalized news recommendation based on click behavior.* Paper presented at the 15th International Conference on Intelligent User Interfaces, Hong Kong.

Liu, L., Mostow, J., & Aist, G. S. (2013). Generating example contexts to help children learn word meaning. *Natural Language Engineering, 19*(2), 187–212.

Liu, X., Croft, W. B., Oh, P., & Hart, D. (2004, July). *Automatic recognition of reading levels from user queries.* Paper presented at the 27th annual International ACM SIGIR Conference on Research and Development in Information Retrieval, Sheffield, UK.

Longman Dictionary of American English. (5th ed.). (2014). Hoboken: Longman.

Lorge, I. (1939). Predicting reading difficulty of selections for children. *Elementary English Review, 16*(6), 229–233.

Lorge, I. (1948). The Lorge and Flesch readability formulas: A correction. *School and Society, 67,* 141–142.

Lund, K., & Burgess, C. (1996). Producing high-dimensional semantic spaces from lexical co-occurrence. *Behavior Research Methods, Instruments, and Computers, 28,* 203–208.

Ma, Q. (2013). Computer assisted vocabulary learning: Framework and tracking user data. In P. Hubbard, M. Schulze, & B. Smith (Eds.), *Learner-computer interaction in language education* (pp. 230–243). San Marcos, TX: Computer Assisted Language Instruction Consortium.

MacGinitie, W. H., MacGinitie, R. K., Maria, K., Dreyer, L. G., & Hughes, K. E. (2000). *Gates–MacGinitie reading tests* (4th ed.). Orlando, FL: Houghton Mifflin Harcourt.

Madnani, N., Burstein, J., Sabatini, J., Biggers, K., & Andreyev, S. (2016). *Language Muse^{TM}: Automated linguistic activity generation for English language learners.* Paper presented at the annual meeting of the Association for Computational Linguistics, Berlin, Germany.

Mair, C. (1997). Parallel corpora: A real-time approach to the study of language change in progress. In M. Ljung (Ed.), *Corpus-based studies in English.*

Proceedings of the Seventeenth International Conference on Language Research on Computerized Corpora (ICAME 17) (pp. 195–209). Amsterdam: Rodopi.

Makni, F. (2014). Applying cognitive linguistics to teaching polysemous vocabulary. *Arab World English Journal, 5*(1), 4–20.

Marcus, M. P., Marcinkiewicz, M. A., & Santorini, B. (1993). Building a large annotated corpus of English: The Penn Treebank. *Computational Linguistics, 19*(2), 313–330.

Marzano, R. J. (2004). *Building background knowledge for academic achievement: Research on what works in schools.* Alexandria, VA: Association for Supervision and Curriculum Development.

Marzano, R. J., & Simms, J. A. (2011). *Vocabulary for the Common Core.* Bloomington, IN: Solution Tree Press.

Mason, J. M., Kniseley, E., & Kendall, J. (1979). Effects of polysemous words on sentence comprehension. *Reading Research Quarterly, 15*(1), 49–65.

Maxwell, L. A. (2014). U.S. school enrollment hits majority–minority milestone. *Education Week, 33*(37). Retrieved from *www.edweek.org/ew/arti cles/2014/08/20/01demographics.h34.html.*

McBride, J. R., & Weiss, D. J. (1974). *A word knowledge pool for adaptive ability measurement* (Research Report 74-2). Minneapolis: Department of Psychology, Minnesota University.

McCutchen, D. (1996). A capacity theory of writing: Working memory in composition. *Educational Psychology Review, 8*(3), 299–325.

McCutchen, D. (2011). From novice to expert: Language and memory processes in the development of writing skill. *Journal of Writing Research, 3*(1), 51–68.

McKeown, M. G. (1985). The acquisition of word meaning from context by children of high and low ability. *Reading Research Quarterly, 20*(4), 482–496.

McKeown, M. G. (1993). Creating effective definitions for young word learners. *Reading Research Quarterly, 28*(1), 16–31.

McKeown, M. G., & Beck, I. L. (2014). Effects of vocabulary instruction on measures of language processing: Comparing two approaches. *Early Childhood Research Quarterly, 29*(4), 520–530.

McKeown, M. G., Beck, I. L., & Apthorp, H. (2011, April). *Examining depth of processing in vocabulary lessons.* Paper presented at the annual conference of the American Educational Research Association, New Orleans, LA.

McKeown, M. G., Beck, I. L., Omanson, R. C., & Pople, M. T. (1985). Some effects of the nature and frequency of vocabulary instruction on the knowledge and use of words. *Reading Research Quarterly, 20*(5), 522–535.

McKeown, M. G., Crosson, A. C., Artz, N. J., Sandora, C., & Beck, I. L. (2013). In the media: Expanding students' experience with academic vocabulary. *The Reading Teacher, 67*(1), 45–53.

McKeown, M. G., Crosson, A., Beck, I., Sandora, C., & Artz, N. (2012). *Robust Academic Vocabulary Encounters (RAVE).* Intervention developed for Robust Instruction of Academic Vocabulary for Middle School

Students grant, Institute of Education Sciences, U.S. Department of Education (No. R305A100440).

McNamara, D. S., Crossley, S. A., & McCarthy, P. M. (2009). Linguistic features of writing quality. *Written Communication, 27*(1), 57–86.

McNamara, D. S., Kintsch, E., Songer, N. B., & Kintsch, W. (1996). Are good texts always better?: Interactions of text coherence, background knowledge, and levels of understanding in learning from text. *Cognition and instruction, 14*(1), 1–43.

McNamara, D. S., Louwerse, M. M., & Graesser, A. C. (2002). *Coh-Metrix: Automated cohesion and coherence scores to predict text readability and facilitate comprehension.* Technical report, Institute for Intelligent Systems, University of Memphis, Memphis, TN.

Meara, P. & Buxton, B. (1987). An alternative to multiple choice vocabulary tests. *Language Testing, 4*, 142–145.

Merriam-Webster's collegiate dictionary (11th ed.). (2014). Springfield, MA: Merriam-Webster.

Mesmer, H. A. E. (2008). *Tools for matching readers to texts: Research-based practices.* New York: Guilford Press.

Meyer, S. (2005). *The twilight saga collection.* New York: Little, Brown.

Mihalcea, R. (2011). Word sense disambiguation. In *Encyclopedia of machine learning* (pp. 1027–1030). New York: Springer.

Miller, G. A. (1995). WordNet: A lexical database for English. *Communications of the ACM, 38*(11), 39–41.

Miller, G. A., & Gildea, P. M. (1985). How to misread a dictionary. *AILA Bulletin*, 13–26.

Miller, G. A., & Gildea, P. M. (1987). How children learn words. *Scientific American, 257*(3), 94–99.

Miller, T. F., Gage-Serio, O., & Scott, J. A. (2010). Word consciousness in practice: Illustrations from a fourth-grade teacher's classroom. In R. T. Jimenez, V. J. Risko, M. Hundley, & D. W. Rowe, (Eds.), *59th annual yearbook of the National Reading Conference* (pp. 171–186). Oak Creek, WI: National Reading Conference.

Millman, J. (1974). Criterion-referenced measurement. In W. J. Popham (Ed.), *Evaluation in Education: Current applications* (pp. 311–387). Berkeley, CA: McCutchan.

Millman, J., & Westman, R. S. (1989). Computer-assisted writing of achievement test items: Toward a future technology. *Journal of Educational Measurement, 26*(2), 177–190.

Milone, M. (2009). *The development of ATOS: The Renaissance readability formula.* Wisconsin Rapids, WI: Renaissance Learning.

Miltsakaki, E. (2009). Matching readers' preferences and reading skills with appropriate web texts. In *Proceedings of the 12th Conference of the European Chapter of the Association for Computational Linguistics: Demonstrations Session* (pp. 49–52). Stroudsburg, PA: Association for Computational Linguistics.

Miltsakaki, E., & Troutt, A. (2008). Real-time web text classification and analysis of reading difficulty. In J. Tetreault, J. Burstein, & R. De Felice (Eds.),

Proceedings of the Third Workshop on Innovative Use of NLP for Building Educational Applications (pp. 89–97). Stroudsburg, PA: Association for Computational Linguistics.

Mislevy, R. J., Almond, R. G., & Lukas, J. F. (2003). A brief introduction to evidence-centered design. *ETS Research Report* (RR-03-16), i–29.

Moloney, K. (2016). Verbum-struct-ion [User blog]. Available at *http://verbumnosvocat.com.*

Monaghan, P., & Ellis, A. W. (2010). Modeling reading development: Cumulative, incremental learning in a computational model of word naming. *Journal of Memory and Language, 63*(4), 506–525.

Moon, R. (1998). Frequencies and forms of phrasal lexemes in English. In A. Cowie (Ed.), *Phraseology: Theory, analysis, and applications* (pp. 79–100). Oxford: Oxford University Press.

Morris, W. (Ed.). (1969). *The American heritage dictionary of the English language.* New York: Houghton Mifflin.

Morrison, C. M., Chappell, T. D., & Ellis, A. W. (1997). Age of acquisition norms for a large set of object names and their relation to adult estimates and other variables. *Quarterly Journal of Experimental Psychology: Section A, 50*(3), 528–559.

Morrison, C. M., & Ellis, A. W. (1995). Roles of word frequency and age-of-acquisition in word naming and lexical decision. *Journal of Experimental Psychology, 21*(1), 116.

Morrison, C. M., & Ellis, A. W. (2000). Real age-of-acquisition effects in word naming and lexical decision. *British Journal of Psychology, 91*(2), 167–180.

Morrison, C. M., Ellis, A. W., & Quinlan, P. T. (1992). Age-of-acquisition, not word frequency, affects object naming, not object recognition. *Memory and Cognition, 20*(6), 705–714.

Mostow, J. (2001). Evaluating tutors that listen: An overview of Project LISTEN. In K. Forbus & P. Feltovich, (Eds.), *Smart Machines in Education: The coming revolution in educational technology* (pp. 169–234). Menlo Park, CA: American Association for Artificial Intelligence.

Mostow, J., Burkhead, P., Corbett, A., Cuneo, A., Eitelman, S., Huang, C., et al. (2003). Evaluation of an automated reading tutor that listens: Comparison to human tutoring and classroom instruction. *Journal of Educational Computing Research, 29*(1), 61–117.

Mostow, J., Hauptmann, A. G., Chase, L. L. & Roth, S. (1993). Towards a reading coach that listens: Automatic detection of oral reading errors. In *Proceedings of the Eleventh Conference on Artificial Intelligence* (pp. 392–397). Burlington, MA: Morgan Kaufmann.

Mostow, J., & Jang, H. (2012). Generating diagnostic multiple choice comprehension cloze questions. In *Proceedings of the Seventh Workshop on Building Educational Applications Using NLP* (pp. 136–146). Stroudsburg, PA: Association for Computational Linguistics.

Mostow, J., Roth, S. F., Hauptmann, A. G., & Kane, M. (1994). A prototype reading coach that listens. In *Proceedings of the National Conference on Artificial Intelligence* (pp. 785–792). Hoboken, NJ: Wiley.

Murray, J. (Ed.). (1884). *Oxford English dictionary.* London: Oxford University Press.

Nagy, W. E. (2007). Metalinguistic awareness and the vocabulary–comprehension connection. In R. K. Wagner, A. E. Muse, & K. R. Tannenbaum (Eds.), *Vocabulary acquisition: Implications for reading comprehension* (pp. 52–77). New York: Guilford Press.

Nagy, W. E., & Anderson, R. C. (1984). How many words are there in printed school English? *Reading Research Quarterly, 19*(3), 304–330.

Nagy, W. E., Anderson, R. C., & Herman, P. A. (1987). Learning word meanings from context during normal reading. *American Educational Research Journal, 24*(2), 237–270.

Nagy, W. E., Anderson, R. C., Schommer, M., Scott, J. A., & Stallman, A. C. (1989). Morphological families in the internal lexicon. *Reading Research Quarterly, 24*(3), 262–282.

Nagy, W. E., Berninger, V. W., & Abbott, R. D. (2006). Contributions of morphology beyond phonology to literacy outcomes of upper elementary and middle-school students. *Journal of Educational Psychology, 98*(1), 134.

Nagy, W. E., & Herman, P. A. (1987). Breadth and depth of vocabulary knowledge: Implications for acquisition and instruction. In M. G. McKeown & M. E. Curtis (Eds.), *The nature of vocabulary acquisition* (pp. 19–36). Hillsdale, NJ: Erlbaum.

Nagy, W. E., & Hiebert, E. H. (2010). Toward a theory of word selection. In M. L. Kamil, P. D. Pearson, E. B. Moje, & P. P. Afflerbach (Eds.), *Handbook of reading research* (Vol. 4, pp. 388–404). New York: Routledge.

Nagy, W. E., & Scott, J. (1990). Word schemas: What do people know about words they don't know. *Cognition and Instruction, 7*(2), 105–127.

Nagy, W. E., & Scott, J. A. (2000). Vocabulary processes. In M. L. Kamil, P. B. Mosenthal, P. D. Pearson, & R. Barr (Eds.), *Handbook of reading research* (Vol. 3, pp. 69–284). Mahwah, NJ: Erlbaum.

Nagy, W. E., & Townsend, D. (2012). Words as tools: Learning academic vocabulary as language acquisition. *Reading Research Quarterly, 47*(1), 91–108.

Nation, I. S. P. (2001). *Learning vocabulary in another language.* Cambridge, UK: Cambridge University Press.

Nation, I. S. P. (2006). How large a vocabulary is needed for reading and listening? *Canadian Modern Language Review/La Revue Canadienne des Langues Vivantes, 63*(1), 59–82.

National Assessment Governing Board. (2008). *Reading Framework for the 2009 National Assessment of Educational Progress* [Developed for the National Assessment Governing Board under contract number ED-02-R-0007 by the American Institutes for Research]. Washington, DC: U.S. Department of Education.

National Governors Association Center for Best Practices & Council of Chief State School Officers. (2010). *Common Core State Standards for English language arts and literacy, history/social studies, science, and technical subjects.* Washington, DC: Author.

Nelson, J., Perfetti, C., Liben, D., & Liben, M. (2012). *Measures of text difficulty: Testing their predictive value for grade levels and student performance*. New York: Student Achievement Partners.

Neuman, S. B., & Wright, T. S. (2015). *All about words: Increasing vocabulary in the Common Core classroom, pre-K–2*. New York: Teachers College Press.

Nishikawa, H., Makino, T., & Matsuo, Y. (2013). A pilot study on readability prediction with reading time. In *Proceedings of the Second Workshop on Predicting and Improving Readability for Target Reader Populations* (pp. 78–84). Stroudsburg, PA: Association for Computational Linguistics.

Nye, B. D., Graesser, A. C., & Hu, X. (2014). AutoTutor and family: A review of 17 years of natural language tutoring. *International Journal of Artificial Intelligence in Education, 24*(4), 427–469.

Olinghouse, N. G., & Graham, S. (2009). The relationship between the discourse knowledge and the writing performance of elementary-grade students. *Journal of Educational Psychology, 101*(1), 37–50.

Olinghouse, N. G., & Wilson, J. (2013). The relationship between vocabulary and writing quality in three genres. *Reading and Writing, 26*(1), 45–65.

Osgood, C. E., Suci, G. J., & Tannenbaum, P. H. (1957). *The measurement of meaning*. Urbana: University of Illinois Press.

Pacheco, M. B., & Goodwin, A. P. (2013). Putting two and two together: Middle school students' morphological problem solving strategies for unknown words. *Journal of Adolescent and Adult Literacy, 56*(7), 541–553.

Palmer, M., Gildea, D., & Kingsbury, P. (2005). The Proposition Bank: A corpus annotated with semantic roles. *Computational Linguistics Journal, 31*(1), 71–106.

Palmeri, T. J., Wong, A. C., & Gauthier, I. (2004). Computational approaches to the development of perceptual expertise. *Trends in Cognitive Sciences, 8*(8), 378–386.

Panman, O. (1982). Homonymy and polysemy. *Lingua, 58*(1–2), 105–136.

Paribakht, T. S., & Wesche, M. (1999). "Incidental" and instructed L2 vocabulary acquisition: Different contexts, common processes. In D. Albrechtsen, B. Henriksen, I. Mees, & E. Poulsen (Eds.), *Perspectives on foreign and second language pedagogy* (pp. 203–220). Copenhagen, Denmark: Odense University Press.

Parish, P. (1963). *Amelia Bedelia*. New York: Holt, Rinehart and Winston.

Parker, R., Graff, D., Kong, J., Chen, K., & Maeda, K. (2011). *English gigaword* (5th ed.). Philadelphia: Linguistic Data Consortium.

Partnership for Assessment of Readiness for College and Careers. (2016). New York: Pearson. Retrieved July 7, 2016, from *https://parcc.pearson.com/resources/practice-tests/english/grade-4/eoy/PC1100538_4ELAPTLP.pdf*.

Paterson, K. (1977). *Bridge to Terabithia*. New York: Thomas Y. Crowell.

Pavlik, P., & Anderson, J. R. (2005). Practice and forgetting effects on vocabulary memory: An activation based model of the spacing effect. *Cognitive Science, 29*(4), 559–586.

Pearson, P. D., Hiebert, E. H., & Kamil, M. L. (2007). Vocabulary assessment:

What we know and what we need to learn. *Reading Research Quarterly, 42*(2), 282–296.

Pearson, P. D., Hiebert, E. H., & Kamil, M. L. (2012). Vocabulary assessment: Making do with what we have while we create the tools we need. In J. Baumann & E. Kame'enui (Eds.), *Vocabulary instruction: Research to practice* (2nd ed., pp. 231–255). New York: Guilford Press.

Pellicer-Sánchez, A., & Schmitt, N. (2012). Scoring yes–no vocabulary tests: Reaction time versus nonword approaches. *Language Testing, 29*(12), 489–509.

Perfetti, C. A. (2007). Reading ability: Lexical quality to comprehension. *Scientific Studies of Reading, 11*(4), 357–383.

Perfetti, C. A., & Adlof, S. M. (2012). Reading comprehension: A conceptual framework from word meaning to text meaning. In J. P. Sabatini, E. R. Alboro, & T. O'Riley (Eds.), *Measuring up: Advances in how to assess reading ability* (pp. 3–20). Lanham, MD: Rowman & Littlefield Education.

Perfetti, C. A., & Hart, L. (2002). The lexical quality hypothesis. In L. Verhoeven, C. Elbro, & P. Reitsma (Eds.), *Precursors of functional literacy* (Published as Vol. 11 of the series Studies in Written Language and Literacy). Philadelphia: John Benjamins.

Perfetti, C. A., & Stafura, J. Z. (2015). Comprehending implicit meanings in text without making inferences. In E. J. O'Brien, A. E. Cook, & R. F. Lorch (Eds.), *Inferences during reading* (pp. 1–18). Cambridge, UK: Cambridge University Press.

Perfetti, C. A., Yang, C. L., & Schmalhofer, F. (2008). Comprehension skill and word-to-text integration processes. *Applied Cognitive Psychology, 22*(3), 303–318.

Pinker, S. (2015). *The sense of style: The thinking person's guide to writing in the 21st century.* New York: Penguin.

Pino, J., & Eskenazi, M. (2009). Semi-automatic generation of cloze question distractors effect of students' L1. In *Proceedings of the SLaTE Workshop on Speech and Language Technology in Education* (pp. 65–68). Retrieved from *www.cs.cmu.edu/~max/mainpage_files/Pino-Eskenazi-SLaTE09.pdf.*

Pino, J., Heilman, M., & Eskenazi, M. (2008, June). *A selection strategy to improve cloze question quality.* Paper presented at the Workshop on Intelligent Tutoring Systems for Ill-Defined Domains, 9th International Conference on Intelligent Tutoring Systems, Montreal, Qubec, Canada.

Pitler, E., & Nenkova, A. (2008). Revisiting readability: A unified framework for predicting text quality. In *Proceedings of the Conference on Empirical Methods in Natural Language Processing* (pp. 186–195). Stroudsburg, PA: Association for Computational Linguistics.

Postman, L., & Keppel, G. (1970). *Norms of word association.* New York: Academic Press.

Pustejovsky, J. (1998). *The Generative Lexicon.* Cambridge, MA: MIT Press.

Qian, D. (1999). Assessing the roles of depth and breadth of vocabulary knowledge in reading comprehension. *Canadian Modern Language Review, 56*(2), 282–308.

RAND Reading Study Group. (2002). *Reading for understanding: Toward a research and development program in reading comprehension*. Washington, DC: U.S. Department of Education.

Rankin, E. F., & Culhane, J. (1969). Comparable cloze and multiple-choice comprehension test scores. *Journal of Reading, 13*(3), 193–198.

Rashidi, N. (2013). Teaching English polysemous words to Iranian EFL learners: Underlying meaning approach and sense selection in comparison. *Journal of Language, Culture, and Translation, 2*(1), 83–101.

Rayner, K. (1998). Eye movements in reading and information processing: 20 years of research. *Psychological Bulletin, 124*(3), 372–422.

Read, J. (1993). The development of a new measure of L2 vocabulary knowledge. *Language Testing, 10*(3), 355–371.

Read, J. (1998). Validating a test to measure depth of vocabulary knowledge. In A. Kunnan (Ed.), *Validation in language assessment* (pp. 41–60). Mahwah, NJ: Erlbaum.

Read, J. (2008). Identifying academic language needs through diagnostic assessment. *Journal of English for Academic Purposes, 7*(3), 180–190.

Read, J., & Chapelle, C. A. (2001). A framework for second language vocabulary assessment. *Language Testing, 18*(1), 1–32.

Reichle, E. D., & Perfetti, C. A. (2003). Morphology in word identification: A word-experience model that accounts for morpheme frequency effects. *Scientific Studies of Reading, 7*(3), 219–237.

Richter, T., Isberner, M. B., Naumann, J., & Neeb, Y. (2013). Lexical quality and reading comprehension in primary school children. *Scientific Studies of Reading, 17*(6), 415–434.

Roid, G. H., & Haladyna, T. M. (1978). A comparison of objective-based and modified-Bormuth item writing techniques. *Educational and Psychological Measurement, 38*(1), 19–28.

Rosa, K. D., & Eskenazi, M. (2013). Self-assessment in the REAP tutor: Knowledge, interest, motivation, and learning. *International Journal of Artificial Intelligence in Education, 21*(4), 237–253.

Rosch, E. (1999). Principles of categorization. In E. Margolis & S. Laurence (Eds.), *Concepts: Core readings* (pp. 189–206). Cambridge, MA: MIT Press.

Rowe, M. L., Raudenbush, S. W., & Goldin-Meadow, S. (2012). The pace of vocabulary growth helps predict later vocabulary skill. *Child Development, 83*(2), 508–525.

Rumelhart, D. E. (1994). *Toward an interactive model of reading*. Newark, DE: International Reading Association.

Ryan, P. M. (2002). *Esperanza rising*. New York: Scholastic.

Sandora, C., Beck, I. L., & McKeown, M. G. (1999). A comparison of two discussion strategies on students' comprehension and interpretation of complex literature. *Reading Psychology, 20*(3), 177–212.

Sasao, Y., & Webb, S. (2017). The Word Part Levels Test. *Language Teaching Research, 21*(1), 12–30.

Scarborough, H. S. (2005). Developmental relationships between language and reading: Reconciling a beautiful hypothesis with some ugly facts. In H.

W. Catts & A. G. Kamhi (Eds.), *The connections between language and learning disabilities* (pp. 3–24). Mahwah, NJ: Erlbaum.

Schmitt, D., Schmitt, N., & Mann, D. (2011). *Focus on vocabulary: Bridging vocabulary.* New York: Longman.

Schmitt, N. (1998a). Quantifying word association responses: What is native-like? *System, 26*(3), 389–401.

Schmitt, N. (1998b). Measuring collocational knowledge: Key issues and an experimental assessment procedure. *Institut voor Togepaste Linguistik, 119*(20), 27–47.

Schmitt, N. (2010). *Researching vocabulary: A vocabulary research manual.* New York: Palgrave Macmillan.

Schmitt, N. (2014). Size and depth of vocabulary knowledge: What the research shows. *Language Learning, 64*(4), 913–951.

Schmitt, N., & Schmitt, D. (2014). A reassessment of frequency and vocabulary size in L2 vocabulary teaching. *Language Teaching, 47*(4), 484–503.

Schmitt, N., & Zimmerman, C. B. (2002) Derivative word forms: What do learners know? *TESOL Quarterly, 36*(2), 145–171.

School Renaissance Institute, Inc. (2000). *The ATOS[TM] readability formula for books and how it compares to other formulas.* Madison, WI: Author.

Schuler, K. K. (2005). *VerbNet: A broad-coverage, comprehensive verb lexicon.* Doctoral dissertation, University of Pennsylvania.

Schwanenflugel, P. J., Stahl, S. A., & McFalls, E. L. (1997). Partial word knowledge and vocabulary growth during reading comprehension. *Journal of Literacy Research, 29*(4), 531–553.

Score, H. B. (1905). *The elephant and the crocodile.* Public domain.

Scott, J., Lubliner, S., & Hiebert, E. H. (2006). Constructs underlying word selection and assessments tasks in the archival research on vocabulary instruction. In C. M. Fairbanks, J. Worthy, B. Maloch, J. Hoffman, & D. Schallert (Eds.), *National Reading Conference yearbook* (pp. 264–275). Oak Creek, WI: National Reading Conference.

Scott, J. A. (2015). Essential, enjoyable and effective: The what, why and how of powerful vocabulary instruction. *Literacy Learning: Middle Years, 23*(1), 14–23.

Scott, J. A., Flinspach, S., & Vevea, J. (2011). *Identifying and teaching vocabulary in fourth- and fifth-grade math and science.* Paper presented at the annual meeting of the National Reading Conference/Literacy Research Association, Jacksonville, FL.

Scott, J. A., Flinspach, S. L., Vevea, J. L., & Castaneda, R. (2015). *Vocabulary knowledge as a multidimensional concept: A six factor model.* Poster at the annual meeting of the Society for the Scientific Study of Reading, Hapuna Beach, HI.

Scott, J. A., Hoover, M., Flinspach, S. L. & Vevea, J. L. (2008). A multiple-level vocabulary assessment tool: Measuring word knowledge based on grade level materials. In Y. Kim, V. J. Risko, D. L. Compton, D. K. Dickinson, M. K. Hundley, R. T. Jimenz, et al. (Eds.), *57th annual yearbook of the National Reading Conference* (pp. 325–340). Oak Creek, WI: National Reading Conference.

Scott, J. A., Jamieson-Noel, D., & Asselin, M. (2003). Vocabulary instruction throughout the day in twenty-three Canadian upper elementary classrooms. *Elementary School Journal, 103*(3), 269–286.

Scott, J. A., Miller, T. F., & Flinspach, S. L. (2012). Developing word consciousness: Lessons from highly diverse fourth-grade classrooms. In J. Baumann & E. Kame'enui (Eds.), *Vocabulary instruction: From research to practice* (2nd ed., pp. 169–188). New York: Guilford Press.

Scott, J. A., & Nagy, W. E. (1997). Understanding the definitions of unfamiliar verbs. *Reading Research Quarterly, 32*(2), 184–200.

Scott, J. A., & Nagy, W. E. (2004). Developing word consciousness. In J. F. Baumann & E. J. Kame'euni (Eds.), *Vocabulary instruction: Research to practice* (pp. 201–217). New York: Guilford Press.

Scott, J. A., Nagy, W. E., & Flinspach, S. L. (2008). More than merely words: Redefining vocabulary learning in a culturally and linguistically diverse society. In A. E. Farstrup & S. J. Samuels (Eds.), *What research has to say about vocabulary instruction* (pp. 182–209). Newark, DE: International Reading Association.

Scott, J. A., Skobel, B. J., & Wells, J. (2008). *The word conscious classroom: Building the vocabulary readers and writers need.* New York: Scholastic.

Scott, J. A., Vevea, J. L., Castaneda, R., & Flinspach, S. L. (2017). *Depth and multidimensionality in vocabulary assessment: A six factor model.* Manuscript under review.

Scott, J. A., & Wells, J. (1998). Readers take responsibility: Literature circles and the growth of critical thinking. In K. Beers & B. Samuels (Eds.), *Into focus: Understanding and supporting middle school readers.* Norwood, MA: Christopher-Gordon.

Shanahan, T., Kamil, M. L., & Tobin, A. W. (1982). Cloze as a measure of intersentential comprehension. *Reading Research Quarterly, 17*(2), 229–255.

Sheehan, K. M., Flor, M., & Napolitano, D. (2013, June). *A two-stage approach for generating unbiased estimates of text complexity.* Paper presented at the Workshop on Natural Language Processing for Improving Textual Accessibility, Atlanta, GA.

Sheehan, K. M., Kostin, I., & Futagi, Y. (2007). *Reading level assessment for literary and expository texts.* Paper presented at the 29th annual conference of the Cognitive Science Society, Nashville, TN.

Sheehan, K. M., Kostin, I., & Futagi, Y. (2008). *When do standard approaches for measuring vocabulary difficulty, syntactic complexity and referential cohesion yield biased estimates of text difficulty?* Paper presented at the 30th annual conference of the Cognitive Science Society, Washington, DC.

Sheehan, K. M., Kostin, I., Futagi, Y., & Flor, M. (2010). Generating automated text complexity classifications that are aligned with targeted text complexity standards. *ETS Research Report* (RR-10-28), i–44.

Shiotsu, T. (2010). *Components of L2 reading: Linguistic and processing factors in the reading test performances of Japanese EFL learners.* Cambridge, UK: Cambridge University Press.

Shore, W. J., & Durso, F. T. (1990). Partial knowledge in vocabulary acquisition:

General constraints and specific detail. *Journal of Educational Psychology, 82*(2), 315–318.

Shute, V. J. (2011). Stealth assessment in computer-based games to support learning. In S. Tobias & J. D. Fletcher (Eds.), *Computer games and instruction* (pp. 503–524). Charlotte, NC: Information Age.

Shute, V. J., Graf, E. A., & Hansen, E. (2006). Designing adaptive, diagnostic math assessments for individuals with and without visual disabilities. *ETS Research Report* (RR-06-01). Princeton, NJ: Educational Testing Service.

Shute, V. J., & Kim, Y. J. (2014). Formative and stealth assessment. In M. Spector, M. D. Merrill, J. Elen, & M. J. Bishop (Eds.), *Handbook of research on educational communications and technology* (pp. 311–321). New York: Springer.

Shute, V. J., Ventura, M., Bauer, M., & Zapata-Rivera, D. (2009). Melding the power of serious games and embedded assessment to monitor and foster learning. In U. Ritterfeld, M. Cody, & P. Vorderer (Eds.), *Serious games: Mechanisms and effects* (pp. 295–321). New York: Routledge.

Shute, V. J., & Zapata-Rivera, D. (2010). Intelligent systems. *International encyclopedia of education* (Vol. 4, pp. 75–80). Oxford, UK: Elsevier.

Simpson, G., & McCarthy, D. (2005) *Corpus linguistics: Readings in a widening discipline*. London: Continuum.

Simpson, R. (2002). *MICASE: The Michigan corpus of academic spoken English*. Ann Arbor: University of Michigan.

Sinclair, J. M. (Ed.). (1987). *Looking up: An account of the COBUILD project in lexical computing and the development of the Collins COBUILD English language dictionary*. London: Collins ELT.

Singley, M. K., & Bennett, R. E. (2002). Item generation and beyond: Applications of schema theory to mathematics assessment. In S. H. Irvine & P. C. Kyllonen (Eds.), *Generating items for cognitive tests: Theory and practice* (pp. 361–384). Mahwah, NJ: Erlbaum.

Sireci, S. G. (2012). *Smarter balanced assessment consortium: Comprehensive research agenda*. Report prepared for the Smarter Balanced Assessment Consortium. Retrieved January 2017, from *https://portal.smarterbalanced.org/library/en/comprehensive-research-agenda.pdf*.

Skory, A., & Eskenazi, M. (2010). Predicting cloze task quality for vocabulary training. In *Proceedings of the NAACL HLT 2010 Fifth Workshop on Innovative Use of NLP for Building Educational Applications* (pp. 49–56). Stroudsburg, PA: Association for Computational Linguistics.

Smeets, D. J., & Bus, A. G. (2012). Interactive electronic storybooks for kindergartners to promote vocabulary growth. *Journal of Experimental Child Psychology, 112*(1), 36–55.

Smith, D. R., Stenner, A. J., Horabin, I., & Smith, M. (1989). *The Lexile scale in theory and practice: Final report*. Washington, DC: Metametrics.

Smith, N. J., & Levy, R. (2013). The effect of word predictability on reading time is logarithmic. *Cognition, 128*(3), 302–319.

Snow, C. E., Lawrence, J. F., & White, C. (2009). Generating knowledge of academic language among urban middle school students. *Journal of Research on Educational Effectiveness, 2*(4), 325–344.

Snow, C. E., Tabors, P. O., Nicholson, P., & Kurland, B. (1995). SHELL: Oral language and early literacy skills in kindergarten and first grade children. *Journal of Research in Childhood Education, 10*, 37–48.

Spache, G. (1953). A new readability formula for primary-grade reading materials. *Elementary School Journal, 53*(7), 410–413.

Spearritt, D. (1972). Identification of subskills of reading comprehension by maximum likelihood factor analysis. *Reading Research Quarterly, 8*(1), 92.

Spira, E. G., Bracken, S. S., & Fischel, J. E. (2005). Predicting improvement after first-grade reading difficulties: The effects of oral language, emergent literacy, and behavior skills. *Developmental Psychology, 41*(1), 225–234.

Stahl, S. A. (1998). Four questions about vocabulary knowledge and reading and some answers. In C. Hynd (Ed.), *Learning from text across conceptual domains* (pp. 15–44). Mahwah, NJ: Erlbaum.

Stahl, S. A. (2003). Vocabulary and readability: How knowing word meanings affects comprehension. *Top Language Disorders, 23*(3), 241–247.

Stahl, S. A. (2009). Words are learned incrementally over multiple exposures. In M. F. Graves (Ed.), *Essential readings on vocabulary instruction* (pp. 69–71). Newark, DE: International Reading Association.

Stahl, S. A., & Nagy, W. E. (2006). *Teaching word meanings*. Mahwah, NJ: Erlbaum.

Stanovich, K. E. (1986). Matthew effects in reading: Some consequences of individual differences in the acquisition of literacy. *Reading Research Quarterly, 21*(4), 360–407.

Stanovich, K. E. (2000). *Progress in understanding reading: Scientific foundations and new frontiers*. New York: Guilford Press.

Stenner, A. J. (1996). *Measuring reading comprehension with the Lexile framework*. Paper presented at the California Comparability Symposium.

Stenner, A. J., Burdick, H., Sanford, E. E., & Burdick, D. S. (2007). *The Lexile framework for reading: Technical report*. Washington, DC: MetaMetrics.

Sternberg, R. J. (1998). Abilities are forms of developing expertise. *Educational Researcher, 27*(3), 11–20.

Stevenson, A. (Ed.). (2010). *Oxford English Dictionary* (3rd ed.). Oxford, UK: Oxford University Press.

Stevenson, M., & Wilks, Y. (2003). Word sense disambiguation. In R. Mitkov (Ed.), *The Oxford handbook of computational linguistics* (pp. 249–265). New York: Oxford University Press.

Steyvers, M., Shiffrin, R. M., & Nelson, D. L. (2004). Word association spaces for predicting semantic similarity effects in episodic memory. *Experimental cognitive psychology and its applications: Festschrift in honor of Lyle Bourne, Walter Kintsch, and Thomas Landauer* (pp. 237–249). Washington, DC: American Psychological Association.

Steyvers, M., & Tenenbaum, J. (2005). The large-scale structure of semantic networks: Statistical analyses and a model of semantic growth. *Cognitive Science, 29*, 41–78.

Stockwell, G. (2007). Vocabulary on the move: Investigating an intelligent mobile phone-based vocabulary tutor. *Computer Assisted Language Learning, 20*(4), 365–383.

Sullivan, J. (2006). *Developing knowledge of polysemous vocabulary.* Doctoral dissertation, University of Waterloo, Waterloo, ON, Canada.

Susanti, Y., Iida, R., & Tokunaga, T. (2015, May). *Automatic generation of English vocabulary tests.* Paper presented at the seventh International Conference on Computer Supported Education.

Svartvik, J. (Ed.). (1991). *Directions in corpus linguistics.* In *Proceedings of Nobel Symposium 82 Stockholm 4–8 August 1991.* Berlin: Mouton de Gruyter

Swanborn, M. S. L., & de Glopper, K. (1999). Incidental word learning while reading: A meta-analysis. *Review of Educational Research, 69*(3), 261–285.

Sweetland, J. (2006). *Teaching writing in the African American classroom: A sociolinguistic approach.* Unpublished doctoral dissertation, Stanford University, Stanford, CA.

Tan, A. H., & Teo, C. (1998). Learning user profiles for personalized information dissemination. In *Proceedings of the 1998 IEEE International Joint Conference on Neural Networks (IJCNN'98)* (Vol. 1, pp. 183–188), Anchorage, Alaska: IEEE.

Taylor, H. U. (1991). *Standard English, Black English, and bidialectalism: A controversy.* New York: Peter Lang.

Taylor, W. L. (1953). Cloze procedure: A new tool for measuring readability. *Journalism Quarterly, 30*(4), 415–433.

Taylor, W. L. (1956). Recent developments in the use of cloze procedure. *Journalism Quarterly, 33*(1), 42–48.

Thissen, D., Steinberg, L., & Mooney, J. (1989). Trace lines for testlets: A use of multiple-categorical response models. *Journal of Educational Measurement, 26*(3), 247–260.

Thompson, P., & Nesi, H. (2001). Research in progress: The British Academic Spoken English (BASE) corpus project. *Language Teaching Research, 5*(3), 263–264.

Thorndike, E. L. (1921). *The teacher's word book* (Vol. 134). New York: Teachers College Press.

Thorndike, E. L., & Lorge, I. (1944). *The teacher's word book of 30,000 words.* New York: Teachers College Press.

Tinkham, T. (1997). The effects of semantic and thematic clustering on the learning of second language vocabulary. *System, 21*, 371–380.

Titone, D. A., & Salisbury, D. F. (2004). Contextual modulation of N400 amplitude to lexically ambiguous words. *Brain and Cognition, 55*(3), 470–478.

Todirascu, A., François, T., Gala, N., Fairon, C., Ligozat, A. L., & Bernhard, D. (2013). Coherence and cohesion for the assessment of text readability. *Natural Language Processing and Cognitive Science, 11*, 11–19.

Tomasello, M., & Tomasello, M. (2009). *Constructing a language: A usage-based theory of language acquisition.* Cambridge, MA: Harvard University Press.

Topkaraoğlu, M., & Dilman, H. (2014). Effects of studying vocabulary enhancement activities on students' vocabulary production levels. *Procedia—Social and Behavioral Sciences, 152,* 931–936.

Tseng, W. T. (2016). Measuring English vocabulary size via computerized adaptive testing. *Computers and Education, 97,* 69–85.

U.S. Department of Education, National Center for Educational Statistics. (2013). *The nation's report card: Vocabulary results from the 2009 and 2011 NAEP reading assessments: National assessment of educational progress at grades 4, 8, and 12.* Washington, DC: Author.

van Daalen-Kapteijns, M. M., & Elshout-Mohr, M. (1981). The acquisition of word meanings as a cognitive learning process. *Journal of Verbal Learning and Verbal Behavior, 20,* 386–399.

Van der Linden, W. J., & Glas, C. A. (Eds.). (2000). *Computerized adaptive testing: Theory and practice.* Dordrecht, The Netherlands: Kluwer Academic.

Van Gelder, T. (2005). Teaching critical thinking: Some lessons from cognitive science. *College Teaching, 53*(1), 41–46.

VanLehn, K. (1988). Toward a theory of impasse-driven learning. In H. Mandl & A. Lesgold (Eds.), *Learning issues for intelligent tutoring systems* (pp. 19–41). New York: Springer Verlag.

VanLehn, K. (1990). *Mind bugs: The origins of procedural misconceptions.* Cambridge, MA: MIT Press.

VanLehn, K., Lynch, C., Schulze, K., Shapiro, J. A., Shelby, R., Taylor, L., et al. (2005). The AndEs Physics Tutoring System: Lessons learned. *International Journal of Artificial Intelligence in Education, 15*(3), 147–204.

Vellutino, F. R., Tunmer, W. E., Jaccard, J. J., & Chen, R. (2007). Components of reading ability: Multivariate evidence for a convergent skills model of reading development. *Scientific Studies of Reading, 11*(1), 3–32.

Verspoor, M., & Lowie, W. (2003). Making sense of polysemous words. *Language Learning, 53*(3), 547–586.

Vevea, J. L., Flinspach, S. L., & Scott, J. A. (2013). *Exploring vocabulary knowledge as a multidimensional construct: Diagnostic information about five aspects of vocabulary understanding.* Paper presented at the annual meeting of the American Educational Research Association, San Francisco, CA.

Voss, E. (2012). *A validity argument for score meaning of a computer-based ESL academic collocational ability test based on a corpus-driven approach to test design.* Graduate Theses and Dissertations, Digital Repository (Paper 12691), Iowa State University, Ames, IA.

Wainer, H., Dorans, N. J., Flaugher, R., Green, B. F., & Mislevy, R. J. (2000). *Computerized adaptive testing: A primer.* New York: Routledge.

Wainer, H., & Kiely, G. L. (1987). Item clusters and computerized adaptive testing: A case for testlets. *Journal of Educational Measurement, 24*(3), 185–201.

Watts, S. M. (1995). Vocabulary instruction during reading lessons in six classrooms. *Journal of Literacy Research, 27*(3), 399–424.

Wauters, K., Desmet, P., & Van Den Noortgate, W. (2010). Adaptive item-based learning environments based on the item response theory: Possibilities and challenges. *Journal of Computer Assisted Learning, 26*(6), 549–562.

Webb, S. (2007). The effects of repetition on vocabulary knowledge. *Applied Linguistics, 28*(1), 46–65.

Weiss, D. J. (1982). Improving measurement quality and efficiency with adaptive testing. *Applied Psychological Measurement, 6*(4), 473–492.

Werner, H., & Kaplan, E. (1952). The acquisition of word meanings: A developmental study. *Monographs of the Society of Research in Child Development, 15*(1, Serial No. 51).

Wesche, M., & Paribakht, T. S. (1996). Assessing second language vocabulary knowledge: Depth versus breadth. *Canadian Modern Language Review, 53*(1), 13–40.

West, M. (Eds.). (1953). *A general service list of English words: With semantic frequencies and a supplementary word-list for the writing of popular science and technology.* London: Longman.

Wheeler, R. S. (2008). Becoming adept at code-switching. *Educational Leadership, 65*(7), 54–58.

Wheeler, R. S., & Swords, R. (2006). *Code-switching: Teaching Standard English in urban classrooms.* Urbana, IL: National Council of Teachers of English.

White, T. G., Sowell, J., & Yanagihara, A. (1989). Teaching elementary students to use word-part clues. *The Reading Teacher, 42*(4), 302–308.

Whitely, S. E. (1977). Relationships in analogy items: A semantic component of a psychometric task. *Educational and Psychological Measurement, 37*(3), 725–739.

Whitmore, J. M., Shore, W. J., & Smith, P. H. (2004). Partial knowledge of word meanings: Thematic and taxonomic representations. *Journal of Psycholinguistic Research, 33*(2), 137–164.

Wild, K. (2001). Phrasal verbs: "A process of the common, relatively uneducated mind"? *English Today, 27*(4), 53–57.

Williams, R., & Morris, R. (2004). Eye movements, word familiarity, and vocabulary acquisition. *European Journal of Cognitive Psychology, 16*(1–2), 312–339.

Wilson, T., Wiebe, J., & Hoffmann, P. (2009). Recognizing contextual polarity: An exploration of features for phrase-level sentiment analysis. *Computational Linguistics, 35*(3), 399–433.

Wixson, K., & Pearson, P. D. (1998). Policy and assessment strategies to support literacy instruction for a new century. *Peabody Journal of Education, 73*(3/4), 202–227.

Wolfe, M. B., Schreiner, M. E., Rehder, B., Laham, D., Foltz, P. W., Kintsch, W., et al. (1998). Learning from text: Matching readers and texts by latent semantic analysis. *Discourse Processes, 25*(2–3), 309–336.

Woodcock, R. N. (1998). *Woodcock Reading Mastery Test—Revised.* Circle Pines, MN: American Guidance Service.

Woolf, B. P. (2009). *Building intelligent interactive tutors: Student centered strategies for revolutionizing e-learning.* Burlington, MA: Morgan Kaufmann.

Worsley-Gough, B. (1932). *Public affairs.* Hamburg, Germany: Albatross.

Wray, A. (2002). *Formulaic language and the lexicon.* Cambridge, UK: Cambridge University Press.

Wright, T. S., & Neuman, S. B. (2014). Paucity and disparity in kindergarten oral vocabulary instruction. *Journal of Literacy Research, 46*(3), 330–357.

Yorio, C. (1989). Idiomaticity as an indicator of second language proficiency. In K. Hyltenstam & L. K. Obler (Eds.), *Bilingualism across the lifespan* (pp. 55–72). Cambridge, UK: Cambridge University Press.

Yoshii, M. (2014). Effects of glosses and reviewing of glossed words on L2 vocabulary learning through reading. *Vocabulary Learning and Instruction, 3*(2), 19–30.

Zeno, S. M., Ivens, S. H., Millard, R. T., & Duvvuri, R. (1995). *The educator's word frequency guide.* Brewster, NY: Touchstone Applied Science.

Zevin, J. D., & Seidenberg, M. S. (2002). Age of acquisition effects in word reading and other tasks. *Journal of Memory and Language, 47*(1), 1–29.

Zhang, D. (2013). Linguistic distance effect on cross-linguistic transfer of morphological awareness. *Applied Psycholinguistics, 34*(5), 917–942.

Zhang, D., & Koda, K. (2012). Contribution of morphological awareness and lexical inferencing ability to L2 vocabulary knowledge and reading comprehension among advanced EFL learners: Testing direct and indirect effects. *Reading and Writing, 25*(5), 1195–1216.

Zipf, G. K. (1935). *The psycho-biology of language.* Boston: Houghton Mifflin.

Zipf, G. K. (1945). The meaning-frequency relationship of words. *Journal of General Psychology, 33*(2), 251–256.

Zwiers, J., & Crawford, M. (2011). *Academic conversations: Classroom talk that fosters critical thinking and content understandings.* Portland, ME: Stenhouse.

Index

Note. "f," following a page number indicates a figure.
Page numbers in bold refer to entries in the Glossary.

Academic vocabulary
    assessment, 31, 36, 41, 55
    collocational knowledge, 88–89
    Common Core State Standards (CCSS),
        47
    grade-level differences, 137–139
    multiword expressions, 65, 125
    overview, 4–5
    word selection for teaching and
        assessment, 55
Academic Word List, 55–56, 101–102,
    156–157, 182, 184. *See also* Word lists
Accents, 140. *See also* Code switching;
    English learners
Accessible words, 61, 69, **197**. *See also* Word
    selection
Accountability, 32, **197**. *See also* Assessment
Acronym, 67, **197**. *See also* Multiword
    expressions (MWEs)
Adaptive spacing, 153, **197**
Affix, 14, 60, 64, 70, 80, 130–132, 135–
    138, 136*f*, **197**. *See also* Morphological
    patterns; Prefix; Suffix
Age of acquisition, 53–60, 157, **197**. See also
    Grade-level word lists; Word frequency
    estimating age of acquisition through
        crowdsourcing, 57, 59
Algorithm, 156, 165–168, **197**
Ambiguity. *See* Polysemy
Annotation, 158, 159, 161, 178, **197**. *See
    also* Crowdsourcing
Antonym, 95. *See also* Semantic networks;
    Synonym

Artificial intelligence, 149, **197**. *See also*
    Natural language processing (NLP);
    Technology
Assessment. *See also* Technology-enhanced
    assessments; Word selection
    adaptive assessment, 79, 150–155
    aligning with instruction, 145–146
    assessing collocations, 88–90
    assessing connotations, 87
    assessing integration of multiple aspects
        of vocabulary knowledge, 95–96
    assessing morphological relatedness,
        86–87, 101
    assessing partial vocabulary knowledge,
        96–102
    assessing role of vocabulary in higher-
        order literacy, 103–104
    assessing semantic knowledge, 94–95
    assessing specific syntactic knowledge,
        85–86
    assessing topical associations, 90–92,
        97–98
    assessing vocabulary knowledge using
        word analogies, 95
    assessing vocabulary to assess reading
        comprehension, 31, 103–104
    automatic item generation, 165–173
    automated passage selection, 162–165
    California English Language
        Development Test, 32
    Cloze Evaluation test (Cloe), 101
    computerized adaptive assessment,
        150–155

conventional vocabulary assessments as assessments of vocabulary size, 33–34
definitional knowledge, 37–38, 37f
depth of lexical knowledge, 82–96
depth of vocabulary knowledge, 44, 50–51
designing tests, 79
digital and online resources, 156–162
dynamic assessment, 80
educational reforms, 45–50, 49f
embedded in instruction, 146
factors not addressed by, 50–51
formative assessment, 31, 75
future of, 40–45
idiomatic associates item types, 96
importance of context in assessment, 19–20
innovative item types, 48–50, 49f
issues associated with, 32–34
limitations of current forms of vocabulary assessment, 32–41
limitations of focusing on definitional knowledge, 37–39, 82
measures of frequency and age of acquisition, 58–60
methods, 79–82
mix of word difficulties in normal text, 36
need for diagnostic assessment, 28
need to measure incremental word learning, 33, 39, 75, 81–82
nonintrusive vocabulary assessment, 173–175
of English language competency, 32
of reading comprehension with cloze items, 41–42
of specific word knowledge, 31, 84–85
of vocabulary size, 31
overview, 8, 30–31, 51, 75–76, 105, 197
partial and incremental knowledge of words, 96–103, 100f
productive and receptive assessment of collocations, 89–90
Productive Vocabulary Levels Test, 95–96
purposes for, 31–32
reliability, 30
Robust Academic Vocabulary Encounters (RAVE), 119–124
role of feedback, 81
role of large-scale assessments, 32
role of reading passage difficulty in assessment design, 41
role of technology, 148–175
selection principles for vocabulary used in an assessment, 68–74
self-assessment, 82–83

semantic associations, 90–92
standards for assessment design, 30–31
stealth assessment, 173–175
summative assessment, 31, 75
test validity, 30
text-completion items, 44
traditional forms of vocabulary assessment, 34–42, 37f
use of contextualized versus decontextualized items, 41, 75
VASE (Vocabulary Assessment Study in Education), 50, 62–63, 70, 99–101, 178–179
vocabulary assessment, 30–41
vocabulary items in Partnership for Assessment of Readiness for College and Careers (PARCC) assessment, 48–49. *See also* Common Core State Standards (CCSS)
vocabulary items in the Graduate Records Exam (GRE), 43–44
vocabulary items in the National Assessment of Educational Progress (NAEP), 44–45
vocabulary items in the Smarter Balanced Assessment, 48. *See also* Common Core State Standards (CCSS)
vocabulary items in the Test of English as a Foreign Language (TOEFL), 42–43
Word Associates Test, 91
word associations, 90–93
word learning, 20, 76–82
word lists, 40–41
Writing Pal, 173–175
Associates (Association), 90–93, 167–168, **197**. *See* Word associations
Automated item generation, 156, 165–173. *See also* Technology
of association items, 167–168
of classroom exercises, 172–173
of cloze items, 169–172
of open-response definitional items, 166–167
of synonym items, 166, 167, 169
use of corpus for automated item generation, 166–169
Automated passage selection, 156, 162–165, 172. *See also* Technology
Automated readability index, 155, 163–164, **198**. *See also* Readability of texts
Automated reading and tutoring systems, 149–155. *See also* Technology
Automated Tutoring Systems, 149–155, 164. *See also* Technology
Autotutor, 164
computer-assisted language learning (CALL), 151

Automated Tutoring Systems *(cont.)*
  computerized adaptive tests (CAT) for
    vocabulary, 150–155
  DSCoVAR, (151–153)
  Project LISTEN, 153–154
  Project REAP, 154–155

Background knowledge, 23, 76
Base word. *See* Morphological patterns;
  Root words
Black English Vernacular (BEV), 140
Books, 112–116, 113*f*–114*f*. *See also*
  Resources
Bound morphemes, 134, **198**. *See also*
  Morphology.
Bound roots, 11, 71, 131, 135, 138, **198**. *See
  also* Latin and Greek roots
Breadth of vocabulary, 33–34, 82–96, **198**.
  See also Vocabulary knowledge
  relationship between vocabulary size and
    total test score, 34–35

Capacity theory of writing, 3, **198**
Categorical relations, 93. *See also* Semantic
  knowledge
Classroom practices. *See* Instruction
Cloze items. *See also* Assessment; Item
  types
  adaptive assessment, 151
  automated generation of, 169–173
  collocational knowledge, 89
  overview, 41–42, 101–102, **198**
Code switching, 139–140, **198**. *See also*
  Dialect; English learners; L1; L2
Collected words and phrases, 109–110,
  115–116. *See also* Word banks
Collocations 13, 21, 28, 76, 84, 169–170.
  See also Multiword expressions
  (MWEs)
  assessing, 88–90
  cloze items for assessment of collocational
    knowledge, 89, 101–102
  depth of vocabulary knowledge, 84
  dictionaries, 25
  idiomatic associates items, 97–98
  overview, 13, 21, 29, 88–90, **198**
  productive assessment, 89
  receptive assessment, 89–90
Combining forms, 11, 131–132, 138, **198**.
  See also Bound roots; Morphology
Common Core State Standards (CCSS), 5,
  22, 41, 45–47. *See also* Assessment
Component words, 10, 14, 28, 88
Compound nouns, 16, **198**
Compound words, 10, 14, 28, 123, **198**
Comprehension, reading. *See* Reading
  comprehension

Computational linguistics, 148, 159,
  193, **198**. *See also* Natural language
  processing (NLP): Technology
Computer adaptive testing, 150, **198**. *See
  also* Technology-enhanced assessments
Computer-assisted language learning
  (CALL) systems, 151–153. *See also*
  Technology
Concreteness, 157, 174, **198**
Congruent word meaning, 39, **198**
Connotations, 13, 21, 24, 38, 50, 76, 84, 87,
  120, 122, 129, 138, **198**
Construct, 28, 30, 31–32, 34, 38, 41, 76,
  83, 84, 101, 163, 165, **199**. *See also*
  Assessment
Construction grammar, 15, 68. *See also*
  Linguistic theory
Context
  assessment, 40, 41–45, 102
  automated identification of useful
    contexts, 170–171
  collocational knowledge, 89
  dictionaries, 27–28
  higher-level literacy, 103–105
  idiomatic associates items, 97–98
  inferring word meaning from, 13, 48–49,
    76, 77–79, 81–82
  instruction, 141–145
  overview, 19–20, 29, **199**
  semantic knowledge, 102
  using a corpus to find contexts for
    instruction, 20
  word associations, 90, 92–93
  word learning from, 77–79, 81–82
  word selection for teaching and
    assessment, 60–61, 67–68, 69, 72,
    73, 74
Co-occurrence of words, 160, **199**. *See also*
  Collocations; Latent semantic analysis
  (LSA); Word associations
Corpus (corpora), 20, 39, 53–54, 58–59,
  69, 89, 91, 123, 152, 156, 159–160,
  167–170, 176–177, **199**
  Abstracts from MEDLINE, 176
  as a resource, 158–159
  available, 54–55, 58, 59, 123, 158–162
  British National Corpus, 54, 176
  Brown Corpus (Kucera & Francis), 54,
    159, 176
  CELEX Corpus, 54
  corpus bias affecting word frequency
    estimates, 58
  Corpus of British Academic Spoken
    English (BASE), 177
  Corpus of Contemporary American
    English (COCA), 123, 176
  digital and online resources for, 158–162

dispersion (frequency across parts of a corpus), 55, 58
Fisher English Training Corpus, 177
generating test items from, 166–168, 170
Gigaword Corpus, 54, 176
HAL Corpus, 54
ICLE corpus (International Corpus of Learner's English), 176
Juris Corpus, 176
Linguistic Data Consortium, 159
LOB Corpus, 159
measures of frequency and age of acquisition, 58–59
Michigan Corpus of Academic Spoken English (MICASE), 177
overview, 20, 176–177, **199**
Switchboard Telephone Speech Corpus, 177
TASA Corpus, 176
using a corpus (corpora) to find contexts for vocabulary instruction,
using a corpus for automatic item generation, 166–169
word associations, 90
word selection for teaching and assessment, 54–55, 56
Crowdsourcing, 59, 157, **199**. *See also* Annotation

Decoding skills, 2, 57, 67, 193, **199**. *See also* Orthographic properties of a word; Reading; Spelling
Denotation, 21. *See also* Connotations; Referential understanding; Semantic knowledge
Depth of vocabulary knowledge, 33, 39, 49–51, 75–76, 82–96. *See also* Lexical quality hypothesis; Vocabulary knowledge
  assessment, 44, 50–51
  components of, 84–85
  lexical knowledge, 82–96
  overview, 33–34, 50, **199**
  relation with polysemy, 72
  VASE (Vocabulary Assessment Study in Education), 50, 62–63, 70, 99–101, 178–179
  word associations, 91
Derivational morphemes, 131–132, **199**. *See also* Morphology
Derived forms, 10, 14, **199**. *See also* Morphology
Determiner, 158, **199**. *See also* Parts of speech; Syntax
Developmental factors. *See* Language development
Dialect, 140

Dictionaries, Thesauri, and Other Lexical Resources, 9, 24–28, 25f, 142–143, 159–161, 183–185
American Heritage Dictionary, 159
and English learners, 142–143
as aids to comprehension, 27
as historical records, 25
as reference tools, 24
Audio English, 186
Collins COBUILD Advanced American English Dictionary, 160
Collins COBUILD Dictionary, 160
complexity of information in a dictionary entry, 25
degree of metalinguistic knowledge needed to use a dictionary effectively, 25–26
differences in ways dictionaries are structured, 26
Edinburgh Associative thesaurus, 158
Learn that Word, 180
Lexipedia, 185
Longman Dictionary of American English, 160
Merriam-Webster Dictionary, 9, 160
MRC Psycholinguistic Database, 158
My Vocabulary Size, 186
online dictionary search, 185
Online Etymological Dictionary, 183
Oxford Advanced Dictionary for Learners of English, 160
Oxford English Dictionary, 160
PropBank, 161
Reverso Dictionary, 184
risk of misinterpreting dictionary entries, 26–27TextProject, 180
VerbNet, 161
Vocabulary.com, 179–180
Vocabulary Spelling City, 180
Word a Day, 186
Word Generation, 121, 179
WordNet, 26, 123, 160
Wordnik, 185
Differentiating definitions item type, 97, 99–103, 100f. *See also* Item types; Semantic knowledge
Difficulty of words, 34–36. *See also* Grade-level vocabulary
relationship with curricular decisions, 36
Digital and online resources, 156–162, 178–185. *See also* Resources; Technology
Discrete item, 103, 167, **199**. *See also* Assessment
Discriminate, 44, **199**. *See also* Assessment
Dispersion, 55–56, 66–67, **199**. *See also* Tier Three vocabulary; Tier Two vocabulary; Word frequency

Distractor (option choice), 45, 167–169,
    171–173, **199**. *See also* Assessment
Domain, 4, **199**. *See also* Background
    knowledge
DSCoVAR system, 151–153, 166–167; *See
    also* Automated tutoring systems
Dynamic assessment, 80–82, **199**. *See also*
    Assessment

Educational reforms, 45–50, 49*f*. *See also*
    Common Core State Standards (CCSS)
Engagement, 119–123, 122
English as a lingua franca (ELF), 140–141
English learners, 20, 32, 62, 65, 69, 76, 101,
    131, 140–145, 150, 172. *See also* L2;
    Second-language teaching
    bilingual, 140
    dictionaries and English learners,
        142–143
    English as a Lingua Franca (ELF), 140
    English as a Second Language (ESL), 140
    Immersion in a second language, 141
    learning from reading, 141–142
    linguistic distance and language learners,
        143–144
    mainstream population, 140
    metonymy as important issue for English
        learners, 144–145
    morphological awareness of English
        learners, 143
    multilingual, 140
    polysemy and English learners, 144–145
    use of glosses by English learners, 142–143
Essential words, 61, 69, **199**. *See also* Word
    selection
Etymologies of words, 125, 133, 183, 185,
    200
Expertise, development of, 4
Eye-tracking, 174

Figurative speech, 144–145. See also
    Metaphor; Metonymy
Fixed expressions. *See* Multiword
    expressions (MWEs)
Foil words, 92, **200**. *See also* Item types
Formulaic language. *See* Multiword
    expressions (MWEs)
Frequency of words, 53–60, 88, **206**. *See
    also* Word frequency
Functional relations, 93–94, **200**. *See also*
    Semantic knowledge

General purpose words. *See* High-frequency
    words
General Service List, 55–56, 156–157, 158,
    182, 184. *See also* High-frequency
    words; Word lists

Generalization, 17, 68–69, 130, **204**. *See
    also* Semantic patterns; Specialization
Generative patterns. *See also* Morphological
    patterns; Semantic patterns; Syntactic
    patterns
    instruction, 126–139, 134*f*, 136*f*
    metalinguistic awareness of, 126–139,
        134*f*, 136*f*
    overview, 13–20, 17*f*, **200**
    productivity of (especially in morphology)
        17, 132
    word selection for teaching and
        assessment, 68, 69
Genre, 3, 22, 41, 163, **200**
Glosses, 142–143, **200**
Grade-level vocabulary, 35–36, 46–47,
    137–139, 186–189
Grade-level word lists, 35–36, 46–47. *See
    also* Living Word Vocabulary (LWV)
Grammatical constructions, 126–127. *See
    also* Construction grammar; Syntactic
    patterns
Graphic organizers, 61, **200**

Higher-level literacy. *See* Word frequency.
High-frequency words, 55–56, 88. *See also*
    General Service List; Word frequency.
High-stakes testing, 41, **200**. *See also*
    Testing
Homonyms, 11, 18, 172, 187, **200**. *See also*
    Phonology; Polysemy
Homophones, 59, 111–112, 187, **200**. *See
    also* Phonology
    effect on word frequency estimates, 59
Hypernym, 84, 99. *See also* Semantic
    networks
    hypernym item type, 97, 98, **200**. *See also*
        Item types
Hyponyms, 85, 93, 185, **200**. *See also*
    Semantic networks

Idioms, 16. 21, 28, 29, 65–66, 88, 97–98,
    200. *See also* Collocations; Multiword
    expressions (MWEs)
Imported words, 61–62, 69, **200**. *See also*
    Word selection
Incidental word learning, 19, **200**. *See also*
    Word learning
Incremental knowledge of words, **200**. *See*
    Partial knowledge of words; Word
    knowledge
Inference
    based on collocational knowledge, 89
    based on context, 77–79
    based on metacognitive knowledge, 23
    based on morphological knowledge,
        80–81, 86–87

in vocabulary assessment, 38–39
to support higher-level literacy, 103–104
Inflectional morphemes, 10–12, 21,
130–137, **201**. *See also* Affix;
Morphological patterns; Suffix
Instruction. *See also* Word selection; Lesson
plans
accessible words, 61
aligning with assessment, 145–146
assessment embedded in instruction, 146
automated tutoring systems, 149–150
best practices, 106–147
constraining contexts, 19, 78, 81–82
depth of lexical knowledge, 82
effective vocabulary instruction and
interpretive inference, 104
English language learners, 140–141
essential words, 61
focused vocabulary instruction, 107,
119–126
generative patterns, 18–20
grammar 172–173
higher-level literacy, 104–105
homophones, 111
impact of large-scale assessment, 32
importance of, 5–8
importance of context in instruction,
19–20
imported words, 61
instruction as cognitive apprenticeship,
147
instructional time focused on vocabulary,
5–7, 119–126
introducing targeted vocabulary in
focused instruction, 119–121
introducing vocabulary prior to reading,
119–121
Language Muse teacher support system,
making definitions useful, 27
metalinguistic awareness of generative
patterns, 126–139, 134*f*, 136*f*
misconceptions, 6–8
multiword expressions, 123–126
overview, 106–107, 146–147
prominence of vocabulary in education,
5–6
providing multiple encounters with
targeted words, 121–123
resources for, 178–181
rich, interactive vocabulary instruction
versus definition-based instruction, 104
role of technology, 148–175
structure of language, 12–13
Structured Word Inquiry (SWI), 132–134,
134*f*
supportive vocabulary interactions with
students, 116–119

teaching in context, 7–8, 19–20, 67–68,
73, 119–126
teaching semantically related words, 61–62
use of definitions, 6–8, 13, 19–20, 27
using a corpus to find contexts for
instruction, 20
valuable words, 61
variations of English, 139–140
vocabulary learning through context,
141–145
vocabulary mega-clusters, 60–61,
word conscious classroom and word
consciousness, 107–119, 108–112,
113*f*–114*f*
word lists, 40–41
word selection based on passage context,
69
word selection for, 68–73
words that emphasize instructional value,
69
Word Zones, 54–55, 73
Intelligent tutoring systems, 149–156,
164,165, 173–175, **201**. *See also*
Automated Tutoring systems
Autotutor, 164
Interactions between semantic,
morphological, and syntactic patterns,
18. *See also* Morphological pattern;
Semantic pattern; Syntactic pattern
Interventions, 121, 132–134, 134*f*, 149–155.
See also Instruction
Intransitive verbs, 21, **201**. *See also* Parts of
speech; Syntax
Item types, 37, 42–45, 68, 97–102, 151,
168–173, **201**. *See also* Assessment.
cloze items, 41–43, 86, 89, 101–102, 151,
163, 169–172
definitional vocabulary items, 95, 99,
166–167
differentiating definitions item type,
97, 99–103, 100*f*. *See also* Semantic
knowledge
hypernym item type, 97, 98, **200**. *See also*
Semantic knowledge
idiomatic associates, 96
synonym, topical associates, 97–98. *See
also* Semantic knowledge

L1, 76, 176, **201**. *See also* Native English
speakers
L2, 76, **201**. *See also* English learners;
Second-language teaching
Language blogs, 181
About Education, 183
Lingholic, 182
Linguist-educator exchange, 182
The English Blog, 183

Language development
    assessment, 33–34, 53–60
    overview, 3–5, 137–139
    resources for, 182–183
    variations of English, 139–140. *See also*
        Dialect
    word consciousness, 108–109
    word selection for teaching and
        assessment, 53–60
Language Muse, 172–173
Language variants, 140.
Latent semantic analysis (LSA), 164, 167,
    201. *See also* Technology; Word
    associations
Latin and Greek roots, 71, 125, 131–132,
    134–138, 136*f*, 143. *See also*
    Morphological patterns
Lesson plans, 178–179. *See also* Instruction
    Exceptional Expressions for Everyday
        Events, 179
    Reading Educator; Vocabulary Strategies,
        179
    Super Synonym Sets for Stories, 179
    VINE (Vocabulary Innovations in
        Education) lesson plans, 178
    Western Washington University
        Linguistics in Education, 179
Lexical access, 83, **201**
Lexical decision task, 83
Lexical diversity, 3. *See also* Word choice
    and writer's craft
Lexical inferencing, 82, **201**. *See also*
    Inference
Lexical knowledge, 82–96, 85–86, 95–96,
    201. *See also* Word knowledge
Lexical morphology. *See* Morphology
Lexical organization, 90–93
Lexical quality hypothesis, 2, 83, **201**. *See
    also* Depth of vocabulary knowledge
Lexical resources. *See* Dictionaries,
    Thesauri, and Other Lexical Resources
Lexicographer, 26, 160, **201**
Lexicon, 11–12, 76–77, **201**. *See also*
    Dictionaries, Thesauri, and Other
    Lexical Resources
Linguistic distance, 143–144, **201**
Linguistic theory, 11–12, 67–68. *See also*
    Construction grammar
Living Word Vocabulary (LWV), 35–36, 57,
    157. *See also* Dictionaries, Thesauri,
    and Other Lexical Resources

Matthew effect, 108, **201**. *See also* Positive
    feedback loop
Memorization, 38, 151. *See also* Rote
    information

Meta-analysis, 19, 40, 130, **201**
Metacognitive skills, 4, 22–23, 139–140
    metacognitive awareness, 22–24, 23*f*,
        107, 109, **202**
    relation to vocabulary acquisition, 22–24,
        47
Metalinguistic skills and awareness, 4,
    22–23, 107, 111, 116–130. *See also*
    Morphological awareness
    ambiguity, 111
    assessments, 75, 83
    dictionaries, 24–28
    of generative patterns, 107, 126–139,
        134*f*, 136*f*
    importance for incidental word learning,
        23–24, 85
    inflectional morphemes, 10, 28, 131
    instruction, 18, 66, 108, 111, 115, 124,
        126–139, 134*f*, 136*f*
    overview, 22–24, 23*f*, **202**
    syntax, 85
    vocabulary knowledge, 75, 106
    word consciousness, 109
Metaphor, 16–17, 129, 144–145, **202**. *See
    also* Figurative speech; Polysemy;
    Semantic patterns
Metonymy, 16, 144–145, **202**. *See also*
    Figurative speech; Polysemy; Semantic
    patterns
Morphology. 10, 16, 18, 22, 65–67, 72–73,
    123–125, 130–139, 134*f*, 136*f*, **202**.
    See also Affix; Bound roots; Derived
    forms; Latin and Greek roots; Prefix;
    Root words; Suffix; Word families
    academic vocabulary and morphemes, 14
    Anglo-Saxon vocabulary and
        morphology, 125, 137
    assessment of morphological inference,
        80–81
    assessment of morphological relatedness,
        86–87, 101
    bound morphemes, 134, **198**
    combining forms 132, 138
    derived words (morphologically complex)/
        derivational morphemes, 10, 131–132,
        199
    dictionaries, 26
    grade-level differences, 137–139
    inflected forms/inflectional morphemes,
        10, 28, 131
    instruction, 69, 70–71, 73, 130–139,
        134*f*, 136*f*
    interactions of with other generative
        patterns, 18–19
    irregular inflections, 131, 137
    lexical morphology, 134–139, 136*f*, **201**

morphemes, 10, 11, 21, 143, 202
morphological awareness, 77, 101, 132, 143–144, 202
morphological awareness as a form of metalinguistic awareness, 70–71, 73, 76, 132, 143–144
morphological awareness of English learners, 143
Morphological inference, 80–81, 202. *See also* Inference
Morphological patterns. 12, 14–15. *See also* Generative patterns; Prefixes; Root words; Suffixes
affix, 14, 60, 64, 70, 80, 130–132, 135–138, 136*f*, **197**
morphological relatedness, 10, 21, 60–61, 84, 86–87, 125–126, 137, **202**
morphology tree, 135–136, 136*f*
overview, 12, 13, 14–15, 29, **202**
polysemy in morphologically complex words, 14–15
prefix, 13, 70, 125, 132, 138
role of morphological vocabulary in growth of vocabulary size, 14, 130–131
root word, 10, 28, 70
spelling of morphological variants, 138l
stress and pronunciation of variants, 138
Structured Word Inquiry (SWI), 132–134, 134*f*
suffix, 13, 125, 132, 138
word-specific vocabulary knowledge, 76–77
Multiword expressions (MWEs), 10, 16, 18, 22, 65–67, 72–73, 123–125. *See also* Collocations; Idioms; Named entity
frequency of multiword expressions, 16, 22
generative patterns, 18–19
instruction, 65–67, 123–126
multiword expressions and the Common Core State Standards, 22
overview, 21, 22, 29, **202**
phrasal verbs, 125, **203**
polysemy, 129
word selection, 64–67, 69, 72–73

NAEP vocabulary framework, 41
Named entity, 22, **202**. *See also* Multiword expressions (MWEs)
National Assessment of Educational Progress (NAEP) Reading Test, 41, 43, 44–45.
Native English speakers, 10, 76, 88, 90, 141–142, 156, 160, 177, 183. *See also* L1

Natural language processing (NLP), 160–173
content matching, 164
overview, 152, 155–156, **198, 202**
Nonintrusive vocabulary assessment, 155–156, 173–175, **204**. *See also* Technology
Norm, 156–158, 165, **202**

Online resources. *See* Digital and online resources
Open-response item, 42, 151, 167, 169–170, **202**. *See also* Item types
Option choice (distractor), 45, 167–169, 171–173, **202**. *See also* Item types
Oral language, 2–3, 6, 9, 33, 131
Orthographic properties of a word, 76–77, **202**. *See also* Spelling

Partial knowledge of words, 96–102. *See also* Depth of vocabulary knowledge; Word knowledge
Partnership for Assessment of Readiness for College and Careers (PARCC), 48–50, 49*f*; *See also* Assessment; Common Core State Standards (CCSS)
Parts of speech, 21, 26–27, 101. *See also* Syntactic patterns; Syntax
articles, 54
conjunctions, 54
count nouns, 21
determiner, 158, **199**
intransitive verb, 21
mass noun, 21
noun, 21
prepositions, 54
transitive verb, 21
verb, 21
Passage reading, 41, 45, 69, **202**
assessment, 41–45
automated passage selection, 162–165, 172
overview, 41
with Cloze items, 41–42
word selection for teaching and assessment, 69
Peabody Picture Vocabulary Test (PPVT), 3, 31. *See also* Assessment
Personalization, 164–165, **203**
Phonology, 133, 138, **203**. *See also* Homonym; Homophone; Pronunciation; Rhymes; Syllables
Phrasal verbs, 16, 22, 66, 84, 125, 172, **203**. *See also* Idioms; Multiword expressions (MWEs)
Phrase collections. *See* Collected words and phrases

Phrases, 20–22, 89–90, 109–110, 125
Polysemy, 4, 9,11–13, 16–18, 21, 47,
    71–72, 101, 111–112, 119–120,
    127–128, 144–145, 169, 203. *See also*
    Generalization; Metaphor; Metonymy;
    Semantic patterns; Specialization;
    Word meaning
  assessment, 68, 69, 71–72, 168–169
  effect on word frequency estimates, 59
  in morphologically complex words, 14–15
  instruction, 68, 69, 71–72, 127–130
  overview, 16–18, 17*f*, 203
  polysemy and English learners, 144
  relation with depth of vocabulary
    knowledge, 72
  role in growth of vocabulary size, 16–18
  role of polysemy in the Common Core
    State Standards, 47
  vocabulary learning through context, 144
  word selection for teaching and
    assessment, 68
  word sense difficulty, 35
Positive feedback loop, 58; *See also* Matthew
    effect
Prefix, 13, 70, 125, 132, 138. *See also* Affix;
    Morphological patterns
  dictionaries, 25
  instruction, 52–53, 70, 130–132
  interactions of with other generative
    patterns, 18–19
  overview, 14–15, 21, 203
  word learning, 10, 11
Productive vocabulary, 7–8, 142, 203.
Productive Vocabulary Levels Test, 95–96.
    See also Assessment
Project LISTEN, 153–154
Project REAP, 153, 154–155
Pronunciation, 21, 25. *See also* Phonology
Prototypical attributes, 28, 68, 72, 91–92,
    94, 97, 101, 120, 203. *See also*
    Semantic knowledge
Pseudowords, 77–78, 203. *See also*
    Orthographic properties of a word
Psycholinguistics, 83, 158, 203
Puns. *See* Word games, wordplay, puns,

RAVE (Robust Academic Vocabulary
    Encounters) program, 119–121,
    122–123. *See also* Instruction
Readability of texts, 42, 46–47, 155,
    162–164, 174, 203
  ATOS readability system
  Degrees of Reading Power (DRP), 164
  Lexile, 164
  readability and genre, 163
  readability and grade level, 163
  readability and text cohesion, 163

  readability measures, 155, 162–164
  Reading Maturity, 164
  role of vocabulary in Common Core
    State Standards' definition of text
    readability, 47
  TASA Open Standard, 164
  TextEvaluator, 164
Reading
  author's craft, 115–116
  interactions around books, 112–116,
    113*f*–114*f*
  vocabulary acquisition, 57–58
  vocabulary knowledge, 10, 108
  vocabulary learning through context,
    141–142
  word learning, 20, 23
Reading-centered automated systems,
    149–150,
  153–155. *See also* Technology
Reading comprehension
  assessment, 32, 34–36
  Cloze technique in assessment, 42
  factors accounting for reading
    comprehension, 1–2
  higher-level literacy, 103–105
  implications for development, 1
  inferring word meaning from context,
    78–79
  morphological awareness, 70, 77
  RAVE (Robust Academic Vocabulary
    Encounters) program, 121
  role of vocabulary knowledge, 1–2, 57
  shared reading, 113
Read's Word Associates Test, 91. *See also*
    Assessment
Receptive vocabulary, 89–90, 203. *See also*
    Breadth of vocabulary
Referential cohesion, 163, 203. *See also* Text
    macrostructure; Topic cohesion
Referential understanding, 103, 203
Register, 21, 87, 139–140, 203
Reliability, 30–31, 205. *See also* Assessment
Resources
  books for developing word awareness,
    185–189
  by conference participants, 192–195
  digital and online resources, 156–162,
    178–185
  novels, 189–192
Rhymes, 21. *See also* Phonology
Rich vocabulary knowledge, 75, 82–96. *See
    also* Depth of vocabulary knowledge;
    Vocabulary knowledge
Root words, 10, 28, 70. *See also*
    Morphological patterns
  dictionaries, 25
  instruction, 131–132

overview, 14–15, 21, **203**
word learning, 10, 11
word selection, 52–53, 70, 73
Rote information, 6, **203**. *See also*
Memorization

Scale, 34–35, 167, **203**. *See also*
Assessment
Second-language teaching, 40–41, 90, 99,
140–141. *See also* English language
learners; L2
Selecting text for readers. *See also*
Readability of texts
content matching, 165
personalization 164–165
Selecting words for teaching and assessment.
See Word selection
Selectional preferences, 21. *See also*
Collocations; Co-occurrence of
words
Semantic association, 84–85, 90–93
Semantic category, 85, 94–95, **204**
Semantic flexibility, 71–72, 122–123,
127–128, 138. *See also* Polysemy
conceptual metaphor, 16
generalization, 16
metaphor, 16, 115, 129, 144–145
metonymy, 16, 129, 144–145
primary or domain senses versus
secondary senses, 72, 116–118, 128
specialization, 16
Semantic knowledge, 94–95, 97, 116–119
assessing, 90–92, 94–95
categorical relations, 94
functional relations, 94
semantic associations, 22, 84, 90–93,
98–99
semantic propositions, 161–162, **204**
semantic relationships, 70, 85, 93,
160–163, **204**
semantic representations, 116–119
taxonomic knowledge, 33, 60–61
Semantic networks. See also Antonym;
Hypernym; Hyponym; Synonym
semantic categories and relations, 21, 33,
60–61, 84–85, 93–94, 101, 109–110,
204
semantic frames, 162, **204**
Semantic patterns, 12, 14, 16–18, 54, 189,
204. *See also* Generative patterns;
Polysemy
assessment, 50, 93–95, 99, 102
interactions with morphological and
syntactic patterns, 18
overview, 12, 13, 16–18, 17*f*, 21
polysemy, 129–130
semantic extension, 129–130

word selection for teaching and
assessment, 61, 68, 70, 71–72
word-specific vocabulary knowledge,
76–77
Semantics, 60, 97, **204**
lexical semantic relationships, 160–161.
See also WordNet
lexical semantics, 128
semantic drift, 128, **204**
SES, 6, **204**
Shared reading, 112–113, 115–116, 119
Simile, 115, **204**. *See also* Figurative
language; Metaphor; Metonymy
Smarter Balanced Assessment, 48. *See also*
Assessment; Common Core State
Standards (CCSS)
Specialization, 17, 130, **204**. *See also*
Generalization; Polysemy; Semantic
patterns
Speech Recognition, 153, 176–177. *See also*
Technology
Spelling, 2, 6–7, 21, 95–96, 132–134
alphabetic writing system, 141
orthography, 76–77, 141
stress and pronunciation of morphological
variants, 138
Standard English, 140. *See also* Code
switching
Standardized assessments, 34–40, 37*f*, **204**.
See also Assessment
Stealth assessment, 173, **204**. *See also*
Nonintrusive vocabulary assessment
Structured Word Inquiry (SWI), 132–134,
134*f*. *See also* Instruction; Morphology
Suffix, 13, 125, 132, 138, *See also* Affix;
Morphological patterns
dictionaries, 25
instruction, 131–132
interactions of with other generative
patterns, 18–19
overview, 14–15, 21, **204**
word learning, 10, 11
word selection for teaching and
assessment, 52–53, 70
Surface factors, 162, **204**
Syllables, 21. *See also* Phonology
Synonym, 43–44, 84, 166, 169, **204**. *See also*
Antonym; Semantic knowledge
Synsets, 93, 102, 160–161, **204**. *See also*
WordNet
Syntactic knowledge, 2, 7, 84, 85–86, **204**
assessing syntactic knowledge, 85–86
Syntactic patterns, 12, 15–16. *See also*
Construction grammar; Generative
patterns
assessment, 44, 50, 101
context, 101

Syntactic patterns *(cont.)*
  instruction, 126–127
  interactions between semantic,
    morphological, syntactic patterns, 18
  overview, 12, 13, 15–16, 21, 205
  word-specific vocabulary knowledge,
    76–77
Syntax, 9, 15, 36, 50, 76, 86, 102–103, 205
  closed-class words, 54
  construction grammar, 15, 68
  grammatical constructions, 15, 68
  part of speech, 21, 26, 85, 101
  syllables, 21

Tacit knowledge
  generative patterns, 9, 11–12, 17*f*, 19, 28,
    67–68, 70–71, 76, 107
  morphological inference and knowledge,
    70–71, 86–87
  overview, 13–18, 205
  word selection for teaching and
    assessment, 70–71
Taxonomic knowledge, 33, 205. *See also*
    Semantic knowledge
Technology, 148–149, 149–156, 156–162,
    173–175. *See also* Nonintrusive
    vocabulary assessment; Technology-
    enhanced assessments
Technology-enhanced assessments. *See also*
    Assessment; Technology
  adaptive assessment, 150–155
  automated item generation, 165–173
  automated passage selection, 162–165
  automated tutoring systems, 149–150
  digital and online resources, 156–162
  nonintrusive vocabulary assessment,
    155–156, 173–175
  overview, 79, 175
  semantic constraints, 21
Test design, 30–31, 151, 165–173. *See also*
    Assessment
Test reliability, 30–31, 205. *See also*
    Assessment
Test validity, 30–31, 205. *See also*
    Assessment
Testing, 32–33, 41. *See also* Assessment
Text macrostructure, 163, 205. *See also*
    Referential cohesion; Topic cohesion.
Text readability, 162–164. *See also* Reading
    comprehension
Tier One vocabulary, 40, 55, 156, 205
Tier Three vocabulary, 40, 55–56, 65,
    91–93, 138, 205
Tier Two vocabulary, 40–41, 47, 55, 61, 73,
    91–93, 205
  relationship to Common Core State
    Standards, 41

TOEFL test of English language proficiency,
    42–43, 167. *See also* English learners;
    Second-language teaching
Topic cohesion, 163, 205. *See also* Referential
    cohesion; Text macrostructure
Topical association, 84–85, 90–93, 97, 98,
    205. *See also* Semantic knowledge;
    Word associations
  assessing, 90–92
Transitive verbs, 21, 26, 205. *See also* Parts
    of speech; Syntax
Tutoring systems, 149–155, 201. *See also*
    Automated item generation; Automated
    passage selection; Automated Tutoring
    Systems; Digital and online resources;
    Nonintrusive vocabulary assessment;
    Technology

Validity, 30–31, 205. *See also* Assessment
Valuable words, 61, 69, 205. *See also* Word
    selection
VASE assessment, 70, 101. *See also* Depth of
    vocabulary knowledge
Verbal fluency, 3
Verbal reasoning. *See also* Inference
  assessing vocabulary knowledge using
    word analogies, 95
Vocabulary. *See also* Developmental factors;
    Language development; Word learning
  acquisition, 33–34, 205
  assessment. *See* Assessment
  construct, 30–31, 205
  development. *See* Developmental factors
  instruction. *See* Instruction
  relation to metacognitive knowledge and
    awareness, 22–24–47
  role of vocabulary in Common Core State
    Standards' definition of literacy, 47
  strategies, 22–24, 47
Vocabulary knowledge. *See also* Assessment;
    Breadth of vocabulary; Depth
    of vocabulary knowledge; Word
    knowledge
  Academic (Tier Two) vocabulary, 4, 55,
    91–93, 138
  assessment, 33–34, 101, 205
  context, 19–20
  conversational (Tier One) vocabulary, 40,
    55, 156, 205. *See also* General Service
    List; High-frequency words
  domain-specific (Tier Three) vocabulary,
    4, 55, 91–93, 138, 205
  growth, 1
  higher-level literacy, 103–105
  importance of, 1, 9–10
  interactions around books, 112–116,
    113*f*–114*f*

metalinguistic and metacognitive
knowledge, 22–24, 23*f*
multidimensionality of vocabulary
knowledge, 33
multiple aspects of, 96–97
overview, 1, 2, 8, 20–22, 28–29, 52–53,
75
partial and incremental knowledge of
words, 96–103, 100*f*
polysemy and role in growth of
vocabulary size, 16–18
reaction time as evidence of vocabulary
knowledge, 83
reading comprehension, 1–2, 57
regularities of language, 11–12
resources for, 185–189
role in argumentation, 4–5
role in critical thinking, 3–5
role in writing quality, 2–3, 115–116
role of feedback, 81
role of word associations in establishing
textual coherence, 92–93
tiers of vocabulary, 40, 55
using to assess other constructs, 31
vocabulary size, 2–3, 9–10, 22, 31,
34–37, 39
vocabulary size and word-learning ability,
79
word selection for teaching and assessment,
54–55, 57–58, 60–61, 69, 73
Vocabulary resources. *See* Dictionaries,
Thesauri, and Other Lexical
Resources
Vocabulary size. *See* Breadth of vocabulary

Word associations, 90–93, 167–168, **197.**
See also Semantic association; Topical
association
Word awareness, 101. *See also*
Metalinguistic skills and awareness
Word banks, 109–110, **205.** *See also*
Collected words and phrases;
Instruction
Word choice and writer's craft, 3, 110,
115–116; *See also* Lexical diversity;
Writing
Word collections. *See* Collected words and
phrases
Word consciousness, 108–112, 124,
127–130, **206.** *See also* Instruction;
Metalinguistic skills and awareness
Word families, 14–15, 60–61, 185, **206.** *See
also* Morphological patterns
Word frequency, 53–56, **206.** *See also*
Breadth of vocabulary
affected by corpus bias, 58
affected by homophones and polysemy, 59

arbitrariness in setting word frequency
cutoffs, 59
American Heritage Word Frequency List,
158
Higher-level literacy, 47, 103–105
of multiword expressions, 16, 22
TASA Word Frequency List, 158
Zipf's law, 53–54
Word games, wordplay, puns, 110–112, 132,
142
Frame Games, 181
Hinky Pinkies, 181
Literal Pictures of Idioms, 181
Vocabular.co.il, 182
Word Sift, 181
Word Tagul Clouds, 181
Word identification, 2
Word introduction, 119–123. *See also*
Instruction
Word knowledge. *See also* Vocabulary
knowledge
assessment of, 33–34, 96–103
confusable words, 96
metalinguistic and metacognitive
knowledge and, 22–24, 23*f*
overview, 20–22
partial and incremental, 96–103, 100*f*,
200
resources for, 185–189
specific knowledge of words and phrases,
20–21, 76
word associations, 90
word selection for teaching and
assessment and, 57–58
Word learning, 9–12, 71, 76 *See also*
Language development
assessment, 20, 33–34, 40, 50–51, 75–77
burden of, 9–10
complexities of, 11
dictionaries, 24–28, 25*f*
effect of variety and number of contexts,
20
emphasis on strategy by the Common
Core State Standards, 46
generative patterns, 13–20, 17*f*
growth, 1
importance of metalinguistic awareness,
23–24, 85
incidental word learning, 13, 19,
112–113
incremental word learning, 19–21, 24, 40,
77–79, 96–102
interactions around books, 112
learning from sentence context, 19, 78,
81–82
link with improving reading
comprehension, 20

Word learning *(cont.)*
  need to assess incremental word learning, 33, 39, 50–51, 75–76, 81–82
  of context, 11
  overview, 47, 50–51, 76–82
  regularities of language, 11–12
  relation to generative patterns, 13, 19, 112–113
  repeated exposures to words from reading, 19, 20, 112–113
  richness of the contexts provided, 20
  role of word-learning skill, 76–82
  self-assessment, 82–83
  vocabulary learning through context, 141–145
Word lists, 35–36, 40–41, 46–47, 55–56, 101–102, 156–157, 158, 182, 184.
  Academic Vocabulary List, 55, 157
  Academic Word List (Coxhead), 40, 55, 73, 101,157, 184
  American Heritage Vocabulary Frequency List, 158
  Biemiller's Words Worth Teaching, 36, 58, 73,156
  by grade level, 35–36, 57–60, 137–138
  General Service List, 55, 157, 184
  New Academic Word List, 157
  New General Service List, 156–157
  TASA Word Frequency List, 158
  Teacher's Handbook of 30,000 Words by Thorndike, 156
  Thorndike's educational word list, 54
  to target instruction, 40–41
Word meaning, 47, 77–81, 90, 111–112, 119–123, 127–130. *See also* Polysemy; Semantics; Vocabulary knowledge
WordNet, 26, 123, 160. *See also* Synsets
Word norm databases, 157–161, **206**. *See also* Dictionaries, Thesauri, and Other Lexical Resources

Word patterns, 67–68, 73, 74, 108, 109–110. *See also* Generative patterns; Morphological patterns; Semantic patterns; Syntactic patterns
Word selection, 52–74, 115–116. *See also* Assessment; Instruction
  accessible words, 61
  based on passage context, 69
  essential words, 61
  for assessment, 68–74
  for instruction, 52–67, 69, 115–116
  imported words, 61
  subjective judgment in, 62–64
  valuable words, 61
  vocabulary mega-clusters, 60–61
  Word Zones, 54–55, 73
Word senses, 51, 64, 71–72, 84, 93, 157, 159–161, 168–169, **206**. *See also* Polysemy; Semantic patterns
  primary or dominant word senses versus secondary senses, 72, 116–118, 128
  word sense disambiguation, 169
Word-centered automated systems, 149–150, 151–153.
Word-conscious classroom, 107–119, 113*f*–114*f*, 146–147, 205. *See also* Classroom practices; Instruction
Wordplay, 110, 128–129, 181–182, **206**. *See also* Word games, wordplay, puns
Word-to-text integration, 79, 104. *See also* Reading comprehension
Writing, 109–110, 115–116. *See also* Word choice and writer's craft
  developmental trends, 2–3
  emphasis on word choice by the Common Core State Standards, 46

Zeugma, 128–129, **206**. *See also* Metonymy; Polysemy
Zipf's law, 53–54. *See also* Word frequency